T0073293

Cloud Computing with AWS

Everything You Need to Know to be an AWS Cloud Practitioner

Pravin Mishra

Apress®

Cloud Computing with AWS: Everything You Need to Know to be an AWS Cloud Practitioner

Pravin Mishra
Espoo, Finland

ISBN-13 (pbk): 978-1-4842-9171-9   ISBN-13 (electronic): 978-1-4842-9172-6
https://doi.org/10.1007/978-1-4842-9172-6

Managing Director, Apress Media LLC: Welmoed Spahr
Acquisitions Editor: James Robinson-Prior
Development Editor: Jim Markham
Coordinating Editor: Gryffin Winkler
Copy Editor: Kezia Endsley

Cover image designed by Freepik (www.freepik.com)

Distributed to the book trade worldwide by Springer Science+Business Media New York, 233 Spring Street, 6th Floor, New York, NY 10013. Phone 1-800-SPRINGER, fax (201) 348-4505, e-mail orders-ny@springer-sbm.com, or visit www.springeronline.com. Apress Media, LLC is a California LLC and the sole member (owner) is Springer Science + Business Media Finance Inc (SSBM Finance Inc). SSBM Finance Inc is a **Delaware** corporation.

For information on translations, please e-mail booktranslations@springernature.com; for reprint, paperback, or audio rights, please e-mail bookpermissions@springernature.com.

Apress titles may be purchased in bulk for academic, corporate, or promotional use. eBook versions and licenses are also available for most titles. For more information, reference our Print and eBook Bulk Sales web page at http://www.apress.com/bulk-sales.

Any source code or other supplementary material referenced by the author in this book is available to readers on GitHub (https://github.com/Apress). For more detailed information, please visit http://www.apress.com/source-code.

Printed on acid-free paper

*To my mother, Mrs. Nayanmati Mishra; my wife,
Neha Mishra; my guru, Amar Singh;
and my dearest friend, the late Bimal Sharma*

Table of Contents

About the Author

Pravin Mishra has more than twelve years of experience in IT and eight years as a course trainer. He specializes in designing and implementing multi-cloud based solutions. As an AWS trainer, Pravin helps students and IT professionals switch careers in AWS Cloud. With a strong belief in "learning by doing," he helps his students grow their cloud-based skills and realize their full potential, from basic concepts and methodologies to getting ready to pursue AWS certification.

Since 2009 he has worked with IT companies like Nordcloud (an IBM company), Eficode, Ericsson, Verizon, and ShepHertz Technologies, helping them build robust cloud IT infrastructures.

About the Technical Reviewers

Florian Rommel is an experienced IT veteran with over 3 decades in professional IT. He has been cloud native for over 9 years and is an expert in cloud infrastructure and cloud technologies. Florian holds multiple AWS certifications and has built and managed extremely large and complex environments with critical application services spanning multiple regions. Florian was also the principle co-architect for the development and deployment of the largest Cloud environment in Europe at the time.

Sudhir Kumar Pradham is a Senior Solutions Architect/Consultant, working in a reputable MNC. Sudhir has extensive experience architecting and designing multi-cloud, multi-account and hybrid cloud solutions using AWS services. As a senior architect, he is always looking for ways to resolve application security, reduce costs, and enhance the operational experience.

CHAPTER 1

Introduction to Cloud Computing

Before you dive into Amazon Web Services, you need a solid foundation of cloud computing. That's the point of this chapter. Without further delay, let's get started.

This chapter covers the following topics:

- What is cloud computing?
- What are the different types of cloud deployment models?
- What are data centers and how did cloud computing come into existence?
- What are the different types of cloud service models?
- What are some important concepts related to the cloud?
- What are the different providers that provide cloud services?
- What are the benefits of cloud computing over traditional methods?

Each of these topics is covered in detail, as they are very important to understand before moving on to AWS.

Once you complete this chapter, you will have a good understanding of cloud computing and its key concepts and benefits, and you will be able to determine when cloud computing is appropriate as well as what models and services to use.

To get the most out of this book, I recommend that you take notes. Notes make learning a lot easier by providing you with quick reference whenever you need it.

I hope you are excited as I am.

Defining Cloud Computing

The concept of cloud computing refers to the on-demand delivery of compute, storage, database, networking, and other services over the Internet (see Figure 1-1).

Figure 1-1. *Cloud computing*

I am assuming that you are a beginner and these terms may be new to you. But don't worry; I am going to explain them shortly.

Let's first look at what on-demand delivery is. On-demand means you get it only when you need it.

You can understand this idea with the help of an example. Suppose you are a "foodie" (see Figure 1-2), so you love cooking and trying new recipes. Imagine how great it would be to get the exact amount of ingredients every time you try a new recipe, so that you get the best taste and don't end up wasting any ingredients.

Figure 1-2. *Pizza*

This may not sound possible when it comes to ingredients, but it is undoubtedly possible in the case of cloud computing. You get exactly what you need and right when you order it.

Another feature that makes cloud computing so simple is its *pay-as-you-go pricing.*

You only pay for what you request and what you use in cloud computing. Once you are done with a service or resource, you can easily delete or deallocate it; hence, you do not need to pay for anything extra. You only pay for what you use and for how long you use it.

There are four core cloud computing services—compute, storage, database, and networking (see Figure 1-3). Let's look at them one by one.

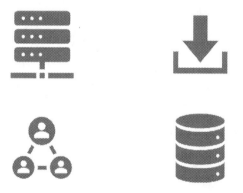

Figure 1-3. *Storage, network, compute, and database services*

Compute

Compute is the processing power of your machine.

For example, suppose you are creating a PowerPoint presentation for your final year project. You need a lot of information for your project, so you open a few web browser tabs. You love music, so you are playing music as well.

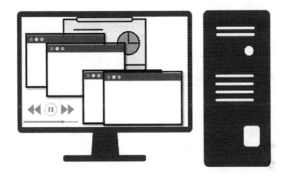

Figure 1-4. *Compute*

As your computer (see Figure 1-4) is performing several tasks simultaneously, you notice that it starts lagging, so you close a couple of tabs and stop the music player. Your computer starts running smoothly again. This happens because your computer has finite compute power and it can process a limited amount of requests at a time. For this reason, a good processor and more RAM are essential to running heavy applications or games.

In the same way, to process your data or run your application on the cloud, you need the compute service that cloud computing offers.

That's enough about compute; the next section looks at another cloud computing service—storage.

Storage

To continue the example, suppose you completed your PowerPoint presentation, and you then saved the PPT file and some other documents on your computer. That means your computer has a storage unit (see Figure 1-5) to store your data. But what happens if your computer's hard disk crashes? You will lose all your data, right? In that case, you can back up your documents on a hard disk drive.

5

Figure 1-5. *Storage units*

By definition, storage enables you to save your data on a data storage device.

You can store data such as videos, music, documents, pictures, and so on. The data that you save on any storage device will remain permanently on that device until you delete it.

Similarly, if you want to store data—either temporarily or permanently—on the cloud, you can use cloud storage.

That is enough about storage, let's now look at database storage.

Database

Again, consider the same example: Suppose, while working on the project, you create an Excel sheet. This sheet has information regarding your projects in rows and columns (see Figure 1-6).

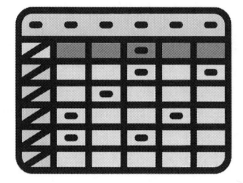

Figure 1-6. *Traditional data*

When you arrange your data or information in certain rows and columns, it is called *structured* data. The data in an Excel sheet is structured data. It is basically in a format that makes it convenient to store or fetch data whenever you want.

Excel sheets are fine for a certain data size, but to store a huge amount of structured data, you need a special type of storage device called a database. There are different types of databases—including MySQL, Oracle, and SQL Server (see Figure 1-7)—which you choose based on the type of data you want to store.

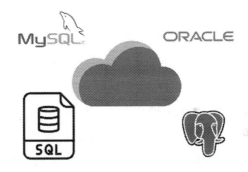

Figure 1-7. *Different types of databases*

A database enables you to store an organized collection of structured information or your application's data. If you need to store structured data in the cloud, you can use a database.

Let's move on to networking services.

Networking

When you use compute, storage, and database in the cloud, these services need to be connected, either privately or over the Internet, and that's where networking comes into the picture.

A networking service provides connectivity among different services.

Networking is an interesting topic (see Figure 1-8) and it's covered in detail in a separate chapter.

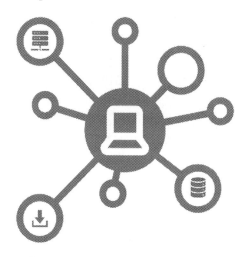

Figure 1-8. *Networking*

Let's return to the definition of cloud computing.

Cloud computing enables on-demand computing services such as database, storage, compute, and networking over the Internet.

Fundamentals of the Cloud

Cloud Deployment Models

In the previous section, you learned about cloud computing; in this section, you learn about different cloud deployment models. But before that, let's consider why you need different types of cloud deployment models.

The answer is simple—different organizations (see Figure 1-9) have different requirements. They want different levels of control over their cloud infrastructure. To cater to their needs, there are different types of cloud deployment models.

Each model offers a different level of management, security, and cost to the users. Once you understand all the cloud deployment models, you can determine which cloud model best suits you and your customers.

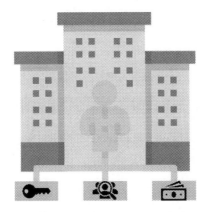

Figure 1-9. *Organizations*

Let's look at the definition of cloud deployment model. It is based on three main attributes (see Figure 1-10).

-   Where is the cloud infrastructure located?

-   Who controls it?

-   Who can access and use it?

Figure 1-10. *Data center attributes*

In addition to all the cloud services like compute, storage, network, and database, cloud infrastructure also involves hardware, building, power, cooling, and so on. Your control on the cloud will vary based on factors like where the infrastructure is located, who maintains it, and who can use it.

Cloud computing offers three cloud deployment models:

- Private clouds

- Public clouds

- Hybrid clouds

Private Clouds

A private cloud is a cloud computing infrastructure that is exclusively dedicated to a particular organization.

In the private cloud (see Figure 1-11) computing model, cloud services—such as compute, storage, database, and network—are available to an organization and its users only.

Private Cloud

Figure 1-11. *Private cloud*

However, the infrastructure can be maintained by the organization itself, or by the third party that is providing the cloud services. Similarly, the hardware can be located on-site or on the third-party site.

When a cloud computing infrastructure is available for a certain organization and to their internal people only, this is called *private cloud*.

Private clouds cost more than public clouds, as companies need to expend a huge upfront capital investment to set them up and maintain them.

They are generally more secure than public clouds. Therefore, organizations that want to run their mission-critical applications prefer private clouds due to security reasons.

Cloud security is covered in Chapter 10. Next up is the public cloud.

Public Clouds

Public clouds are cloud computing infrastructures that are maintained and operated by cloud service providers and that are available for public use.

The public cloud is available from a number of providers, including Amazon Web Services (AWS), IBM, Alibaba, Google Cloud, and Microsoft Azure.

In the public cloud computing model, cloud services such as compute, storage, database, and network are available over the Internet, and anyone can use them. It means a startup, a big organization, or even an individual can use public cloud services (see Figure 1-12).

Public Cloud

Figure 1-12. *Public cloud*

It is the cloud service provider's responsibility to maintain the physical infrastructure that supports their cloud services, such as the building, its power and cooling systems, as well as those that encounter hardware failures. You learn about these public cloud providers in detail later in this chapter.

Now, let's discuss the hybrid cloud.

Hybrid Clouds

The term hybrid refers to the combination of two or more elements.

A *hybrid cloud* is a cloud computing infrastructure that benefits from the public and private models and enables organizations to use both.

When an organization uses a public cloud along with their private cloud, that's called hybrid cloud (see Figure 1-13). In other words, a hybrid cloud incorporates a private cloud and a public cloud and allows applications and data to be shared among the two.

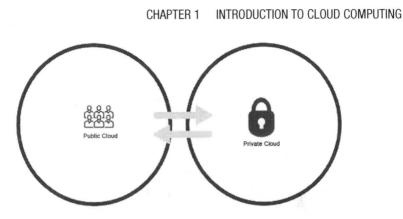

Figure 1-13. *Hybrid cloud*

You now have an idea about the three deployment models of cloud computing and what makes them different from each other.

Traditional Data Centers

This section covers data centers, their components, and some common challenges associated with on-premise data centers. Let's get started.

To understand what a data center is, let's go back 20 years and consider how traditional IT used to work. You might know that a lot of companies started either in a study room or a garage, including Amazon, Apple, and Google, which all started in garages (see Figure 1-14).

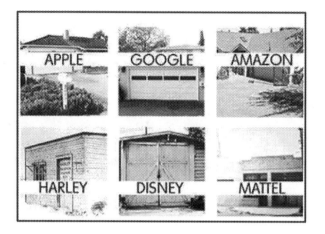

Figure 1-14. *Garage start-ups*

The founders of these companies got a computer, put it in their garage or study room, and deployed these websites on the Internet. These computers provided the website with underlying hardware required to run it. As their businesses grew, they added more computers (see Figure 1-15) to meet demand.

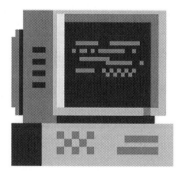

Figure 1-15. *Old computer*

This worked well in the beginning, but there came a time when the garages became packed with computers and there was no space left to accommodate new ones. They moved these computers to a bigger space or a building that could accommodate the hardware based on the demand.

The physical space where organizations keep computer systems and related hardware required for their websites, apps, or IT infrastructure is known as a *data center.*

You will hear about traditional data centers and on-premises data centers. Don't worry, these are the same. The terms data center, on-premises, and traditional data center are used interchangeably.

A data center is all about big computers and related hardware required to run a website or an app. You can add more systems and hardware based on the growth of your company. This works well at first, but there are challenges with traditional data centers, which is why organizations eventually move to the cloud. Let's talk about these challenges now.

Cost

First and foremost, cost is a major challenge with the traditional data center. Setting up a data center involves a huge upfront investment in building, hardware, cooling, power, ventilation equipment, and so on (see Figure 1-16). It doesn't end there; you have to spend a significant amount on maintenance as well.

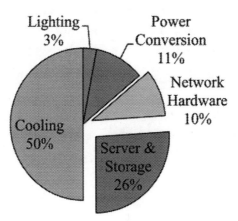

Figure 1-16. *Data center cost component*

Capacity Planning

Another big problem with the data center is capacity planning. They should always be ready to meet the demand. It's hard to predict the actual hardware requirement. If businesses grow five times, you need five times more servers. If businesses grow eight times, you need eight times more servers. Also, if it doesn't grow at the expected rate, you will have extra servers. Due to this unexpected demand, most of the time, developers end up over-provisioning the servers, which leads to wasted computing space, cooling, electricity, and so on. At the end of the day, it is all about cost.

Staffing and Technical Skill Sets

In addition to the servers and storage, data centers also include network connectivity, connecting cables, power, cooling systems, applications, and many other things.

To monitor the data centers and troubleshoot them, you need a skilled staff, which leads to additional cost.

Now you understand the data center and the challenges of maintaining and running the data center. Is there a way to reduce this hassle of setting up and maintaining a data center? Is it possible to outsource this to a third party? The answer to both of these questions is yes. Many organizations outsource these tasks, as maintaining and running a data center is not their core business.

They work with third-party data center service providers (see Figure 1-17) to rent space on the provider's facility, where they either keep their servers or rent servers from them. They pay the service provider for managing their servers.

Figure 1-17. *Third-party data center providers*

That's a better way to offload some challenges, like staffing and training; however, capacity planning and upfront investment would still be major issues.

That's where cloud computing comes to the rescue, because you no longer need to spend money and resources on physical space and maintenance. Hosting applications and storing data has now become handy. You can get compute, storage, database, and network on demand without having to worry about setting up and maintaining data centers.

Cloud Service Models

As part of this section, you learn how cloud service models work.

This is an important concept in cloud computing that will help you understand how cloud provides you with flexible ways to deploy your applications. Cloud computing is offered in three service models, each satisfying a unique business requirement:

- IaaS (Infrastructure as a Service)

- PaaS (Platform as a Service)

- SaaS (Software as a Service)

Let's start.

Do you know what organizations have to manage if they decide to host an application on their on-premise data centers (see Figure 1-18)?

- The application itself.

- This application's database for the data.

- It must be developed in a programming language, right? So they need a web or application server, called a *runtime*.

- A programming language and some middleware software to run the application.

- An operating system (OS).

- The physical server, which is virtualized with a hypervisor to run multiple operating systems. That helps run multiple applications on a single physical server. Virtualization is covered in Chapter 5.

- Storage, for saving data.

- Networking to connect IT systems like routers, switches, other computers, and the Internet.

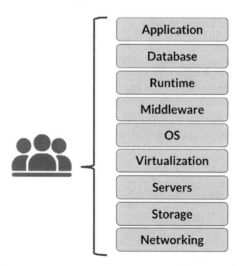

Figure 1-18. Application hosting on their on-premise data

These teams have to manage many things.

It's similar to making the whole pizza at home (see Figure 1-19). You have to get everything that's needed to make the pizza, from pizza dough to toppings, an oven, the gas, and more.

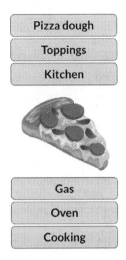

Figure 1-19. *Making pizza at home*

There are other ways you can enjoy a pizza, without having to do everything yourself. Similarly, cloud computing also offers different models to host your applications. Let's take a look at these models.

IaaS (Infrastructure as a Service)

The first cloud service model is Infrastructure as a Service, also known as IaaS.

This cloud service model provides the fundamental building blocks for hosting applications, such as networking, storage, compute and virtualization.

As an application developer, you do not need to think about the underlying core services; your team can now focus on the things that matter the most for your application.

If you compare this to the pizza example, you get a well-equipped kitchen, with a mixer, gas, baking sheet, and oven. Now all you need to do is make the pizza dough, top it with your favorite toppings, and cook it.

Platform as a Service (PaaS)

The next cloud service model is Platform as a Service, or PaaS.

This model adds an additional layer on top of IaaS, which includes the operating system, middleware, and runtime.

In this model, cloud providers take care of the runtime, middleware, and operating systems, along with core services like networking, storage, servers, and virtualization.

This model provides even more flexibility to the application development team, so they can focus on application development, deployment, and management.

Take the pizza example again: you get readymade pizza dough. You simply add toppings of your choice and cook it.

Software as a Service (SaaS)

The final cloud service model is Software as a Service (SaaS).

The SaaS model allows organizations to purchase complete software services from third-party providers.

Cloud providers are responsible for everything that is required to develop and deploy an application. In an SaaS offering, you don't have to worry about anything at all. One of the most common examples of SaaS is Gmail, where you only care about sending and receiving emails.

There are many more SaaS applications, including Google Drive, Dropbox, and so on. Surprisingly, we have been using SaaS all this time.

Note that, by definition, SaaS applications work on a pay-as-you-go basis. You pay a subscription price to use these services.

If you compare this again to the pizza example: SaaS is basically Kotipizza, Dominos, Pizza Hut, and so on. They are well known for pizza-as-a-service. You order and pay for a pizza and get it with no hassle.

To sum up, let's take a quick look at what these cloud services models have to offer:

- The *IaaS* model offers the computing resources to host, build, and run applications.

- The *PaaS* model provides an environment for application developers to build and deploy applications.

- The *SaaS* model delivers paid software to users and companies over the Internet.

Key Cloud Concepts

As part of this section, you learn about some key concepts in cloud computing:

- – Scalability (vertical and horizontal scaling)

- – Elasticity

- – Agility

- – High availability

- – Fault tolerance

Scalability

Let's assume you have a web application running on a virtual machine. If *virtual machine* is a new term for you, don't worry. You learn more about this in Chapter 6. For the time being, think of it as your laptop or desktop with computing power to process any request or command.

21

When more people access your application, it will require more computing power, which is nothing but CPU and memory, to serve all the users. You have to scale up this virtual machine by increasing its computing power.

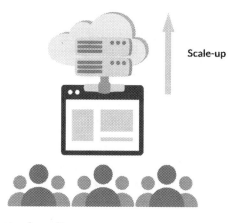

Figure 1-20. *Vertical scaling*

If you decide to increase the size of your existing virtual machine, you are moving along the vertical line, which is why this is called "vertical scaling" (see Figure 1-20). Increasing the size of the resource is called "scaling up." If you decrease the size or power of the machine, this is known as "scaling down."

Instead of increasing the size of your virtual machine, you can also scale up your resources by adding more virtual machines to your infrastructure.

In this case, you are moving along the horizontal line, hence, this type of scaling is called "horizontal scaling" (see Figure 1-21). If you increase the number of your virtual machines, this is called "scaling out." And if you decrease the number of the virtual machines, this is called "scaling in."

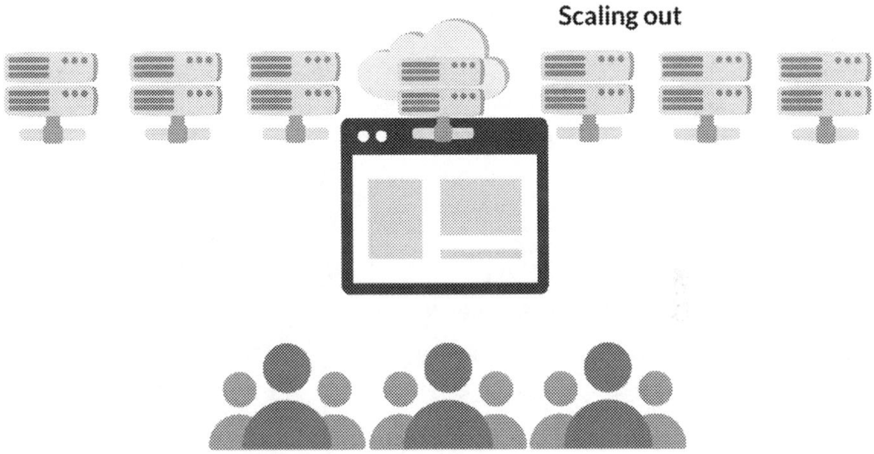

Scaling out

Figure 1-21. *Horizontal scaling*

To summarize, scalability is the ability of the system to adjust in size and power. In this case, scaling is a process of increasing or decreasing the compute power.

Elasticity

Let's assume your application is working fine, but you notice that the load on your application varies throughout the day. There is more traffic during the daytime and less at night.

As the day progresses, your application needs more power, but you don't need the same amount of resources during the night. The ability to scale the virtual machines based on the demand of the application is known as *elasticity*.

Basically, you design the system so that it can allocate and deallocate virtual machines whenever necessary. When the process is automated, this is called automatic scaling. Elasticity is the ability of the system to scale dynamically.

Agility

Let's take the same application example again. Whether you want to achieve scalability or elasticity for your application, you need more virtual machines. Right?

The question is how quickly can you get virtual machines when you need them. One of the major differences between the cloud and on-premises is that requesting resources in the on-premises environment usually takes days, weeks, or even months, whereas in the cloud, this could be done in minutes or even seconds.

Hence, *agility* is the ability to react quickly.

High Availability

Again, going back to the example application. You are running an application on one virtual machine. Your security team needs to update security patches to the operating system, which will take around an hour or so, and during this time, your application will be down.

That's not a good user experience, right? Your users won't be able to use your application for around an hour. In IT terms, you could say the application is not highly available.

High availability is the ability of a system to operate continuously without failure for a designated period.

In this case, to make the application available to your users, you can run the application on two virtual machines. While your security team is patching on one virtual machine, another machine is available and serves requests to your users.

Fault Tolerance

Let's continue with the same example; your application is now highly available, as you are running your application on two virtual machines. You have a strict requirement that your application runs on two virtual machines all the time.

Let's assume there is a hard disk crash on one virtual machine, so your application stops working on that virtual machine. In simpler terms, your virtual machine cannot tolerate hard disk failure. To cope with such situations, you need a fault-tolerant system.

Tolerance is the ability of a virtual machine to remain up and running during component and service failures.

As a result, a failure in a single point will not cause the whole system to fail. A fault-tolerant system can continue to run at a useable, and most importantly, reasonable level.

A fault-tolerant system takes care of any failure, repairs it, and keeps the application running.

Fault tolerance refers to the ability of a system (computer, network, storage, etc.) to continue operating without interruption when one or more of its components fail.

Alright, I hope you now understand the meaning of these cloud-specific terms, as they are important. Make sure you can explain them to others.

The Benefits of Cloud Computing[1]

So far in this chapter, you have learned about the traditional data center, cloud computing, and different elements and features of cloud computing. This section looks at the main advantages of using cloud computing, since these benefits help you decide whether cloud computing is right for you.

---

[1] https://docs.aws.amazon.com/whitepapers/latest/aws-overview/six-advantages-of-cloud-computing.html

Trade Fixed Expenses for Variable Expenses

When you trade fixed expenses for variable expenses, it means that you can eliminate the upfront cost of setting up a data center. With "traditional" data centers or "traditional" data centers with hardware, you incur a large financial investment in acquiring physical space to set up your data center, acquire the hardware, and hire employees to rack and stack this hardware. This upfront investment is called *CAPEX*, for capital expense or fixed expense.

On top of that, you need a technical team to keep the data center running. This cost is known as *OPEX*, for operational expense or variable expense.

Combining CAPEX and OPEX can be hundreds of thousands of dollars for a medium to large data center. For a small organization or start-up, that's a significant amount.

Another challenge is the utilization of the data center. It does not matter whether you use the full capacity of the data center or not; you have already invested CAPEX amount and will have to bear a regular OPEX.

One of the main benefits of cloud computing is its low cost. Billing with the cloud is fundamentally different from the traditional data center. With a cloud setup, you pay monthly, based on the resources you consume. That's the great part! If you are just starting your venture, there's no need to invest thousands of dollars to set up the data centers. Instead, you can opt for a cloud setup and pay only for what you use.

If your bill exceeds the budget you allocated, you can save money on the cloud by shutting down unused resources, purging old resources, and optimizing your applications.

Benefit from Massive Economies of Scale

Now let's move onto the next advantage, that is, you benefit from massive economies of scale (see Figure 1-22).

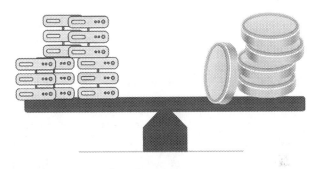

Figure 1-22. *Economies of scale*

You get the cloud at a very low price. That's because of the economies of scale that come with cloud setups. Simply put, when you do something at large scale, the cost goes down (just ask Walmart or Costco). Cloud providers use big data centers all around the world and invest in huge amounts of hardware and cloud experts. Due to this, they get everything at a lower price, yet they install and operate efficiently.

Due to all of these reasons, you get cloud facilities at a lower cost than if you operate your own data center.

Stop Guessing at Capacity

Another advantage of cloud computing is that you don't have to make assumptions about capacity. In order to run your business effectively, you must estimate how much capacity you will need when building a traditional data center.

Consider the case where you estimate that you will have five million subscribers in two years. You purchase a sufficient amount of hardware to sustain that demand in the future. However, it turns out that you only have about one million users, which is a lot less than you expected. With a traditional setup, you would have to live with all the hardware and cost that you bought to support five million users.

On the other hand, if you underestimate the capacity, you will have to expand your capacity and add more hardware to handle the growth before you lose customers. That takes time.

The bottom line is that estimating your capacity beforehand is problematic, and you are very likely to be wrong.

With cloud computing, you don't have to guess the capacity. You can simply allocate resources based on your current business needs and use the simple scaling mechanisms of cloud computing to add and/or remove resources as your needs change. Isn't that great?! Let's move on to the next benefit, which is one of my favorites.

Increased Speed and Agility

If you are someone who loves trying new things, cloud computing can make it very easy for you to experiment with new ideas and products. You can quickly spin up new environments based on your requirement, and once you are done, simply delete those resources to avoid any additional costs.

I hope, by now, you see that you don't have the same flexibility with an on-premise data center. Scaling up requires buying new hardware and installing it, which sometimes take weeks and even months.

The flexibility of cloud computing helps you focus on the things that matter the most and drive innovation for your business.

Don't Spend Money on Running and Maintaining Data Centers

Another advantage of cloud computing is that you don't have to spend money on data centers and their maintenance (see Figure 1-23).

Figure 1-23. *Maintaining data centers*

If you need a server or an application for your business, you don't need to spend your time and money on running and maintaining data centers. Instead, you can opt for the cloud setup and focus on your core business. You just get what you require from the cloud and let the cloud providers take care of the servers and data centers. You can put all your efforts and energy into growing your business.

Go Global in Minutes

Finally, with cloud computing, you can go global in minutes (see Figure 1-24), which is one of its most exciting features.

Let's assume you own a company in India and want to expand into Japan. You have data centers in India to serve your customers in India. But to operate in Japan, you need data centers in Japan. One way is to set up the data centers in Japan, but that's time-consuming and expensive.

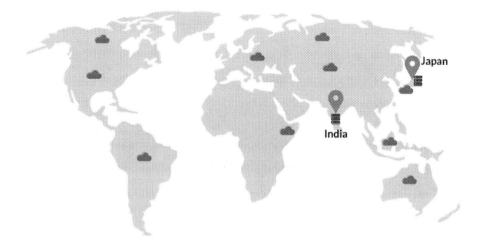

Figure 1-24. *Go global in minutes*

Cloud providers have data centers all over the world. If you are using cloud computing in India, you can start and run your application in almost any region of the world in just a few clicks. You learn about this process in detail in Chapter 2.

You can take advantage of the global presence of cloud providers and replicate your application in Japan or any part of the world. Using the traditional approach would take several months or even years, whereas using the cloud, it takes a matter of minutes.

These are six of the main advantages of cloud computing, and I recommend that you study more about these advantages and look for companies that are operating globally using cloud computing.

The Different Cloud Providers

This section talks about the different cloud service providers currently in the market.

As you know, this book is all about Amazon Web Services (AWS); however, there are other cloud providers available in the market as well. Before you fully dive into AWS, let's briefly explore how cloud computing began and the different key players in the cloud computing industry.

Let's start by looking at a couple of other computing models that worked for many decades.

One of them is client-server computing (see Figure 1-25).

In the client-server computing model, the client requests the resources from the server and the server uses centralized storage hosting to serve the resources. The server uses this centralized storage to store software applications and data on the server side.

Now suppose a client wants to access some data. They will connect to the server, gain appropriate access, and then execute the task.

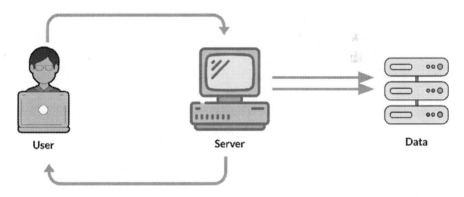

Figure 1-25. *Client-server computing mode*

Shortly after client-server computing, a distributed computing system (see Figure 1-26) was developed, in which computers could share resources. The concept of shared computing was a revolution. That revolution is what you are learning about in this book—cloud computing.

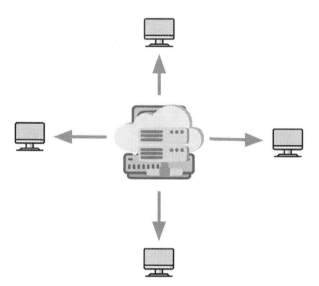

Figure 1-26. *Distributed computing model*

Around 1961, John McCarthy, an American computer scientist, suggested that computing can be sold like a utility, just like water or electricity. It was a thoughtful idea, but it was ahead of its time like all brilliant ideas.[2]

Time passed, and in 1999, Salesforce.com began delivering its application through a simple website. Customers could access the Salesforce application over the Internet. As a result, computing became a utility for the first time.

In 2002, Amazon started Amazon Web Services. It was a wing of Amazon.com itself, but its purpose was to provide Amazon.com with the storage and compute services required to run the e-commerce website. After successfully using it for four years, in 2006, Amazon Web Services decided to sell compute as a service to the general public. That was when the public cloud came into existence.

---

[2] https://en.wikipedia.org/wiki/John_McCarthy_(computer_scientist)

In 2009, Google started Google Apps as a Platform as a Service (PaaS) offering. By this time, all the other cloud computing contenders began to enter the cloud computing field.

In the same year, Microsoft announced Windows Azure, and after that other companies like HP, VMWare, Oracle, and Rackspace also joined the game. That's how cloud computing started and these are the main players in the cloud computing market.

I recommend that you learn more about these service providers, as this will help you understand their offerings, strengths, and limitations. Knowing all this will help you during your interviews.

Summary

The chapter began with the fundamentals of cloud and cloud computing, which is defined as on-demand compute, storage, database, networking, and many more services over the Internet. Cloud services are available on a pay-per-use basis, so you are only charged for the services you use.

The chapter also explored the different deployment models of the cloud, including private, public, and hybrid. I hope you can now decide whether to use public cloud, private cloud, or hybrid cloud for your application.

You should now be aware of the fact that setting up your own data center and maintaining it is not easy. It requires a huge amount of money, time, and expertise and doesn't guarantee success in the long run. Earlier, organizations used to spend a good amount of their time and money setting up and maintaining these data centers, which meant they could not focus on their core business as well. After the emergence of cloud computing, this problem no longer exists.

You also learned how cloud service models work, and how you can use IaaS, PaaS, and SaaS to create the infrastructure and to deploy and run the application. SaaS is delivered to organizations over the Internet.

You then learned about the key concepts of cloud computing, which give it an edge over traditional methods. These are scalability, elasticity, agility, high availability, and fault tolerance. It's no wonder that cloud computing is beneficial to IT, and that companies are moving their dependency from traditional data centers to cloud services. When companies use cloud services, they pay only for what they use, which directly helps in cost savings.

Cloud services are global and mobile. Cloud providers have a presence all around the world, so companies can reach any part of the world in just a few clicks. How great is that?!

You have gained so much knowledge about cloud and cloud computing, and I recommend reviewing what you have learned in this chapter, as these concepts are very important from an interview point of view. If anything is unclear, read the chapter again or go through your notes, if you prepared them.

That's all for this chapter; let's meet up in the next chapter.

CHAPTER 2

Getting Started with AWS

This chapter discusses AWS accounts and explains how to create an AWS account. It also covers the following topics:

- What is the AWS free tier?

- How do you configure Multi-Factor Authentication (MFA) and password policies?

- How do you secure an AWS account?

- How do you set up a budget and an alert?

The chapter covers each topic in great detail so that you get a clear understanding, as these topics are very important to understanding the basics of AWS and its account.

After completing this chapter, you will have a thorough understanding of the AWS account, its creation concepts, and its security aspects.

You also learn how to create an Amazon Web Services account and how you can use its free tier resources.

To get the most out of this training, I recommend that you take notes throughout this chapter. Taking notes makes the learning process a lot easier and provides you with quick support whenever you need it.

© Pravin Mishra 2023
P. Mishra, *Cloud Computing with AWS*, https://doi.org/10.1007/978-1-4842-9172-6_2

AWS Accounts

Before you move to AWS and start exploring its services, the very first thing that you need is an AWS account. But before you create your AWS account, there are a few things that you need to know. This section covers the elements of an AWS account and the things you need to create an account. Let's get right into it. (I am assuming that you don't have an account already, so you are going to create one in the next section.)

An AWS account serves as a container where you create and manage all your AWS resources and services.

The first thing you need to create and manage an AWS account is an identity. I cover identity in Chapter 3, so for now, you can think of it as a user. This user will control and manage the entire account. When you create an account for yourself, you will act as an identity.

As a user, you will create some resources in your account that will eventually generate some bills, so you can manage all types of billing in the same account. Each account has AWS resources, identity, and billing (see Figure 2-1).

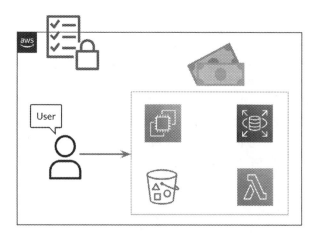

Figure 2-1. *An AWS account*

An AWS account is a naturally secure environment. No one outside your account can access your resources and you will get the bills only for the resources you provision in your account.

You can start your AWS journey with a single account, but when your organization grows in size and complexity, it might be difficult to manage everything on a single account. That's why AWS recommends using multiple accounts. For instance, you can create separate accounts for development, test, and production teams in your organization. This simplifies the security, control, and billing process for each team and provides different teams with the required flexibility to focus on innovation.

Let's look at what you need to set up an account with AWS. First, you need a unique email ID, which means that it should not be used in any other AWS account. You also need a credit card or debit card, which is required for billing purposes. You also need a cell phone number, where you will receive a verification code. With these three pieces of information, you can create an AWS account (see Figure 2-2).

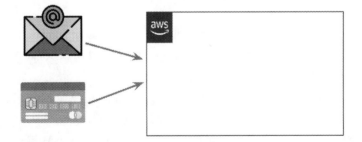

Figure 2-2. *Creating an AWS account*

As soon as you create your AWS account, you are basically creating a user who has control over all the resources available in your account. It is this identity or user that is known as the *AWS account root user.*

The root user can log in with the email and password you used when you created the account. (I talk about the root user in detail in Chapter 10.)

When you sign in to your AWS account, the first screen that you see is known as the AWS Management Console (see Figure 2-3).

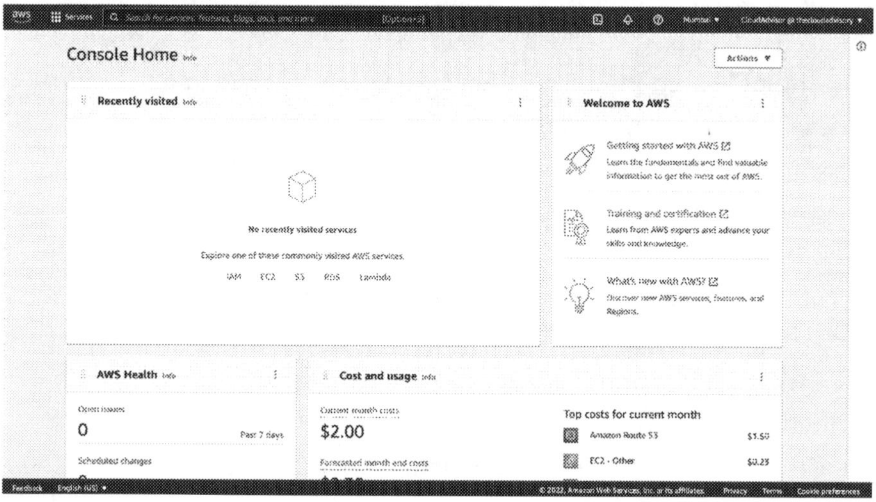

Figure 2-3. *The AWS Management Console*

It's a browser-based console that users can access through an Internet browser. Additionally, AWS accounts can be accessed in other ways, which you will see in the next chapter.

You will also be asked to authenticate your identity when you log in the first time. That's basically the Identity and Access Management, commonly known as the IAM Service. It ensures secure access to your AWS accounts and the resources in them. You learn more about IAM in Chapter 3.

AWS Free Tier

In this section, you learn about AWS Free Tier services and their limitations. Let's get started.

The AWS Free Tier lets customers try some AWS services for a limited period without having to pay anything.

This means AWS provides a selection of services free of charge on the AWS platform, to gain some hands-on experience.

AWS Free Tier is classified into three categories:

- The first category is "Free Trials." Under this offering, you can use some AWS services for a short period. Amazon Redshift falls into this category. You can try DC2.Large node 750 hours per month for two months.

- The second category is "12 Months Free." That means you have 12 months to try these services for free. Amazon EC2 falls into the 12 Months Free category. AWS offers a free 12-month trial with 750 hours of usage every month for the t2.micro instance type. You can run your application free for 12 months. This is a significant period to master AWS, and you can try out and learn almost all the core services. I hope you make the best use of it.

- The last category is "Always Free." These services are available to you forever, but there is a limit to how much you can use these services. They never expire until you cross the available limit. AWS Lambda falls into the Always Free category. It is a serverless compute option, which you will learn about later in the book. As of today, this category allows for one million free invocations per month. That means if you stay under one million invocations, it will always be free, and this category never expires.

That's all for this lesson. I recommend checking this page before and while using AWS services: `https://aws.amazon.com/free/`. There are so many services you can try for free, but make sure you know about the free tier availability of a service before you use it.

Securing an AWS Account

This section explains how to secure your AWS account with a password policy and using Multi-Factor Authentication (MFA). It also looks at access keys and secret keys.

Let's get started with MFA.

Multi-Factor Authentication (MFA)

You have an email ID and password to log in to your AWS account. After logging in, you can access the AWS Management Console and perform different operations.

Say that someone steals your password. This person can log in and do anything in your account. Right? Especially if they have administrator access, they can delete production resources, transfer confidential data, change the application configuration, and whatnot.

How do you protect your account on top of a password? Well, MFA, or multi-factor authentication, can do the trick.

MFA is a method of authentication that requests that the user provide at least two verification types, which are known as *factors*, to get access to an account or resource such as a website, a mobile phone app, or services.

So, apart from the username and password, users have to enter a one-time password, or OTP, delivered via SMS, email, or authenticator apps such as Google and Microsoft Authenticator.

The two-factor authentication method can be seen when you try to log in to Gmail from a new device. If someone tries to log in to your Gmail account, it asks for the password and sends a one-time password (OTP) to the registered mobile number.

MFA is used in the combination of your password and a security device you own, like your phone.

After configuring MFA on AWS, you have to verify your account. As a result, you have to provide an MFA token every time you log in to your AWS account. MFA basically adds another level of security over your password. So even if someone steals your password, they still won't be able to log in to it. Hence, it is a good practice to configure MFA into your AWS account.

MFA and security in general are important topics from both the interview and exam points of view. You should expect questions like, how do you add an extra layer of security to your AWS root or IAM user? The answer to this question is using Multi-Factor Authentication (MFA).

Access Key and Secret Key

Apart from the Management Console, you can also access AWS through the CLI and the SDK. You will learn more about this in a following section, titled "Interacting with AWS."

When you access AWS using any of these methods, you must provide a secret key and an access key (see Figure 2-4).

Figure 2-4. *Access key and secret key*

Using these keys might not be as user-friendly as using a username and password, but you have to use them in your code to log in to your AWS account, either through CLI or SDK.

These are known as access keys, and they're used for programmatic access. You'll create some access keys later in the book and learn how to use them to log in. For now, let's move on to the next topic, which is using password policies.

Password Policy

This is a way to enforce strong passwords for your AWS account users, because accounts are more secure when you use strong passwords. Password policies set rules that you want your users to follow when creating or resetting their passwords. Using a password policy, you can:

- Enforce a minimum password length.[1]

- Enforce at least one uppercase letter from the Latin alphabet (A-Z).

---

[1] https://docs.aws.amazon.com/IAM/latest/UserGuide/id_credentials_passwords_account-policy.html

- Enforce at least one lowercase letter from the Latin alphabet (a-z).

- Enforce at least one number.

- Enforce at least one non-alphanumeric character (! @ # $ % ^ & * ( ) _ + - = [ ] { } | ').

- Enable password expiration.

- Make the password expiration require an administrator reset.

- Allow users to change their passwords.

- Prevent password reuse.

It is possible to set a minimum password length rule. Then, you can enforce specific character types. For example, you may want to have an uppercase letter, a lowercase letter, and a number.

Other than that, you can also specify that non-alphanumeric characters, such as percentages, pound signs, and so on, to be included.

You can also enable password expiration, which means users need to rotate their passwords after a certain time. For example, after 90 days, 120 days, and so on.

You can give users the option to change their passwords, or you can also opt for only the administrator to be able to change passwords.

Finally, you can prevent password reuse so that users, when they change their passwords, can't use a previous password.

A password policy is a guard against any malign attempts on your accounts. A password policy is also an important topic under AWS security from the certification exam or interview point of view.

AWS Budgets and Alerts

You now have our own Free Tier account, and you know how to secure it with Multi-Factor Authentication and password policies. You also understand the AWS Free Tier and the different offerings under it.

Ideally, you will only be using Free Tier services for hands-on practice in AWS, and if you stick to these free offerings only, you will not be charged. In case you accidentally use a paid service or forget to delete a service that could be paid after a certain time, it is essential to set a budget and a billing alert, so that you get notification via email or SMS when you reach the set limit.

Interacting with AWS

In Chapter 1, you learned about the different cloud deployment models, which were IaaS, PaaS, and SaaS. But did you know that you can also use AWS services as any of these models? This section explains the different methods needed to interact with your AWS account and services.

So far, you have been interacting with AWS through the Management Console, which is a web interface. In addition to that, there are two other ways to interact with AWS:

- Using the AWS CLI (command-line interface). Basically, this is a tool that you install and configure on your computer that allows you to access the AWS services and automate them through your computer terminal scripts.

- Using the SDK (software development kit). This is used by programmers and developers to interact with AWS services directly from the application code.

If this all doesn't make complete sense, don't worry, I cover them both in detail.

The AWS Management Console

Let's start with the AWS Console again. It is a web interface for interacting with AWS services. Since it can be accessed through your web browser, it is the easiest way to manage resources on AWS. Just log in to your AWS account and do whatever you want.

What's more, a mobile version of the AWS Management Console is also available. You can install it on your phone and access almost all the AWS services from your phone. Isn't that great?!

Let's look at some advantages of using the AWS Management Console:

- It's excellent for beginners.

- It's easy to interact with AWS services.

- It provides a step-by-step user interface.

- It is great for performing administrative tasks.

- It is *not* suitable for automating tasks, as operations are performed manually.

If you are a beginner, the AWS Management Console is the right start, as you can very easily interact with AWS services. It's like navigating just another website, but as discussed, it's easier because of its very clean, step-by-step user interface. For all these reasons, the Management Console is the best choice for beginners.

Now, why only for beginners? That's because some operations in the AWS Console are manual and take time. Hence, it's not possible to automate everything through the Management Console, and that's why developers use a command-line interface (CLI). Let's look at it next.

AWS CLI

The AWS CLI (command-line interface) is a unified tool that lets you manage your AWS services. It allows you to manage your AWS services using your computer terminal. You can easily install this tool on your computer. It supports Windows, Mac, and Linux operating systems.

You can do everything that you can do with the AWS Management Console. For example, if you want to list all the users in your account, you simply open a terminal in your computer and type the following:

```
AWS list-users
```

This will show you a list of all available users in your account. To delete users, you can use this command:

```
aws delete-user --user-name UserName
```

This will delete that user from your account.

You can also combine these two commands to execute both tasks in one step. That's a significant advantage of using the AWS CLI over the Management Console. You can automate tasks in CLI.

Let's assume you have 50 users in your account and you want to delete users whose names start with M. In order to do this from the AWS Management Console, you would have to find each user and delete them one by one.

But that's not the case with CLI. You can write the script and use the two commands to perform the same task. This will be done quickly. Similarly, you can manage multiple AWS services using the same script.

To access AWS through CLI, you need to authenticate yourself just like in the AWS Management Console, but instead of using a username and password, you provide an access key and secret key.

The access key acts like the username and the secret key is your password. (If any of this sounds confusing, worry not, as you are going to learn how to install and configure the AWS CLI in the next section.)

Let's look at some advantages of using the AWS CLI:

- It is a great way to interact with AWS through a computer terminal.

- It is an excellent way to automate tasks and achieve Infrastructure as a Code.

Finally, there is the SDK.

The Software Development Kit (SDK)

This is also called a devkit, or a software development kit.

As the name suggests, it is a collection of tools and programs used by developers to develop a cloud-based application.

Although it might seem similar to using the AWS CLI, you *cannot* use the AWS SDK in your computer terminal. It is only used with or within your application code, which allows your application to interact with AWS services.

SDK supports many types of programming languages, including C++, Go, Java, JavaScript, .NET, Node.Js, PHP, Python, Ruby, and many others.

There are also mobile SDKs for Android and iOS. Let's look at this with an example. Assume that you are designing a mobile application that will allow people to share their photos. For that, you will be using Amazon S3 as the storage. Your application needs to interact with the AWS Amazon S3 Service, right?

It is not possible to use the AWS Management Console nor the AWS CLI in this scenario, because you want your application code to access AWS resources. Therefore, you need to use the AWS SDK. It will allow you to access and manage your AWS services through your application code.

You might already know about the advantages of using SDK. It is a perfect tool to interact with AWS through application code.

I hope you now understand all three methods of interacting with AWS.

Using the AWS Console

In the last section, you learned about different ways to interact with AWS services. This section dives deep into the AWS Management Console and explains the following:

- The different ways to access the AWS Management Console

- How to create an alias for an account

- How to select an AWS Region in an account

- How to navigate to various AWS services and their dashboards

Let's get right into it. First, you need to log in to get access to the AWS Management Console and the credentials you use determine what type of user you are. As of now, you are the *root user*, who is the owner of the account. This person has full access to all the resources and services within the account.

There are other types of users in your account, called *IAM users.* These users have limited access to resources and services.

Let's look at the difference between the root user and IAM users.

The root user is the user you created when you created the account. If you log in using root credentials, you will have full access to the account.

On the other hand, root users create IAM users. You will read more about them in the later chapter.

To log in to AWS as a root user, you need the email ID and password that you used and the MFA that you enabled. However, to log in as an IAM user, you need a username, a password, and either a 12-digit AWS account ID or an account alias. As you have neither, you can log in as the root user that you already created and create an account alias.

Go to the AWS sign-in[2] page. Enter the email ID and click Next. Then, you need to pass the security check by entering the correct CAPTCHA. Enter your password, then click Sign In. (see Figure 2-5).

Figure 2-5. *Signing in*

If you have configured MFA (see Figure 2-6), you have to enter a unique code in addition to your password to be able to log in.

---

[2] https://console.aws.amazon.com/console/home?nc2=h_ct&src=header-signin

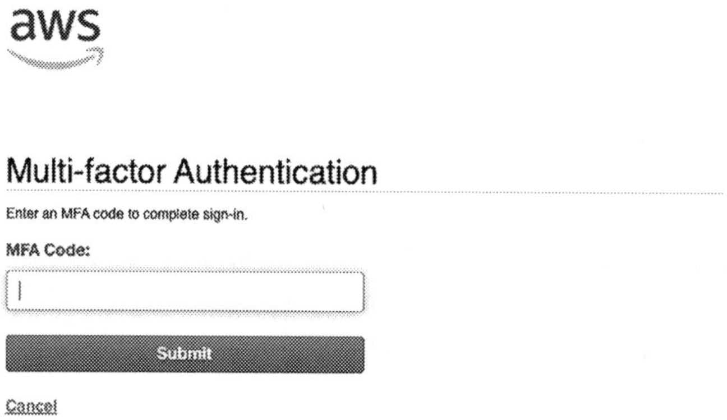

Figure 2-6. *Multi-Factor authentication in action*

Once you enter the correct MFA code, you will be logged in to the AWS Console.

Now that you are in the console, there are a few things you should quickly check. One of them is the Account. (see Figure 2-7). Here, you can see the account settings, which contains details of your account, like contact information and alternate contact for billing, operation, and security.

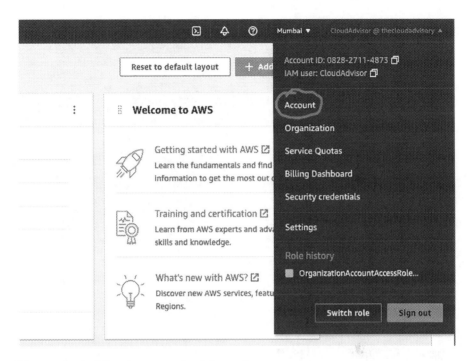

Figure 2-7. *The Account dashboard*

You can also check the billing dashboard. Click Billing Dashboard
(see Figure 2-8), and you will see the billing summary and other details,
including the bill for the current month, previous bills, and budget control.

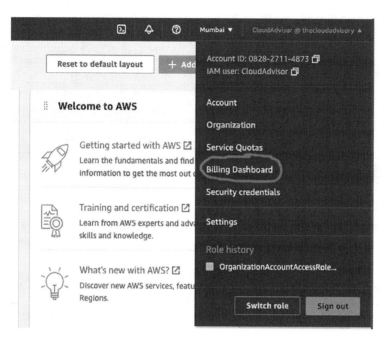

Figure 2-8. *The Billing dashboard*

I recommend regularly checking this page to see if you have any unwanted bills. Now let's go back and create an account alias.

Creating an Account Alias

Type IAM in the search box and click IAM (see Figure 2-9).

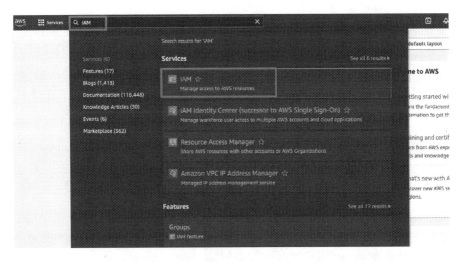

Figure 2-9. *The IAM dashboard*

Figure 2-9 shows the Identity and Access Management service dashboard. As you can see on the right side, you have an account ID and the account alias. Note that the account alias is the same as the account ID (see Figure 2-10).

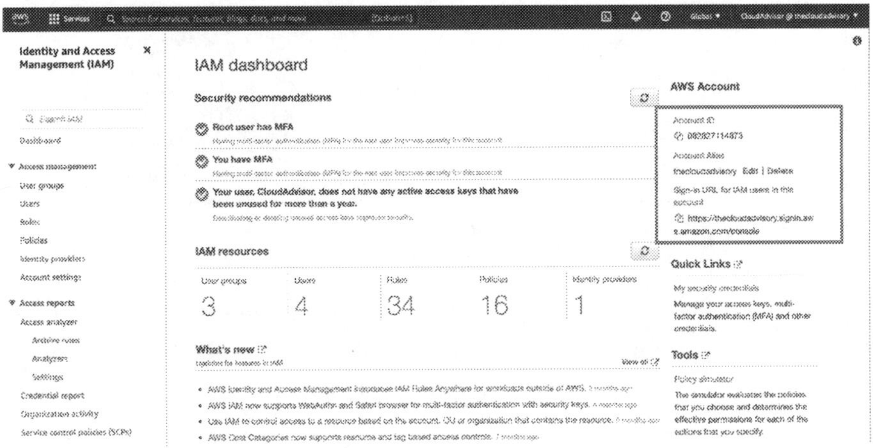

Figure 2-10. *Account ID*

53

This is the 12-digit account ID. Remembering it might be a challenge, so you can create an alias that's much easier to remember. For that, click Create, add your ID, *"something you like,"* and then choose Save Changes. That will create an alias for you. You can use this ID or alias every time you log in using the IAM user.

Now go back to home page again. To do that, simply click the AWS logo.

AWS Region

We have another drop-down for selecting the AWS Region. Let's select a region for your account (see Figure 2-11).

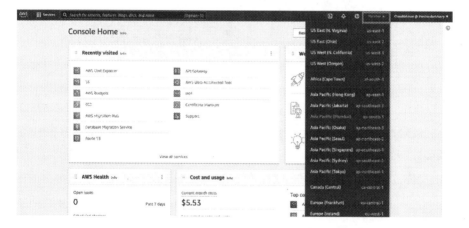

Figure 2-11. *Selecting a AWS Region*

Figure 2-11 shows that you are currently in Mumbai, and ap-south-1 is the region code. Each region has a specific code, and you use this code when using the AWS CLI and SDK. You will learn more about this in the upcoming sections.

This is discussed in detail in the section entitled "The AWS Global Infrastructure" later in this chapter, and you can see that there are many regions and supported regions in AWS.

When logging in to the AWS Management Console, select an AWS Region to create services in a specific region. This is the first thing you do when you create any new service, except a few that are not region-sensitive. It is crucial to decide and select the region where you want to create your AWS services.

An important tip: If you create some AWS resources and you don't see those resources in the console, that means you created them in a different region and you will have to switch to their region to see them.

Let's move forward and see how to navigate to AWS services.

Search AWS Services

The AWS Management Console provides multiple ways for navigating to individual service dashboards.

In the search box on the navigation bar, enter the name of the service. You will see the results; simply choose the service you want from the search results list.

Figure 2-12. *IAM*

For example, to go to the IAM service (see Figure 2-12), you simply type that in, and you will get a list of all the services that include IAM. If you click IAM, it will take you to the dashboard. You can go back to the home page by clicking the AWS logo.

Next, choose Services to open a full list of services (see Figure 2-13). The services are listed by category. Select the service that you want.

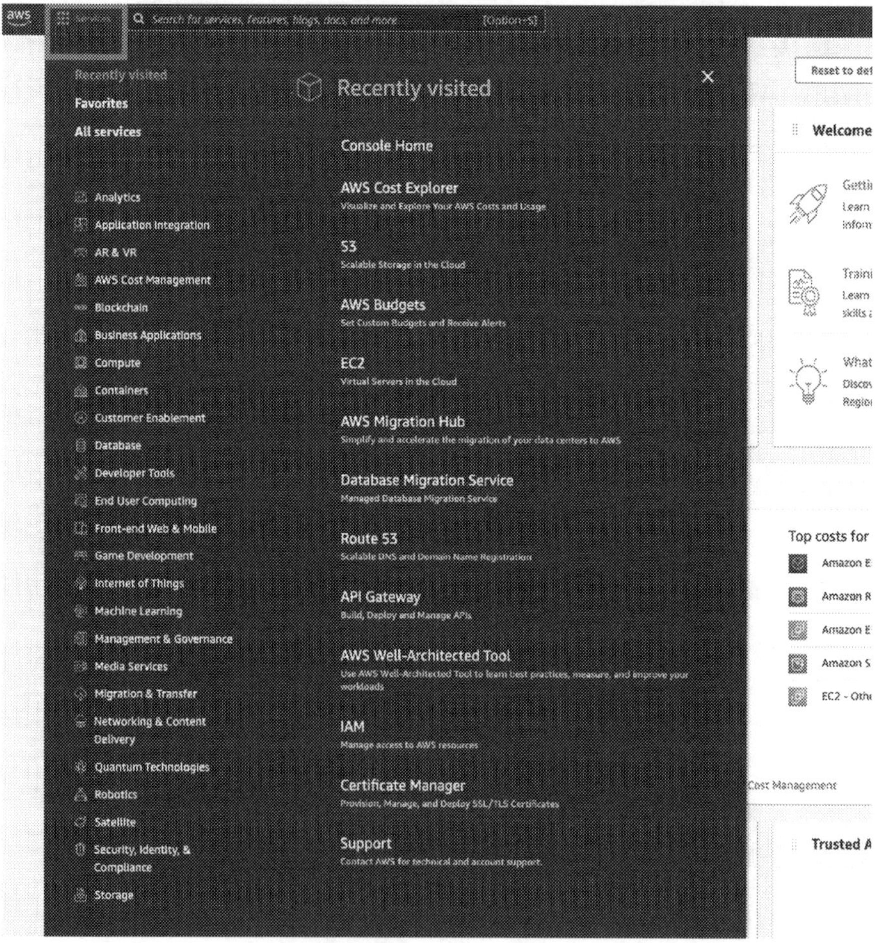

Figure 2-13. *AWS services (Find AWS Services)*

For example, scroll down and select the Storage category, which includes AWS Backup, EFS, S3, and many more. I cover those services in later chapters. This gives you a high-level way of looking at the services based on their categories.

Next is the Recently Visited tab. Go to home page again, by clicking the AWS logo. You can then see the recent services (see Figure 2-14) I have visited within the console, including S3, EC2, and AWS Cost Explorer.

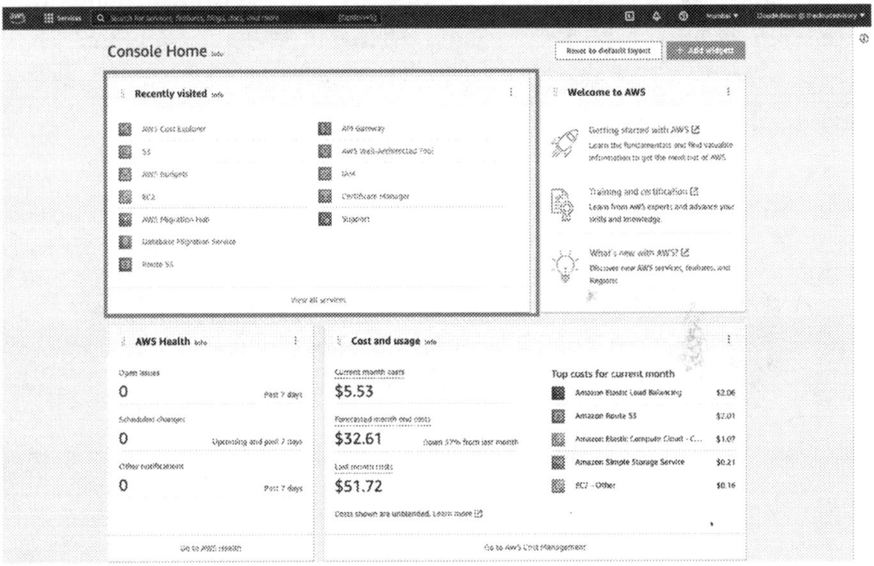

Figure 2-14. *Recent used services*

These are the services that I recently worked with.

If you work with only a handful of services, this can be a very quick way to access the specific dashboards.

Installing the AWS CLI

In this section, you learn how to install the AWS CLI on your system.

Since I have a Mac, I use Mac installation instructions; however, the process remains the same for other operating systems, including Windows and Linux.

Go to the browser and find the installation documentation. In the search bar, type **Install AWS CLI on Mac** (see Figure 2-15). You can also search for your operating system, such as "Install AWS CLI on Linux" or "Install AWS CLI on Windows". I will open the first link, "Installing and Updating the Latest Version of AWS CLI."

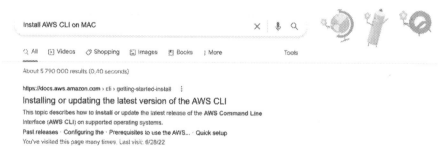

Figure 2-15. *Searching the AWS CLI*

This page has installation instructions for all three operating systems—Linux, macOS, and Windows (see Figure 2-16).

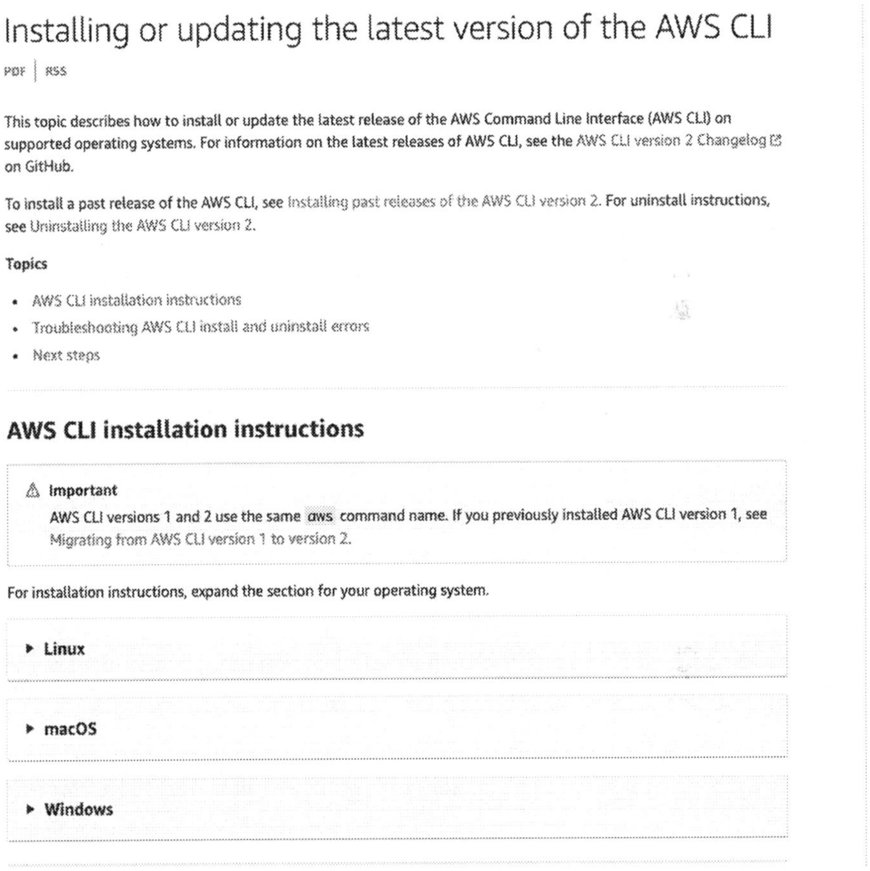

Installing or updating the latest version of the AWS CLI

PDF | RSS

This topic describes how to install or update the latest release of the AWS Command Line Interface (AWS CLI) on supported operating systems. For information on the latest releases of AWS CLI, see the AWS CLI version 2 Changelog ☒ on GitHub.

To install a past release of the AWS CLI, see Installing past releases of the AWS CLI version 2. For uninstall instructions, see Uninstalling the AWS CLI version 2.

Topics

- AWS CLI installation instructions
- Troubleshooting AWS CLI install and uninstall errors
- Next steps

AWS CLI installation instructions

⚠ **Important**

AWS CLI versions 1 and 2 use the same `aws` command name. If you previously installed AWS CLI version 1, see Migrating from AWS CLI version 1 to version 2.

For installation instructions, expand the section for your operating system.

▸ **Linux**

▸ **macOS**

▸ **Windows**

Figure 2-16. *The AWS CLI installation instructions*

I will follow this process for macOS. First download the `.pkg` file. Once it's downloaded, open it and click Continue, Continue, Continue, and Agree. You will then be asked for permission to install for all users "on this computer." Click Continue and then click Install. The CLI will be installed on your system.

Wait for everything to complete. The system writes the files. Eventually, you should see that the installation is successful. Once you are done with the installer, move it to the trash.

To verify the installation, open a terminal, go to the Search option, type **terminal**, and then add this:

```
aws -- version
```

If you have a running CLI on your system, it should return the version of the AWS executable. In this case, AWS CLI 2.4.28 is installed (see Figure 2-17). It shows that everything has been installed correctly.

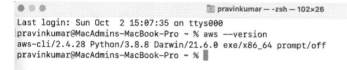

```
Last login: Sun Oct  2 15:07:35 on ttys000
pravinkumar@MacAdmins-MacBook-Pro ~ % aws --version
aws-cli/2.4.28 Python/3.8.8 Darwin/21.6.0 exe/x86_64 prompt/off
pravinkumar@MacAdmins-MacBook-Pro ~ %
```

Figure 2-17. *The AWS CLI version is displayed*

Download the CLI on your system, as you will be using it in future lessons. If you have any issues, have a look at the above mentioned AWS documentation.

The next section explains how to interact with AWS services using the CLI.

Using the AWS CLI

You will continue learning how to interact with AWS services by using the AWS CLI.

Let's get started. Open the terminal on your laptop. First of all, make sure you have installed the AWS CLI. You can check by typing the following command on your terminal:

```
aws --version
```

You should get the version of the AWS CLI. Second, it is necessary to authenticate the AWS CLI to access AWS services, and as discussed, the AWS CLI uses access keys for authentication. (I cover authorization and authentication in detail in Chapter 3.) For this demo, you need to create an access key in the AWS Management Console. Click Account, then choose Security Credentials. (see Figure 2-18).

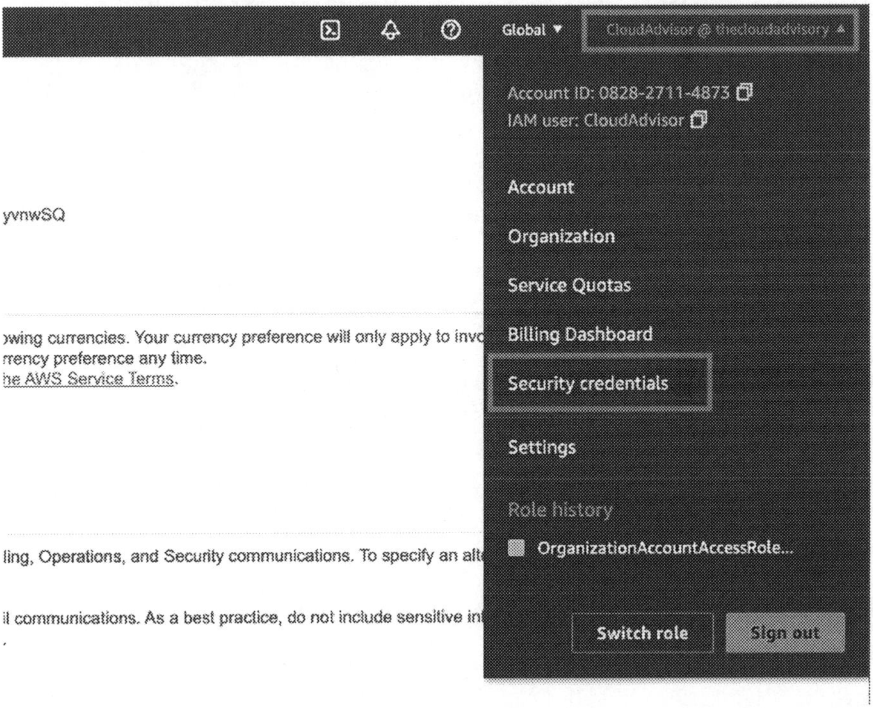

Figure 2-18. *AWS Security Credentials*

Once you are in My Security Credentials, expand the Access Key. You can create new access keys, which are critical since they govern authentication and authorization when using the CLI and SDK to access AWS.

As a note, you will be creating access keys here. However, I am going to delete these keys immediately after this demo. You should also not use root user access keys on a day-to-day basis and delete these as well. This is not a good practice.

For now, click Create New Access Key and then choose Show Access Key.

You have both the access key and secret access key (see Figure 2-19). This is what you will use to access your AWS resources through the CLI. Copy both the keys to a text file. You can download them as well by clicking Download and then Allow.

Figure 2-19. *Creating an access key*

Now go back to the AWS CLI and type the following in the terminal:

```
aws configure
```

Enter the secret access key first, followed by the secret access key. Now enter the default region name, and in this case, choose the ap-south-1 one. See Figure 2-20.

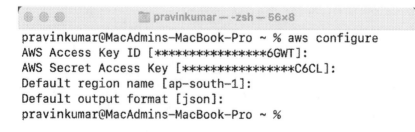

Figure 2-20. *Configure the AWS CLI*

62

Now choose the default output format. In this case, choose the JSON format. Once you have all of that in place, press Enter. You have successfully configured the AWS CLI, which means you should be able to run it and get information about the AWS resources.

Let's quickly check it by running a command that will list the S3 buckets. Type the following:

```
aws s3 list
```

This will return a list of all of the different S3 buckets that you created in this account. If you don't have any buckets, it will not return anything.

To quickly review what you've done in this lesson, you created root user access keys, ignoring for now the caution that you should not generally create access keys for the root user. Still, you created one for this demo. As long as you delete them, it should be fine. Go ahead and delete the keys now. Finally, you accessed the S3 to verify that you could access the AWS resources.

The AWS Global Infrastructure

This section covers the AWS global infrastructure, which includes AWS Regions, Availability Zones, and Edge Locations.

After completing this topic, you will have an understanding of the AWS Regions, Edge Locations, and their global infrastructure. Ensure that you follow the lessons and practice in your account.

AWS Regions and Availability Zones

In this section, you learn about

- AWS Regions

- Different Availability Zones

- The importance of regions and Availability Zones

Suppose you want to host a web application. For that, you need your own data center, right? Now that you know about AWS and other cloud services, you don't need to set up a data center and can easily host your application in the AWS cloud.

Let's assume that you are still using an on-premise data center. What if a disaster hits your data center? That's a valid question, right? Anything can happen, and since you own and manage the data center, you have to figure out what you will do in such extreme situations. One way to avoid a complete shutdown of your application is by running a second data center at some other location. When one goes down, the other will be there as a backup. But maintaining another data center is double the hardware and maintenance costs.

Don't worry, that was just an example and AWS has a better solution— AWS Regions.

An AWS Region is nothing but the geographic location worldwide where different data centers are clustered. That means AWS maintains multiple data centers in one place.

According to AWS standards, there must be at least two data centers in one region and each data center should have redundant electricity, cooling, heating, networking, and connectivity.

Once again, all these regions are connected through the AWS backbone network, which is basically a very high-speed network. Each of these regions has different names and codes. These names are based on their worldwide geographical location.

Geographic location refers to the physical location, like Mumbai, Tokyo, Frankfurt, North America, China, South America, and the Middle East.

These are some examples:

- Mumbai -> `ap-south-1`

  - Mumbai is a physical location. They call it Mumbai Region and it has the `ap-south-1` code. The same goes for Singapore and other locations.

- Singapore -> `ap-southeast-1`

- Sidney -> `ap-southeast-2`

- Cape Town -> `af-south-1`

When you have an AWS account, you can choose in which region you want to deploy your AWS services, whether you want to launch it in Mumbai or in Tokyo. This also depends on different factors that I will talk about going forward.

In simple words, you can say that AWS is a cloud service provider, and it has data centers around the world.

As of now, there are 27 geographic regions with 87 Availability Zones across the world. AWS keeps adding new regions. By the time you are reading this chapter, these numbers may have changed, so you can look at the link[3] provided in the resources section under this topic to check the latest number of AWS Regions. Let's move forward and talk about Availability Zones.

What Are Availability Zones?

Availability Zones are one or more individually separated and distinct data centers with redundant power, networking, and connectivity in an AWS Region.[4]

---

[3] `https://aws.amazon.com/about-aws/global-infrastructure/`

[4] `https://aws.amazon.com/about-aws/global-infrastructure/`

In other words, they are nothing but an isolated data center within a region. The only difference is that they have redundant power, networking, and connectivity. Each Availability Zone (AZ) has a set of data centers isolated from other AZs. An Availability Zone (AZ) is nothing but a group of data centers. As per the AWS Standard, an AWS Region must have two Availability Zones.

Take the example of the Mumbai region, which has three Availability Zones. As you saw earlier, every region had specific code. Similarly, the Availability Zones also have corresponding code, which consists of a region code followed by an alphabetic descriptor.

The Mumbai region code is `ap-south-1`.

Availability Zone 1 use the code `ap-south-1a`. Similarly, Availability Zone code 2 is `ap-south-1b` and the third Availability Zone has the code `ap-south-1c`. I hope it's now clear that the region code followed by an alphabetic descriptor is the Availability Zone code.

Every AWS Region has two or more Availability Zones. Mumbai has three Availability Zones, North Virginia has six Availability Zones, and so on.

Why these Availability Zones are important? So, you know that one region has multiple Availability Zones. The Availability Zones are not single data centers, but instead consist of clusters of data centers.

Some Availability Zones have two data centers while others have three or more. All these Availability Zones are located somewhere between 50 to 100 km (30 to 60 miles) apart.

Suppose one of them goes down; the entire cluster of data centers would also go down. However, data centers in other Availability Zones will continue working. Hence, you will not face a complete shutdown of your application or website.

AWS infrastructure is designed to ensure the high availability of the applications. If you wonder how this matters to you, let me tell you.

Suppose you want to deploy your application in the Mumbai Region, and as you know, the Mumbai region has three Availability Zones. The first thing you would do is launch a server in any of the zones as per your requirement.

Once the server is launched, you can access it over the Internet. You don't need to worry about in which Availability Zone you have launched your server as long as you can access it over the Internet.

But suppose the Availability Zone in which you launched your server goes down completely. That means your application will also be down. But that's not it; you also will not be able to access your application data. And if you don't have that data, you won't be able to revive your application. To avoid such situations, AWS uses Availability Zones.

Let's take a look at the advantages of Availability Zones. The first benefit is the *higher availability.*

When you design your applications, you make sure that you put all your servers and databases in multiple Availability Zones. That way, if one goes down, you have another zone to cover.

Second, if you remember, we talked about the distance between two zones being somewhere between 50-100 km (30 to 60 miles). Suppose you set up a primary database in one zone. You can have the replica of this database in the secondary zones. It is also possible to have synchronous replication between two databases; this will copy all your data in both the databases simultaneously.

If one zone goes down, you have another one to operate normally, which is called *fault tolerance*. Note that this is not a default design by AWS; you have to architect your applications in multiple Availability Zones to achieve high availability and fault tolerance. I hope the Availability Zone idea is clear to you now.

Now you'll look at scenarios in which you will learn how to use Availability Zones to make your applications highly available.

Suppose in an AWS Region, you have two Availability Zones, called AZ-1 and AZ-2.

The first thing you do is launch an EC2 server and a corresponding database in AZ-1. Similarly, you could launch another web server and corresponding database in AZ-2.

Your application and database both are highly available, and they can sustain if one zone goes down.

In a nutshell, the AWS Region is the geographic location across the globe, and the Availability Zone is the cluster of data centers in a particular region.

So, why is there a need for so many regions today?

Of course, this gives you the flexibility to deploy your application in any AWS Region that is beneficial to you. Other than that, consider these reasons:

- The main reason is the *low latency* access to applications. If your user base is in the United States, deploying your application in the United States only makes sense. Similarly, if you have your user base in India, you will choose the Mumbai region.

- The second reason is *regulatory compliance.* Different countries have different rules for regulating the data; therefore, having multiple region gives you the liberty to choose what works best for you.

- The third reason is to sustain *any types of disaster.* All these AWS Regions are across the globe and the minimum distance between any two regions should be 300 km, which we call the disaster recovery site. This is to make sure that your application runs in one of the sites, and the other site should be at least 300 km apart to ensure they are not a part of the same system. Hence, you can also leverage the benefit of multiple regions.

Apart from the latency requirement, regulatory compliance, and disaster recovery, there are some additional considerations that you can also look at when using multiple regions.

For example, for the global applications, organizations want to provide the best user experience to their users across the globe. One way to achieve that is by deploying your application in the regions closer to your audience. For example, a United States based application uses the Mumbai Region to provide the Indian user a better experience.

Cost is another benefit of using multiple regions. Since every country has a different economy, the pricing of using AWS varies from country to country. Therefore, you get cheaper services in some countries and, as an organization, that's a great way to save money.

Next, you have a *reduced blast radius*. Many people and organizations want that in case a region goes down. They may want to leverage another region as disaster recovery. Many times, they also distribute their workloads across the regions. In case something happens to one region, another region is active and that's how they reduce the blast radius of the disaster.

That was all about the AWS Regions and Availability Zones. Make sure that you understand everything well, as they are important from an interview point of view.

AWS Edge Locations

In the last section, you learned about the AWS Regions and Availability Zones. In this section, you learn about another important aspect of the Amazon Global Infrastructure, which is the Edge Location.

Let's start with an understanding of the AWS Region and how to choose a region for your application.

There are many factors behind choosing an AWS Region, but the primary criteria is the distance to your target customers. Always choose a region that is nearest to your target customers. But what if you have customers worldwide?

Let's assume you have a video-streaming application on which users can publish the time-lapse of the Indian landscape. You hosted your application and its data in the Mumbai Region, since your customers are from India. But after a few months, you see a good amount of traffic coming from Japan.

As of now, you are serving all the Japanese customer requests from the Mumbai Region only. But due to the large distance between India and Japan, your Japanese users may not have a good user experience because of low latency issues.

You can properly roll out your application in Japan, by copying your data in a cloud region in Japan, which is Tokyo in the case of AWS. That's how you can serve your customers there. This is an example of *caching*.

By definition, caching is keeping a copy of data in a temporary or cache location. In this way, the data can be accessed more quickly when needed.

In this case, you can cache your data in the Tokyo data center and provide a smooth user experience to your Japanese customers.

Another concept that you need to understand is the Content Delivery Network, commonly known as a CDN. It is nothing but a technical term for caching copies of data in a data center closer to the customers. Note that CDN is not an AWS-specific term.

Content Delivery Networks (CDNs) are used to cache content (such as images, videos, and websites) on proxy servers that are closer to end users than the origin servers, thus allowing the content to be accessed faster.

Again, these proxy servers reside in data center, and these data centers are called *Edge Locations*.

What is the difference between regions and Edge Locations, as both are data centers? Consider this:

- Edge Locations are smaller data centers, and they are available across all big cities in the world. If you compare, the total number of Edge Location is more than 12 times of number of regions. You have more options to cache your data and serve it quickly to your customers.

- Edge Locations are separate from regions and are located at other locations. This allows you to push your content from a region to Edge Locations in different parts of the world.

- An AWS Edge Location hosts a special service to deliver this content faster, which is called Amazon CloudFront. Whereas an AWS Region hosts almost all AWS services. Other than CloudFront, AWS Edge Locations also operate a DNS service called Route 53. I cover CloudFront and Route 53 in a later chapter.

Alright, there is so much more than this about Amazon Web Services' global infrastructure, so let's keep things simple and take a quick look at the key points about the AWS global infrastructure:

- An Amazon Web Services (AWS) Region is a geographically isolated location, from which you can access the AWS services required to run the application.

- Regions consist of Availability Zones, which are physically separated buildings with their power, heating, cooling, and networks. By utilizing Availability Zones, you can minimize the amount of effort you need to expend in solving high-availability and disaster recovery scenarios.

- Amazon CloudFront is available at AWS Edge Locations to help deliver content to your customers no matter where they are in the world.

Summary

In this chapter, you learned about the different ways to interact with AWS services. AWS can be used through the Management Console, which is a web interface. It is an easy way to manage your services. You also learned about two more ways to interact with AWS: using the AWS CLI (the command-line interface) and using the SDK (the software development tool).

The AWS Console will likely be the primary method for interacting with the platform for first-time users and beginners.

This topic was full of hands-on example to ensure that you get practical experience as much as possible and simplify learning by doing.

It might be helpful for you to revisit this chapter if there is any confusion or you need more clarity on any specific section.

CHAPTER 3

AWS Identity and Access Management

This chapter covers how identity and access management (IAM) works, focusing on users, groups, and roles in IAM with a hands-on lab. You'll also learn about the IAM policy and other types of policies and review some IAM best practices.

What Is Identity and Access Management?

Do you know why educational institutions provide students with ID cards? Because an institution's ID cards give them control over who can access their facilities. This ID card acts as proof of identity. Similarly, AWS has a service that helps companies manage their identity in the cloud. The IAM framework ensures that the right people in your organization can access only the services they need to do their jobs.

Remember, it is not good practice to use your root account for everything you and your team do, as it could lead to some serious security issues. Let's consider an analogy here.

Suppose you are working in an organization, and every day when you enter the main entrance, you have to show your ID card to the security guard, or you need to swipe your login card. In this way, your organization ensures that you are the right person who can access the organization's premises. This is exactly how IAM works. When you show your ID card, you prove that you are the right person. As a person, you are an IDENTITY.

Now, when you show your ID card to the security guard, they look at the photo and your face and verify that they match. Once you're verified successfully, you get ACCESS.

Through this whole process, you as a PERSON gets ACCESS to the right premises. That's not it; this ID card serves as proof to access a lot of other services and facilities in your organization. For instance, some people can only use the account section, while others can only use Human Resources, and so on. There is a well-defined system of who can use what. In the same way, IAM is an AWS service that makes sure that the right person has access to the right resource.

AWS IAM provides access control across all of its services and resources. It is possible to specify who can access which services and resources, and under which conditions. There is also the concept of the IAM policy, which you can use to manage permissions to your workforce and systems to ensure least-privilege permissions.

If this does not yet make sense, don't worry. This chapter covers these issues in more detail. For now, let's look at three important concepts of Identity and Access Management:

- Identification

- Authorization

- Authentication

These three terms are closely related, but they are not the same. Let's look at each.

Identification

Identification is the ability to identify a user uniquely. It defines how a person or system can be identified. In the last example, you identified yourself with an ID card. That varies from system to system.

When you log in to your bank account, you use a username and password. You identify yourself to the bank portal with your username and password. In other words, your identification is your username and password. Identification basically is the process of identifying every unique user who is accessing your services or facilities.

The second concept is *authentication*.

Authentication

Authentication is the process of recognizing a user's identity. When you show your ID card to the security guard, they compare your photo to your face. That's authentication.

When you log in to your bank account, you provide your username and password. The banking backend system matches your username and password with the username and password stored in their system. The system makes sure you are providing the right username and password. If you know the correct username and password, you are the owner of the account.

If you have been given a unique identity, there has to be a system to recognize it every time you use your unique identity. That process of recognizing the authenticity of your identity is known as *authentication*.

Authorization

Finally, *authorization* is the process of giving someone permission to access something. Once you are authorized, you can enter the premises and go to your office. But you can't go to the canteen kitchen, because you are not allowed (or we can say you are not *authorized* to access the canteen kitchen area, based on your job function).

75

Next, let's look at Identity and Access Management with respect to AWS.

A Closer Look at AWS Identity and Access Management (AWS IAM)

AWS IAM is an AWS service that helps an organization manage access of their AWS accounts and services. It provides fine-grained access control across all AWS services, meaning you can specify who can access which services and resources and under which conditions.

If you want person X to only access the AWS EC2 service and person Y to only access the S3 service, that's completely possible. This is achieved with an IAM policy. You are going to learn about IAM policies later in this chapter.

IAM Users, Groups, and Roles

This section, covers the elements of IAM, which include:

- – Users

- – Groups

- – Roles

Let's start with users. A *user* is a person who utilizes an AWS service in an AWS account. As discussed in the previous chapter, AWS has two types of users: the root user and an IAM user.

Root User[1]

The root user name itself gives a you clue that this is the special user. It is created when the AWS account was created.

When you create an AWS account, AWS will create one identity (user) for you. That identity (user) is called the AWS root user. This user has access to all AWS services and resources in the account. Some important points about AWS root users include:

- To log in as the root user, use the email address and password you created when creating the account.

- AWS's root user has full access to all of the account's resources and services.

- It is not good practice to use the root user for everyday tasks, and you should never ever share the root user credentials with anyone. Only a very few reliable people should have the root credentials.

IAM User[2]

Now that you know that you can't use the root user for your day-to-day job, that's where the IAM user comes into the picture.

The IAM user is an entity that you (the root user) create in an AWS account to represent the user who interacts with AWS resources in your account.

Now, let's look at this with an example. Let's say you are the team leader in an organization, and you have an AWS account. You have two developers—Ram and Shyam—and two administrators—Sita and Gita—on your team. Your team needs access to an AWS account to host an application.

---

[1] https://docs.aws.amazon.com/IAM/latest/UserGuide/id_root-user.html
[2] https://docs.aws.amazon.com/IAM/latest/UserGuide/id_root-user.html

Because you don't want to give them access to your root account, you can create IAM users for your team members and provide them with the access to the services that they need. Each team member represents one IAM user, as each team member needs to interact with an AWS account to do their job. So, you need to create four IAM users for Ram, Sita, Shyam, and Gita.

Now that you understand the IAM user, let's look at the way IAM user works and how to assign permissions to different IAM users.

When you create a user, the user has a username, password, and access keys that you share with the person to access the AWS account.

The username and password will be used to access the AWS Management Console and access key for programmatic access with the AWS CLI.

Every user has been added to the same AWS account. Users have their own credentials to access AWS accounts. The important question is what kind of AWS resources they can use.

New IAM users do not have default permission to access your AWS resources. To provide your IAM users with the necessary permissions, you need to give them these permissions. You can do this by adding IAM policies to each IAM user.

An IAM policy defines the permissions that are given to any user interacting with an AWS account. IAM policies are covered in the next section.

In a nutshell, you create IAM users and attach policies to provide permissions, and the users can use these credentials to access these resources. An important point here to note is that IAM users don't have to represent an actual person. This could be an application. Let's say you have an application on-premises that needs to access an AWS service. You can configure the access key inside the application to access AWS services. That is another important use of the access key.

Okay, let's now look at IAM groups.

IAM Groups

As the name implies, an IAM group is a collection of users and permissions assigned to those users.

Let's go back to the same example. On your team, you have two developers (Ram, Shyam) and two administrators (Sita, Gita). Both developers will be accessing the same AWS services and the same goes for the administrators.

Instead of assigning permissions to individual users, you can group these users and assign permissions to that group at once. In this case, you can create two groups. A group called Developers and a group called Administrators. IAM groups provide an easy way to manage permissions for users according to their job functions.

When you create a user, you assign a policy to the individual user. But in the case of a group. You add a policy to the group and the permissions will apply to all users in that group. Let's look at another good use case for an IAM group.

As you know, every user in a specific group has the permissions defined for that group. Adding a new user to the administrator user group can assign them administrator privileges once they join your organization. Similarly, you can remove an existing employee from the old user groups and add them to the appropriate new user groups if he or she is moving to a new project or role in the same organization.

In other words, the IAM group lets you attach policies to multiple users at once. Whenever you attach a policy to a user group, all members of the group receive the policy's permissions.

Now let's look at IAM roles.

IAM Role[3]

An IAM role is an IAM identity that you can create in your account that has specific permissions.

Similar to IAM users, IAM roles are attached to an IAM policy defining what they are allowed to do. You must be thinking, what is the difference between an IAM role and a user?

An IAM user is a unique person who has a username, password, and access key with the permissions attached to it. However, IAM roles don't require a username, password, or access key. The IAM role can't be directly linked to a person or a service. Instead, it can be assumed by a person or resource for a definite session. What does that mean?

Let's say your application runs on an EC2 instance and an EC2 instance needs to access an image from S3. In this case, EC2 assumes the role. Based on the policy, it will access images from S3 (see Figure 3-1). As mentioned, roles don't have any access keys or credentials associated with them. The credentials are temporary and dynamically assigned by AWS. AWS gives the temporary credential to the role to complete the task, when it is needed.

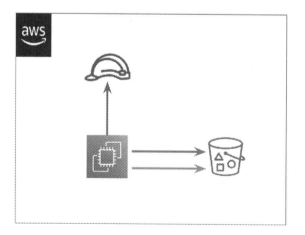

Figure 3-1. *The IAM policy to access AWS S3*

---

[3] https://docs.aws.amazon.com/IAM/latest/UserGuide/id_roles.html

Creating an IAM User, Group, and Role

In this section, you learn how to create IAM users and groups. By the end of this lab, you will be able to create these IAM entities and comfortably navigate through the AWS IAM Console. Let's get started.

Creating Users

Let's start by creating two users, named Ram and Shyam. In this example, Ram is a developer and Shyam is an AWS administrator.

1. You can navigate to the Users page by clicking the User option in the IAM dashboard. This shows the Users page, where you will see all the users created for your account (see Figure 3-2).

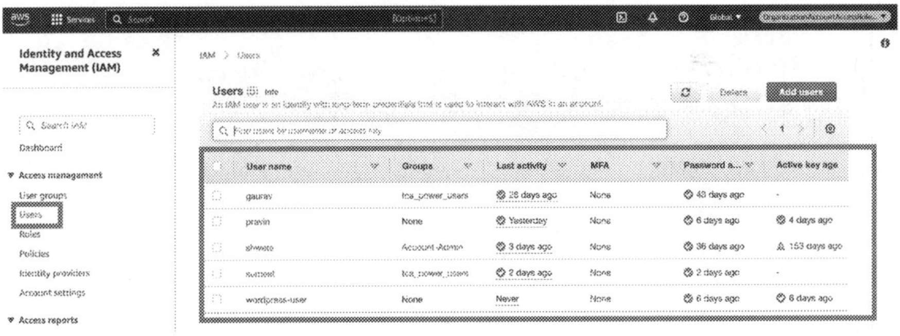

Figure 3-2. *The Users page*

2. Now create your first AWS user by clicking the Add Users button. Start by giving a username to your user. Call this user **Ram** (see Figure 3-3). When creating more than one user with the same properties, you can simply add another username by clicking the Add Another User button. However, in this example, you will add users one by one.

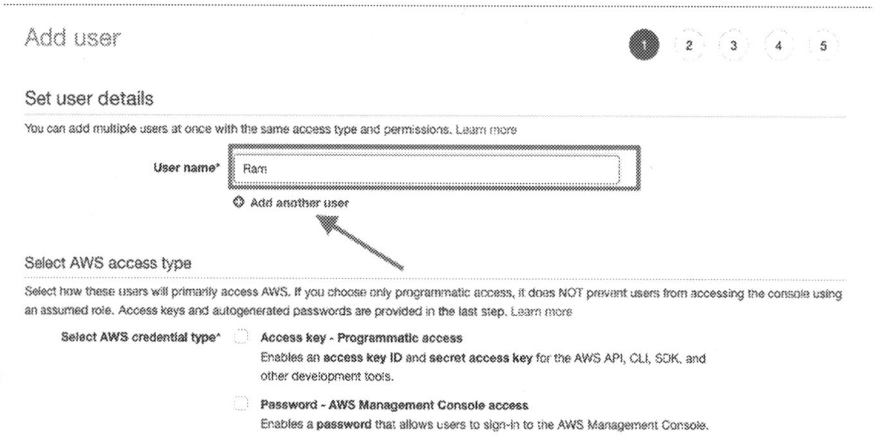

Add user

Set user details

You can add multiple users at once with the same access type and permissions. Learn more

User name*   Ram

⊕ Add another user

Select AWS access type

Select how these users will primarily access AWS. If you choose only programmatic access, it does NOT prevent users from accessing the console using an assumed role. Access keys and autogenerated passwords are provided in the last step. Learn more

Select AWS credential type*   ☐   **Access key - Programmatic access**
Enables an **access key ID** and **secret access key** for the AWS API, CLI, SDK, and other development tools.

☐   **Password - AWS Management Console access**
Enables a **password** that allows users to sign-in to the AWS Management Console.

Figure 3-3. *User called Ram*

3.   The next option is AWS Credential Type. You should select Access Key - Programmatic Access to allow this user to access the AWS CLI commands or use the AWS SDK and the AWS API. You do not need this for this example, so select only the Password - AWS Management Console Access option (see Figure 3-4), which will give Ram access to the AWS via the Management Console.

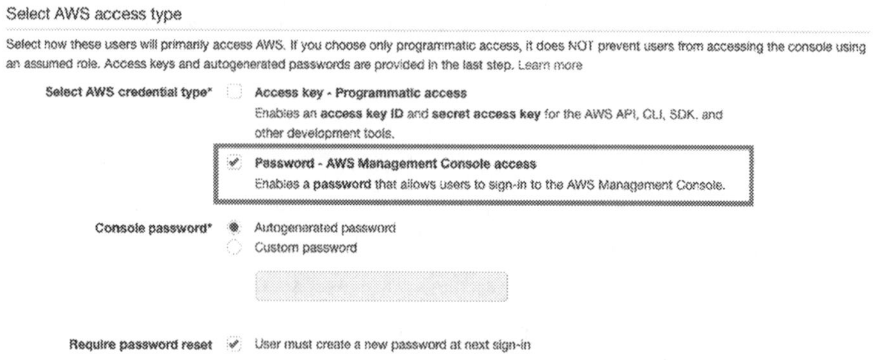

Select AWS access type

Select how these users will primarily access AWS. If you choose only programmatic access, it does NOT prevent users from accessing the console using an assumed role. Access keys and autogenerated passwords are provided in the last step. Learn more

Select AWS credential type*   ☐   **Access key - Programmatic access**
Enables an **access key ID** and **secret access key** for the AWS API, CLI, SDK, and other development tools.

☑   **Password - AWS Management Console access**
Enables a **password** that allows users to sign-in to the AWS Management Console.

Console password*   ● Autogenerated password
○ Custom password

Require password reset   ☑ User must create a new password at next sign-in

Figure 3-4. *AWS access*

4. Selecting this provides more options. You can
    have AWS create an auto-generated password
    (see Figure 3-5) or you can manually add a simple
    password for this user. For this example, let AWS
    provide an auto-generated password.

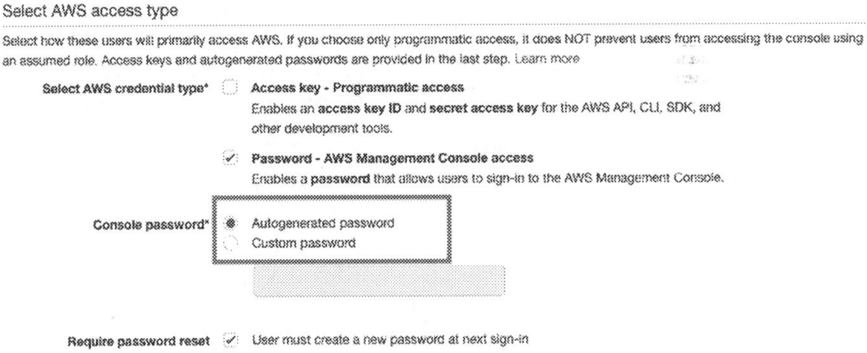

Figure 3-5. *Password creation*

5. The next option is Require Password Reset (see
    Figure 3-6). You should check this box if you want
    your users to reset their passwords when they
    first access the console. Uncheck this option for
    this demo.

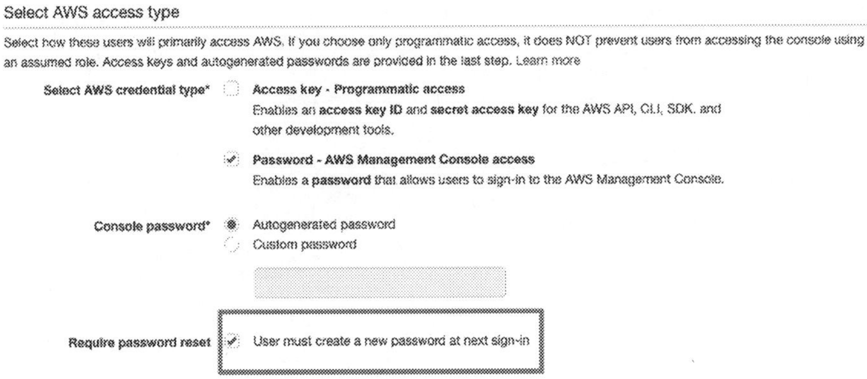

Figure 3-6. *Password reset*

6. Click Next: Permissions. Here, you have three options:

- You can add users to a user group.

- You can copy permissions from an existing user that you already have in your account.

- You can attach policies directly.

There are no users or user groups in this account, so you have no options. But if you click the third option, Attach Existing Policies Directly (see Figure 3-7), you will see a list of policies, even if you have never created a policy in your account.

▾ Set permissions

Add user to group	Copy permissions from existing user	Attach existing policies directly

Create policy   ⟳

Filter policies ∨	Q Search		Showing 824 results
Policy name ▾		**Type**	**Used as**
▸ ☷ AdministratorAccess		Job function	Permissions policy (7)
▸ ☷ AdministratorAccess-Amplify		AWS managed	None
▸ ☷ AdministratorAccess-AWSElasticBeanstalk		AWS managed	None
▸ ☷ AlexaForBusinessDeviceSetup		AWS managed	None
▸ ☷ AlexaForBusinessFullAccess		AWS managed	None
▸ ☷ AlexaForBusinessGatewayExecution		AWS managed	None
▸ ☷ AlexaForBusinessLifesizeDelegatedAccessPolicy		AWS managed	None
▸ ☷ AlexaForBusinessPolyDelegatedAccessPolicy		AWS managed	None
▸ ☷ AlexaForBusinessReadOnlyAccess		AWS managed	None
▸ ☷ AmazonAPIGatewayAdministrator		AWS managed	None
▸ ☷ AmazonAPIGatewayInvokeFullAccess		AWS managed	None
▸ ☷ AmazonAPIGatewayPushToCloudWatchLogs		AWS managed	None
▸ ☷ AmazonAppFlowFullAccess		AWS managed	None
▸ ☷ AmazonAppFlowReadOnlyAccess		AWS managed	None

Cancel   Previous   Next: Tags

Figure 3-7. *Policy list*

7. These are the AWS Managed policies, which
    means that these policies are managed by AWS
    and that if any change is required, it will be
    made by AWS. These are highly useful for simple
    applications where you don't want to create and
    maintain your own policies and let AWS handle
    all this for you. Select a policy here, such as
    AmazonS3ReadOnlyAccess (see Figure 3-8) and give
    this permission to your user. Let's first create a user
    with no permissions.

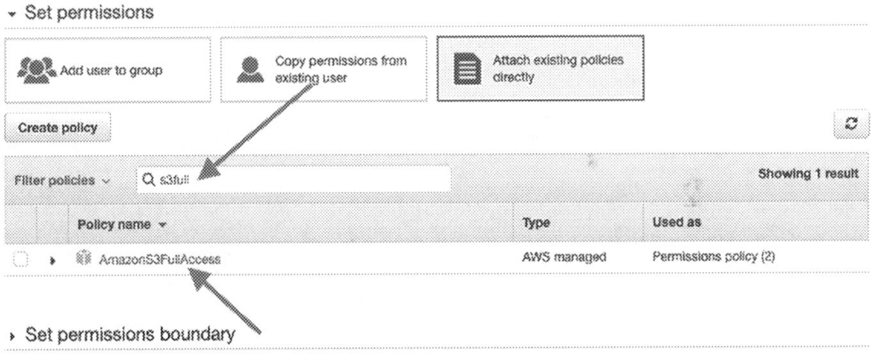

Figure 3-8. *AmazonS3ReadOnlyAccess policy*

8. Click Next: Tags (see Figure 3-9) to add tags to
    your users.

- Set permissions

Add user to group	Copy permissions from existing user	Attach existing policies directly

Create policy

Filter policies ˅	Q s3full		Showing 1 result
Policy name ˅		**Type**	**Used as**
✓ ▸ AmazonS3FullAccess		AWS managed	Permissions policy (2)

▸ Set permissions boundary

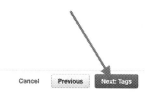

Cancel   Previous   Next: Tags

Figure 3-9. *Adding tags*

9. Add an example tag with a Key called Department
    and a Value of Finance (see Figure 3-10). Then click
    Next, which will open the review page, where you
    can see the final details about your user.

Add tags (optional)

IAM tags are key-value pairs you can add to your user. Tags can include user information, such as an email address, or can be descriptive, such as a job title. You can use the tags to organize, track, or control access for this user. Learn more

Key	Value (optional)	Remove
Department	Finance	✕
Add new key		

You can add 49 more tags.

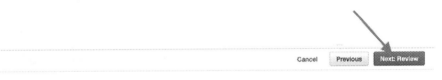

Cancel   Previous   Next: Review

Figure 3-10. *IAM tags*

10.   Click Create User (see Figure 3-11). This takes you
to the final step of creating an AWS user. You can see
that the user Ram was created. You can even view
the password of this user.

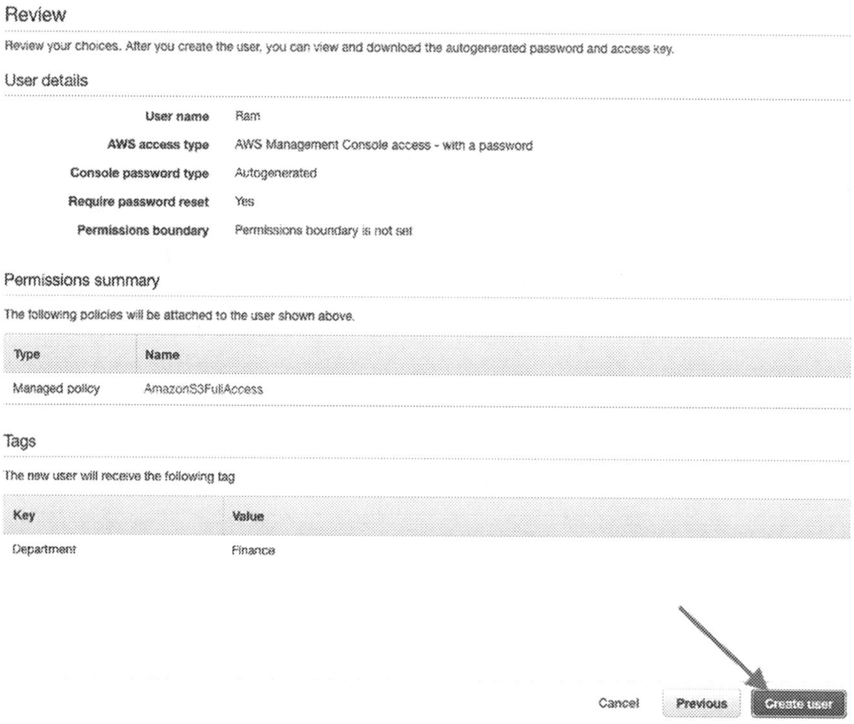

Review

Review your choices. After you create the user, you can view and download the autogenerated password and access key.

User details

User name	Ram
AWS access type	AWS Management Console access - with a password
Console password type	Autogenerated
Require password reset	Yes
Permissions boundary	Permissions boundary is not set

Permissions summary

The following policies will be attached to the user shown above.

Type	Name
Managed policy	AmazonS3FullAccess

Tags

The new user will receive the following tag

Key	Value
Department	Finance

Cancel   Previous   Create user

Figure 3-11. *Creating a user*

11. Click Download CSV (see Figure 3-12), which will download a CSV file with user credentials to your computer. You should save these credentials somewhere after creating the user. If you navigate away from this page, you will no longer be able to get these credentials again.

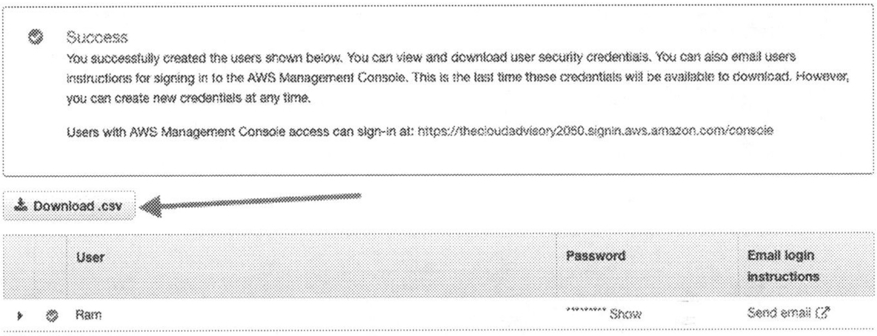

Figure 3-12. *Downloading the CSV of the credentials*

12.   Click Close. You can see that the user called Ram has been added to the Users page.

Let's create another user, named Shyam.

1.   Follow the same process. Add the username **Shyam**. Allow AWS access via the console, leave all values at their defaults, except Require Password Reset, and click Next.

2.   Don't add any permissions; just click Next. Add the sample tag the same as you did for Ram— Department and Finance.

3.   Click Next and then choose Create a User.

4.   Download the CSV file to save credentials. Remember that you won't be able to get these credentials back after closing this page.

You have created the two users named Ram and Shyam, so you can now create user groups.

Creating Groups

1. Click User Groups and then choose Create Group (see Figure 3-13) to create your first user group.

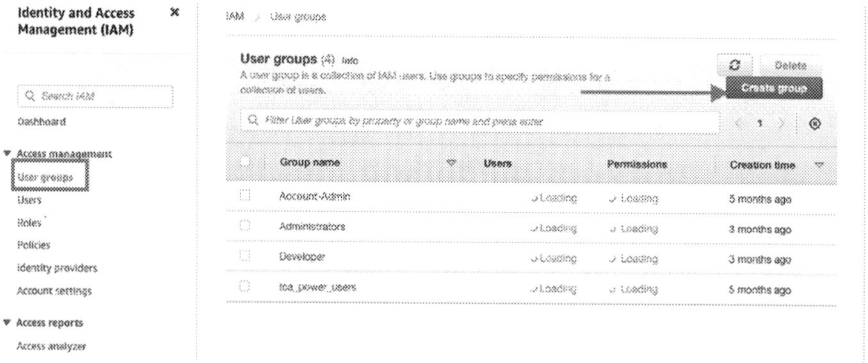

Figure 3-13. *Group creation*

2. Name the group Developers (see Figure 3-14). You can add users to this group from the table. Add Ram, who is a developer, to this group.

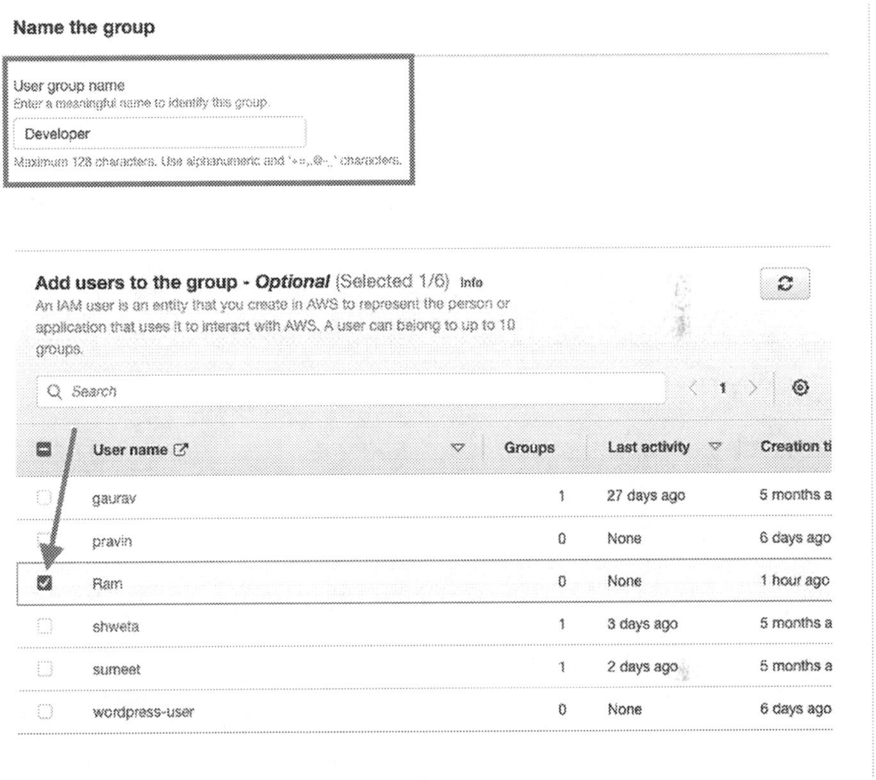

Name the group

User group name
Enter a meaningful name to identify this group.

Developer

Maximum 128 characters. Use alphanumeric and `+=,.@-_` characters.

Add users to the group - *Optional* (Selected 1/6) Info
An IAM user is an entity that you create in AWS to represent the person or application that uses it to interact with AWS. A user can belong to up to 10 groups.

	User name ⭧		Groups	Last activity		Creation ti
☐	gaurav		1	27 days ago		5 months a
☐	pravin		0	None		6 days ago
☑	Ram		0	None		1 hour ago
☐	shweta		1	3 days ago		5 months a
☐	sumeet		1	2 days ago		5 months a
☐	wordpress-user		0	None		6 days ago

Figure 3-14. *Naming the group*

3. The next step is to add policies to this group. You want your developers to be able to fully access EC2 and S3, so you need to check AmazonS3FullAccess (see Figure 3-15) from the Policies table and then click Create Group.

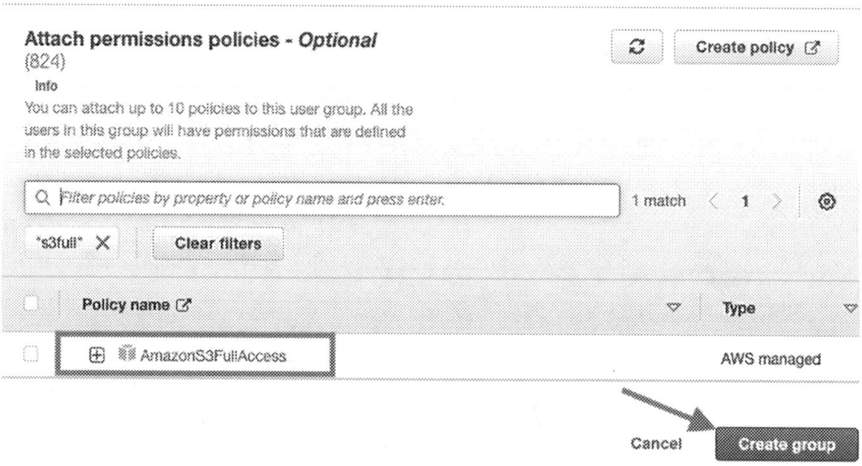

Attach permissions policies - *Optional*
(824)
Info
You can attach up to 10 policies to this user group. All the
users in this group will have permissions that are defined
in the selected policies.

Policy name ☑			▽	Type	▽
	⊕ ▓ AmazonS3FullAccess			AWS managed	

Figure 3-15. Group creation

You now have a Developers group with only one user. Let's create an
Administrators group as well. Follow the previous steps. Next, you can
attach policies to this group. You will attach the AdministratorAccess
policy. Click Create Group to see that your groups have been created.

In the next section, you will log in as the IAM user and create roles.

Logging In with the IAM User and Creating Roles

In this lesson, you will log in with the IAM user to the AWS Console and
create a role. (I assume you have completed the last demo, so you have a
user named Shyam and his password.) Let's get started.

1. First log in as the administrator named Shyam and
    use that user to create a role. Open the CSV file (see
    Figure 3-16) you downloaded when creating Shyam.
    This includes the Username, Password, Access Key
    ID, and Secret Key ID fields, and the Console Login
    link. Because you did not select programmatic
    access, the Access and Secret Key are empty.

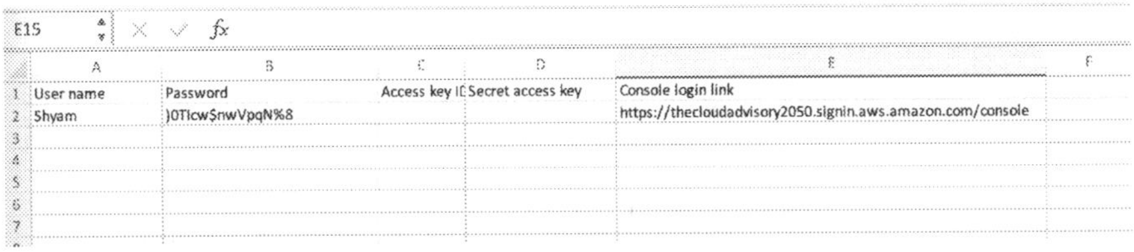

	A	B	C	D	E	F
1	User name	Password	Access key ID	Secret access key	Console login link	
2	Shyam	)0TIcw$nwVpqN%8			https://thecloudadvisory2050.signin.aws.amazon.com/console	
3						
4						
5						
6						
7						

Figure 3-16. *Role creation*

2. Copy the Console Login link and open it in the browser. You'll see that the account alias (see Figure 3-17) is already filled; this is something you created in another demo. You can also use the Account ID.

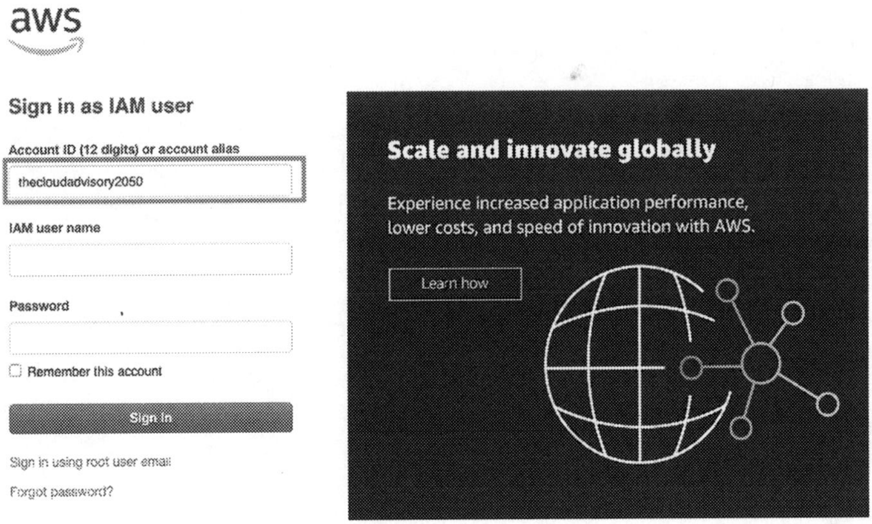

Figure 3-17. *Filling in the Account ID*

3. Add your username and password, as shown in the CSV file, and click Sign In (see Figure 3-18).

Sign in as IAM user

Account ID (12 digits) or account alias

thecloudadvisory2050

IAM user name

Shyam

Password

••••••••••••

☐ Remember this account

Sign In

Sign in using root user email

Forgot password?

Apache Kafka Made Easy

Set up and scale Kafka clusters with ease using Amazon MSK

aws

Figure 3-18. *Logging in*

4. This will take you to the AWS Console. You can see
    the AWS Console as before, but in the top-right
    corner of your screen, you can see that you are
    logged in as Shyam (see Figure 3-19).

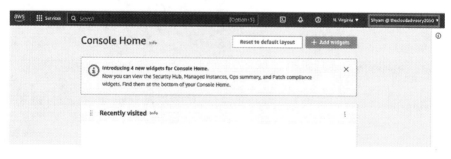

Figure 3-19. *Logged in as Shyam*

5. Navigate to the IAM Console again. Click the Roles
    option on the left dashboard and select Create Role
    (see Figure 3-20).

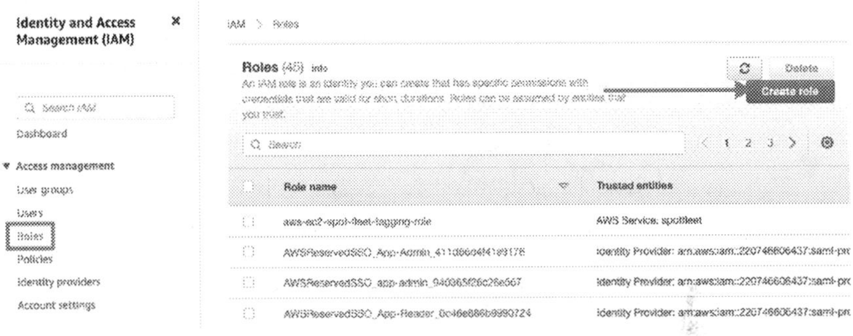

Figure 3-20. *Creating a role*

6. The first option you have is to select the trusted
    entity. This means you should select what this role is
    for. Who or which service is going to use this role?

    -   The first option is the AWS service. You should
        choose this when you want to assign this role to
        AWS services like EC2, Lambda, or ECS, which is
        what you will do here.

    -   The next option is the AWS account, which is used
        to create a role that can be accessed from other
        AWS accounts. If you want someone to be able to
        log in from another account, choose this option.

    -   The next option is Web Entity, which is when you
        want users to be able to assume this role and access
        the AWS Console via a web entity like Google
        Facebook login.

    -   The next option is SAML 2.0 Federation. SAML
        is a user maintenance service that is used by big
        organizations to allow their employees access to
        different services in the organization. This can
        be integrated with AWS to give access to the AWS
        Console.

- The final option is a custom trust policy. You can use this to define a custom JSON trust policy. Don't worry if the last three options didn't make sense to you. Only the first two options are important for this course.

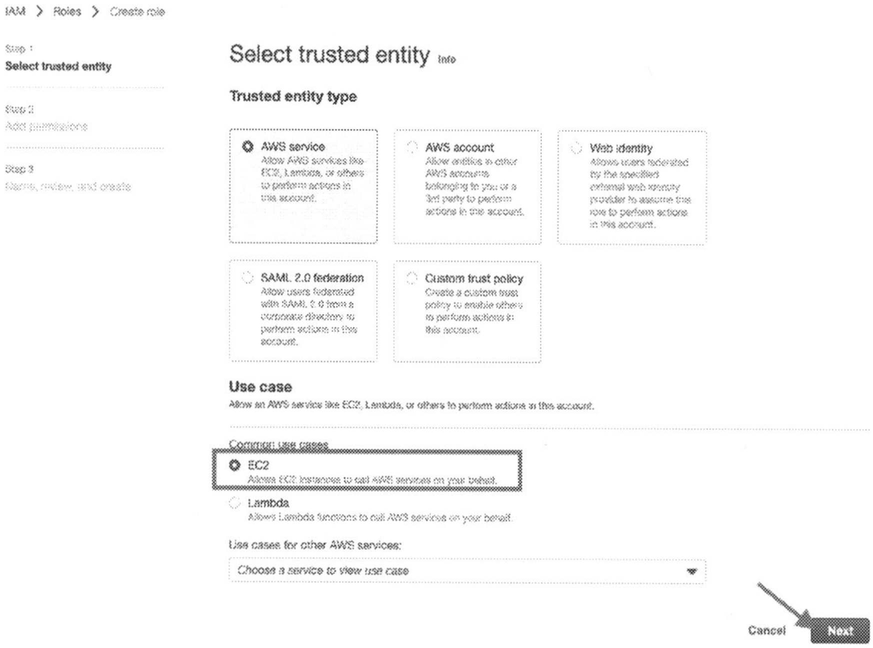

Figure 3-21. *Creating a role*

7. Choose AWS Service and select EC2 from the options. Now you will create a role that can be attached to an EC2 instance. Click Next. You'll see the list of policies that you can attach to this role. Attach the AmazonS3FullAccess (see Figure 3-22) policy and click Next.

Add permissions Info

Permissions policies (Selected 1/824) Info

Choose one or more policies to attach to your new role.

C   Create policy

Q *Filter policies by property or policy name and press enter.*   1 match   < 1 >   ⚙

"s3full" ✕   Clear filters

☑	Policy name ☑	▽	Type ▽	Description
☑	⊞ AmazonS3FullAccess		AWS m...	Provides full access to all buckets via the AWS Manage...

▶ **Set permissions boundary - optional** Info

Set a permissions boundary to control the maximum permissions this role can have. This is not a common setting, but you can use it to delegate permission management to others.

Cancel   Previous   Next

***Figure 3-22.** Adding permissions*

8. Enter the role name. You see a description already filled with a meaningful message: "Allows EC2 instances to call AWS services on your behalf." Review the role and click Create Role. It will take a few seconds. Now you can see the role you created on the Roles page. You will use this role in upcoming demos.

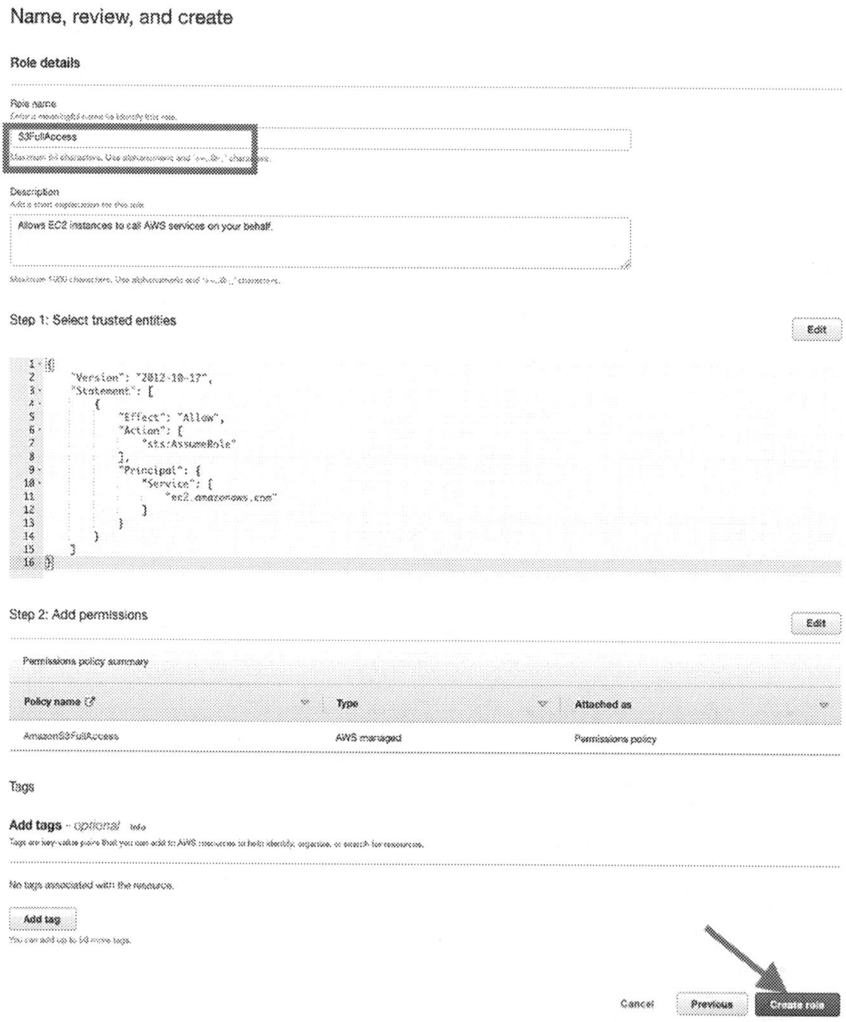

Name, review, and create

Role details

Role name

Enter a meaningful name to identify this role.

S3FullAccess

Maximum 64 characters. Use alphanumeric and '+=,.@-_' characters.

Description

Add a short explanation for this role.

Allows EC2 instances to call AWS services on your behalf.

Maximum 1000 characters. Use alphanumeric and '+=,.@-_' characters.

Step 1: Select trusted entities   Edit

```
1  {
2    "Version": "2012-10-17",
3    "Statement": [
4      {
5        "Effect": "Allow",
6        "Action": [
7          "sts:AssumeRole"
8        ],
9        "Principal": {
10         "Service": [
11           "ec2.amazonaws.com"
12         ]
13       }
14     }
15   ]
16 }
```

Step 2: Add permissions   Edit

Permissions policy summary

Policy name	Type	Attached as
AmazonS3FullAccess	AWS managed	Permissions policy

Tags

Add tags – *optional* Info

Tags are key-value pairs that you can add to AWS resources to help identity, organize, or search for resources.

No tags associated with the resource.

Add tag

You can add up to 50 more tags.

Cancel   Previous   Create role

Figure 3-23. *Finalizing the role*

IAM users are the best to give access to your AWS account. I recommend creating an IAM user for yourself with Administrator permission and use it going forward. Make sure to enable MFA for IAM users as well.

I believe you already deleted the access key and the secret key for the root user, which you created in the last demo. At this stage, you can also create an access and secret key for your IAM as well. You can find the link in the Resource section. In the next lesson, you learn about IAM policies.

IAM Policies and Features

The last section was all about IAM users, groups, and roles. It also briefly discussed IAM policies to give permissions, but that's not enough. Understanding policies is crucial to effectively working with IAM. This section covers IAM policies in detail, including their definition and types.

What comes to your mind when you hear the word *policy*? If you think rules or guidelines, you got it right. An IAM policy is more or less the same thing. In the previous section, you gave certain permissions to users, groups, and roles that you created, and then only they could perform the actions as per those permissions granted. These permissions are nothing but policies.

By definition, IAM policies are entities that define an identity's permissions.

As mentioned earlier, policies contain permissions that determine whether a request is allowed or denied. It means whatever action is performed by an identity, the permission is given by its policy. So the IAM policy can be used when you have to set the permission for an identity in IAM.

Let's look at the same example. You have a team of two developers, Ram and Shyam, and two administrators, Sita and Gita. You created two groups—the Developer group and the Administrator group.

As per the job role and permissions, the developers in your organization can list, start, and stop the EC2 instance and the administrators can create and delete the EC2 instance. EC2 is nothing but a compute service in AWS. I talk about it in the coming chapters.

You will create two policies—one for the developers, which will allow them to list, start, and stop EC2 instances, and another for administrators, which will enable them to create and delete EC2 instances. You will attach these policies to the respective groups and the policy will be applied to everyone in these groups. That means that Ram and Shyam will have permissions as developers and Sita and Gita will have permissions as administrators.

Hence, in this example, by attaching the developer policy to the Developer group, you are allowing the members in that group to perform specified actions and nothing more. Let's look next at the different types of IAM policies.

Types of Policies

IAM policies are entities that define an identity's permissions. According to that definition, a policy can be attached to identities or resources. As you already know, an identity is nothing but IAM users, groups, and roles, and the resource refers to AWS services such as EC2 instances, S3 buckets, or Lambda. Based on the two ways a policy can be attached, it is of two types:

- Identity-based policy

- Resource-based policy

Identity-Based Policy[4]

Identity-based policies are attached to an IAM user, group, or role. These policies let you specify what that identity can do (its permissions).

This policy controls which actions can be performed by an identity, on which resources, and under what circumstances.

---

[4]https://docs.aws.amazon.com/IAM/latest/UserGuide/access_policies_identity-vs-resource.html

It is important to note that these policies are specific to each individual user, which allows users to access the AWS resources in their own accounts. IAM users, groups, and roles can have multiple policies that together define their permissions.

For example, the IAM user named Ram can be assigned the policy stating that they are allowed to perform Amazon EC2 `RunInstances` actions. It is also possible to specify that Ram is allowed to retrieve items from an Amazon S3 bucket named `mybucket`. Based on both of these permissions, Ram is only able to launch EC2 instances and access `mybucket`.

The other type of policy is the resource-based kind.

Resource-Based Policy[5]

These policies are attach with an AWS resource, such as Lambda, ECS, EC2 instances, and so on.

These policies control which actions a specified AWS service can perform on other resources and under what conditions. Consider this example: At times, there will be scenarios where the EC2 instance would like to access the S3 bucket. You need to attach the policy to the EC2 instance and give it the required permission to access S3.

Identity-based policies are of two types—managed policies and inline policies.

Managed Policies[6]

The managed policy is further classified in AWS as a Managed Policy and a Customer Managed Policy. Let's take a closer look at each of them.

---

[5] https://docs.aws.amazon.com/IAM/latest/UserGuide/access_policies_identity-vs-resource.html

[6] https://docs.aws.amazon.com/IAM/latest/UserGuide/access_policies_managed-vs-inline.html

AWS Managed Policy

Managed policies are policies that are created and managed by AWS.

As the name suggests, this policy is created and managed by AWS and you cannot make any changes to it.

For example, Amazon S3 read-only access or S3 full access. Essentially, they're designed to align closely with commonly used IT industry job functions like administrator, developer, or reader.

You can give S3 full access permission to the administrator and S3 read-only access to the auditor. The objective is to make granting permissions for these standard job functions easy. AWS-managed policies cannot be changed and AWS will manage and update the policies as necessary.

Customer-Managed Policies

Customer-managed policies are created and managed by the customer.

Basically, as a customer, you can create and manage these policies. If you want a fully controlled policy that you can maintain, you can use a customer-managed policy, which you create and manage in your AWS account. They provide more precise control over your policies than AWS-managed policies.

Another advantage of customer-managed policies is that you can attach multiple entities to your account, making it much easier to scale. For example, say you have four reader users in your account for a different team that all need the same type of Amazon EC2 read-only access.

You can create one customer-managed policy and attach it to all four users. If you need to change that policy, you can change it in one place, which applies to all those users. It provides you a built-in, centralized change-management process for those managed policies. You have complete control and you can manage permissions at any level you feel is necessary.

Next and last is the inline policy.

Inline Policy

Inline policies are directly attached to the user or group. They maintain a strict one-to-one relationship with the policy and identity.

That means an inline policy is attached to a single entity. It is generally created when you create an identity and deleted when you delete the identity. It is beneficial when you have to give permission to a temporary user or group. You create an inline policy while creating a user or group. When you will delete the user, the policy will also be deleted.

Alright, so that's pretty much about the policies. Let's quickly summarize what you learned in this topic. A policy is basically permission that decides which actions should be taken in the AWS accounts. You learned about the different types of IAM policies, which are identity-based policies and resource-based policies. Identities-based policies can be further divided into two categories—managed policies and inline policies. Managed policies can be AWS Managed or Customer Managed.

The next section looks at important IAM best practices. This is a very important topic for Cloud Practitioner certification.

IAM Best Practices

This section discusses a few IAM best practices to ensure the security of your AWS accounts.

User

The first IAM best practice is to avoid sharing login credentials. Instead of sharing root user credentials with different users in your organization, you should create IAM users for individuals who are going to use your AWS resources.

Let's look at an example. Suppose you have two developers and two administrators on your team. What people sometimes do is create one IAM user and share user credentials with all these people. But this is not a good practice. Instead, you should create four different users according to the roles of these team members and share the user credentials with them.

The objective is that every user should have their own IAM credentials to access your account, regardless of whether they use the Management Console, the AWS CLI, or an SDK.

Group

It is always best to create groups and assign only the required permissions to these groups.

That means if there are multiple users in your organization with the same job role, instead of assigning permissions to individual users, you create a group, assign a permission to this group, and add all the users who have the same job role in the group. Every user will assume these permissions.

Let's look at this with the same example. Suppose you have two developers and two administrators on the team. Instead of giving permission to these four individual users, you should create two groups (one for the administrators and another for the developers) and grant them the required permissions. New users can now be added to their respective groups. The users will automatically assume the permissions assigned to their respective groups. This practice helps you manage the permissions at the group label instead of at the user level.

Permissions

AWS recommends you always create permission for what the user needs according to their role; these are known as *least privilege permissions*.

For instance, if a user's job is to start and stop the EC2 instances, instead of giving them full access to EC2, you should only give permission to start and stop the EC2 instance. You should always create least-privilege permissions when designing permissions.

Auditing

AWS says that you should always enable CloudTrail inside each and every AWS account.

If you don't know what CloudTrail is, it is an AWS service that's free except for storage. Whenever a user interacts with your AWS account, the cloud trail will log every activity, which eventually will help you during an audit. You learn CloudTrail in detail in Chapter 10.

Say a user logged in to your AWS account, created an EC2 instance, and then terminated it. AWS CloudTrail will log all the three activities. This way, you will have a record of all the activities that users are doing inside your account.

Password Policy

AWS says that you should always configure password policies, which were discussed in the previous chapter. Password policies ensure that every user has a strong password.

MFA

You should always enable multi-factor authentication for privileged users.

I recommend that you enforce MFA for every user. You can create a policy and attach that policy to all groups. Whenever any users log in to an AWS account, they will have to authenticate their identity twice. This is a very good practice to ensure your account and AWS resources are secure.

Rotate

Everyone accessing your AWS account needs to change their user credentials every now and then.

You can require users to rotate their credentials every two months or three months or six months. This is a part of the password policy inside your AWS account. Using this policy, users have to rotate their passwords, access keys, and secret keys.

Root User

In general, you shouldn't use the root user for your day-to-day activities, as it might expose your root user credentials.

Additionally, you should also not limit the access of the root user. Immediately after signing up for an AWS account, you should store the root user credentials somewhere private, and you should create an IAM user for yourself as well.

I hope you now understand that account security is a real issue and you should employ these practices to safeguard your account from any possible threat.

AWS Core Services

AWS core services are fundamental to all applications, which is why they are known as *core* services. With AWS, you can access a broad range of global cloud services, which are the building blocks of any cloud architecture. You need to understand some of these services that are important for this book. The first category is storage.

Storage Services

AWS offers various storage services like S3, EBS, and EFS. These storage services are used for different purposes and can also be integrated with other services.

Compute Services

AWS offers many computing services like virtual machines, containers, and serverless. I cover these in Chapter 6. It is important to understand all compute offerings so you can design secure, cost-effective, and highly available architecture.

Database Services

AWS offers many database services like SQL, NoSQL, Caching, and data warehouse offerings like RDS, DynamoDB, Redshift, and so on. You will learn them in Chapter 8.

Networking Services

Virtual private clouds (VPCs) are part of AWS cloud networking, and VPNs and Direct Connect are also available for connecting on-premises data centers to the cloud network.

Summary

This chapter explained how identity and access management (IAM) works, focusing on users, groups, and roles in IAM with a hands-on lab. You also learned about the IAM policy and other types of policies and reviewed some of the IAM best practices. The next chapter covers AWS Storage services.

CHAPTER 4

AWS Storage Services

This chapter covers one of the core AWS services, the Amazon simple storage service (S3). It starts with a basic explanation of the Amazon S3 service and its use case. You'll learn about its different features, like S3 availability, durability, and data replication. You will also go through the storage classes and do the hands-on lab, where you will create an S3 bucket and folder and then upload the data.

Overview of Amazon S3

This section starts with an overview of S3 and then looks at some of its important components, buckets, folders, and objects.

S3 allows you to store, retrieve, access, and back up any amount of data at any time, from anywhere over the Internet. S3 is a perfect storage solution for storing massive amounts of data, such as audio files, movies, large-scale photo storage, big data sets, and so on.

You can access S3 from the Management Console, the AWS CLI, or the AWS SDK. Let's talk about how to store data in S3. To store data inside S3, you need to create a bucket inside an AWS account.

© Pravin Mishra 2023
P. Mishra, *Cloud Computing with AWS*, https://doi.org/10.1007/978-1-4842-9172-6_4

S3 Buckets

An S3 bucket is a logical container in which data is stored inside S3, so to store data in S3, you need to create a bucket. You can also create multiple buckets to organize your data.

A bucket is distinguished by its name, and it should be globally unique across all regions and accounts.

For example, if I create a bucket and name it my-bucket, no one else can use this name in any AWS account. In other words, once an S3 bucket is created, no other AWS account can create the S3 bucket with a similar name.

An S3 bucket simply works as storage, in which you can store unlimited data, either directly inside the bucket or by creating a folder and putting the data in that folder.

Folders[1]

Folders are used for grouping and organizing files. Unlike a traditional file system, Amazon S3 doesn't use a hierarchy to organize its files. For the sake of organizational simplicity, the Amazon S3 console supports the folder concept as a means of grouping data.

You can have multiple folders or files inside a single bucket. Basically, the folder is a namespace inside the bucket. Let's look at this with an example.

Inside the AWS account, you have the S3 service. In this service, you can create buckets as you have learned so far; inside this bucket, you can store files, images, videos, or data.

Moreover, if you want to organize your data, you can create folders inside the bucket, and also folders inside folders. Then you can store the data inside these folders as well. It will make more sense when you run the demo in the next section.

---

[1] https://docs.aws.amazon.com/AmazonS3/latest/userguide/using-folders.html

S3 Objects

Another important concept in S3 is the object. When you store data that could be files, documents, images, or videos, they are known as *objects* in AWS. Hence, the object is nothing but your file, document, image, video, and so on.

Anything sitting on your hard drive is known as a file, but when you upload this file into S3, it is known as an object, and the bucket in S3 is similar to the file directory on your hard drive.

The following sections cover the characteristics of objects that you need to know.

Maximum Object Size

The maximum size of a single object that you can upload to S3 is 5 TB (terabytes). Note that 5 TB is not the size of total data that you can upload, instead, it's the maximum size of a single file that S3 allows you to upload.

That doesn't mean that you can't upload objects bigger than 5 TB. If you have a bigger object, you have to split it into multiple parts, and then use something called a *multi-part upload* to upload the parts.

Object Versioning

Object versioning is nothing but keeping multiple variants of the same object when you are making some changes to it.

In S3, you can version objects to protect them from any unintended actions or even being accidentally deleted. This means that you always retain the previous versions of an object.

Storage Class

You can create multiple buckets and store them across different classes or tiers of data, called storage classes.

Classes are different levels of storage with different costs. Based on how frequently you use your data, you can choose a class. If you don't use your data much, you could choose a cheaper class and leave your data there. This is covered in detail in an upcoming chapter.

Permissions

Last but not least, you can create permissions to limit who can access or see your objects. One of the most common policies in the bucket policy is a resource-based policy, which you can use to grant permissions to your bucket and its objects.

In this section, you looked at the S3 bucket, folder, objects, and their characteristics. In the next section, you learn how to create an S3 bucket and folder and upload data into it.

Amazon S3 Demo

Let's go to the AWS Management Console:

1. Select the AWS Region. In this example, I select the Mumbai region. After that, go to the S3 Console. There are three ways you can find the S3 service in the console:

    - The first method is by searching for S3 in the search box, and it will give you S3 in the result.

    - The second method is by finding the S3 in the All Services menu. Just expand the menu, locate the S3 service, and click to open it.

    - Finally, if you have previously used S3 in your account, it will be listed under the recently visited services.

2. Type S3 in the search box and click to confirm. When you first arrive at the S3 console, you will see a list of buckets in this AWS account.

3. Since S3 uses a global namespace, you don't have to select a region while using the console. Now, if you are thinking why did you select the region if S3 is a global service? Well, selecting the right region every time when you are working in your account is a good practice. It doesn't matter whether the service is global or region-sensitive.

4. Create an S3 bucket. To do that, click Create Bucket and choose a name.

5. One thing to note here is that the bucket name should be unique. To make this name unique, add some random numbers at the end. There are some rules that you need to follow when naming buckets. The first rule is that the bucket name should be between 3 and 63 characters. Second, the name must have lowercase letters, numbers, dots, and hyphens. It should begin and end with either a letter or a number. Last, your bucket name should be unique across AWS.

6. Select the region where you want your bucket to be created and leave the rest of the default settings as they are. Go ahead and create the bucket. The bucket has been created and it didn't take more than a second. On this page, you can see the bucket name, the region where you created the bucket, and access to the bucket object.

7. Go to the bucket where you can see the different tabs, including Properties, Permission, Metrics, Management, and Access Points. There is an object inside this bucket. This is where you upload your files. You can upload objects in the S3 bucket or you can create folders inside the bucket to organize your data. Go ahead and create a folder called Demo.

8. You can upload your object to the bucket or to this folder. Click Upload. You have two options—you can upload files or folders. You will upload a file here, so click Add Files.

9. You can add some additional settings to the object. Just click Properties and you will see the storage class. It is Standard by default. This topic is covered in detail later in this chapter. For now, skip this and click Upload. Verify that the file has been uploaded successfully.

10. You can exit by clicking Close. Now you have one object in the S3 bucket called demo.jpg. If you click the demo.jpg object, it will take you to the object's dashboard, where you will see the object's properties, permissions, and version.

11. Go to the Properties tab. You can find all the details about the object, like who the owner is, in which region the object is uploaded, when the object was last modified, the size of the object, the type, object key, the S3 URL, the Amazon resource name, any Etag, and the object's URL.

12. It is the link to the file. You can open it by clicking it, but let's open it in a new tab. As you can see, I get "access denied" because this bucket is not public and I don't have the right to access it. If the bucket is not public and you try to open the file using its public URL, it will not open.

13. Go back to the object's dashboard. There is another way to open this object, by clicking Open. It will open a new tab and show you the demo picture.

14. Now you must be thinking, why does this work even when the bucket is not public? Well, when you open an object through the Open command, it opens, because this is a unique URL. As you can see, the URL is much, much longer and not similar to a public URL. This is a special URL for me as an owner of this object, and I am authorized to access this object through this URL.

15. The last thing I want to show you is how to delete an object from S3. For that, go back to the bucket and select the object. Then click Delete.

16. You have to type **delete** to confirm that you want to delete the object. Then click Delete Object. This will permanently delete this object.

I hope you now have confidence in S3 and its scope. In this section, you went through a demo, where you created an S3 bucket and folder, uploaded objects successfully, and then deleted them. If you haven't already, go ahead and try this yourself.

Availability, Durability, and Data Replication

This section looks at three important concepts—availability, durability, and data replication—that will be used a lot in the next section when discussing different storage classes.

Availability

Availability refers to the system uptime. This simply indicates how long the system is available. In other words, it's the time during which the system is operational and able to deliver data upon request. It's measured as a percentage. It is also known as SLA, which stands for Service Level Agreement. It is basically a promise that service providers have with their customers for the availability of their services or systems. If they keep their promise and customers get everything within the promised time, that means the SLA is completed.

Let's look at an example. If supermarkets say they are open 24*7, that means they are available around the clock for you. If they keep their promise and are open all the time, you can say that their availability is 100 percent and they fulfil the SLA.

Durability

Durability refers to long-term data protection. That simply measures how well your data is protected from any possible loss or corruption. In addition to availability, your data should not be lost or corrupted if you store it in a storage device for a long time. Durability is also measured as a percentage.

Let's look at this with an example as well. Suppose you stored 1,000 kilograms of potatoes in cold storage for six months. When you got them back, there are only 800 KGs. It means that 200 KGs of potatoes were rotten or eaten by rats. That means the cold storage service was not durable. Next time, you will make sure to store your potatoes in a well-equipped cold storage so there will be no loss. This is called durability.

Now you understand what data durability and availability are, it's important to know how data is stored in S3. It is based on a concept called *data replication*, discussed next.

Data Replication

If you remember from the last lab, you created an S3 bucket inside the Mumbai region and uploaded an image.

When you upload data to your bucket, this data will go into one of the Availability Zones in the region. In this case, you created a bucket in the Mumbai region, so the image was uploaded into one of its Availability Zones. But to secure this data, AWS makes additional copies of the data and replicates it in other Availability Zones. As a result, all Availability Zones within the same region store and replicate the data.

Why does AWS do that? You need to remember that AWS promised 11 nines of data durability. This simply means that AWS has a 99.99999999999 percent data durability guarantee.

AWS doesn't ensure 100 percent data durability, but they say that there is a 99.999999999 percent chance that your data won't be lost. How does AWS make sure when you are uploading any data inside S3 that it won't suffer any loss?

AWS maintains copies of your data in each Availability Zone in the same region. In the case of data loss at one zone, they recover the data from other Availability Zones.

That's how your data is always present in all the Availability Zones of one region and that's the reason AWS promises 11 nines of durability. In extreme cases, if a Availability Zone goes down, your data will still be available in other Availability Zones of that particular region.

This is one of the significant benefits of using Amazon S3. This is a simple example of when you upload new data. Now, let's look at what happens when you make changes to your data.

Suppose you have an image in three Availability Zones, and you change the color of the image and uploaded it. AWS automatically updates the remaining two copies of your data in the other zones.

The same goes for delete actions as well. When you delete data from one zone, it will be deleted from all Availability Zones in the region.

Storage Classes

This section looks at different storage classes. This section is full of facts, so I recommend you take notes. In one of the previous chapters, you stored an image in an Amazon S3 bucket. When uploading the object, you noticed that the storage classes appeared under the properties. AWS offers you various options to store your data in the cloud. These options are known as storage classes and you can choose any class based on how frequently you access your data (see Figure 4-1).

▼ **Properties**
Specify storage class, encryption settings, tags, and more.

Storage class
Amazon S3 offers a range of storage classes designed for different use cases. Learn more ☑ or see Amazon S3 pricing ☑

	Storage class	Designed for	Availability Zones	Min storage duration	
◉	Standard	Frequently accessed data (more than once a month) with milliseconds access	≥ 3	-	-
○	Intelligent-Tiering	Data with changing or unknown access patterns	≥ 3	-	-
○	Standard-IA	Infrequently accessed data (once a month) with milliseconds access	≥ 3	30 days	1
○	One Zone-IA	Recreatable, infrequently accessed data (once a month) stored in a single Availability Zone with milliseconds access	1	30 days	1
○	Glacier Instant Retrieval	Long-lived archive data accessed once a quarter with instant retrieval in milliseconds	≥ 3	90 days	1
○	Glacier Flexible Retrieval (formerly Glacier)	Long-lived archive data accessed once a year with retrieval of minutes to hours	≥ 3	90 days	-
○	Glacier Deep Archive	Long-lived archive data accessed less than once a year with retrieval of hours	≥ 3	180 days	-
○	Reduced redundancy	Noncritical, frequently accessed data with milliseconds access (not recommended as S3 Standard is more cost effective)	≥ 3	-	-

Figure 4-1. *S3 classes*

These S3 storage classes are purpose-built to provide the lowest cost storage for different access patterns.

This means different types of storage classes are designed to fulfill different purposes of storing data. As a cloud engineer, it is very important to understand these classes, as they can save you time and money. Let's look at them one by one.

S3 Standard

S3 Standard is a general-purpose storage class used for data that's frequently accessed. The storage class is known for its high durability, availability, and performance. S3 Standard is designed for 99.999 percent availability and 11 nines percent (99.999999999) durability.

In other words, there is just a 0.001 percent chance that your data will be lost. This gives you high throughput with low latency. In addition, it can sustain up to two concurrent facility failures. That means if two Availability Zones have problems, your data is still safe.

The S3 Standard delivers low latency and high throughput, making it suitable for a wide range of use cases, including:

- Applications based on the cloud

- Websites with dynamic content

- Distribution of content

- Applications for mobile devices and gaming

- Analyzing Big Data

Amazon S3 Intelligent-Tiering (S3 Intelligent-Tiering)[2]

The next storage class is S3 intelligent tiering. As its name suggests, this storage class automatically moves data to the most cost-effective access tier according to the users' access patterns. Here, the access pattern indicates how frequently one data set is accessed.

---

[2] https://aws.amazon.com/s3/storage-classes/intelligent-tiering/

The objects move automatically from one storage class to another storage class based on the changing access patterns of these objects. As a result, frequent access data will be moved to the frequently accessed storage and infrequently accessed data will be moved by S3 intelligent tiering to the correct category.

In terms of latency and throughput, it is similar to the S3 Standard. But this is highly cost-optimized. For example, if data is moved to the Infrequent Access class, that will save up to 40 percent on storage costs. If it is moved to the Glacier class, that will save up to 68 percent on storage costs.

It is also designed for eleven nines 99.999999999 percent durability and three nines 99.9 percent availability over a given year, across multiple Availability Zones.

As a user of this service, you only have to pay a small monthly monitoring and auto-tiering charge. This gives you the most cost optimization without thinking too much about it. It is also resilient against events that can affect an entire Availability Zone.

Standard IA (Infrequent Access)

The next storage class is Infrequent Access. As the name suggests, this storage class is used for less frequently accessed data. This is data that you only access once in a while, but you also want to be immediately available whenever you need it. If that's the case, you can use the Infrequent Access storage class.

It is designed for 99.9 percent availability and eleven nines 99.999999999 percent durability.

Availability of infrequent classes is lower than the S3 Standard. Because you don't access these files very frequently, it is cheaper than the Amazon S3 Standard. But when you do access these files, you pay a per GB retrieval charge. This is the tradeoff in this class.

You pay less for storage but need to pay a retrieval fee every time you access your data.

This low-cost and high-performance combination makes S3 Standard-IA ideal for long-term storage, backups, and disaster recovery. This data class is also resilient to failures in entire Availability Zones.

One Zone-Infrequent Access (S3 One Zone-IA)[3]

This storage class is very similar to the Infrequent Access storage class, the only difference being that in One Zone-IA, the data is stored in a single Availability Zone, whereas in the Infrequent Access class, it is stored in at least three Availability Zones.

Basically, your data is less available, because it is present in just one Availability Zone. The best part is that you still have low latency and high throughput performance. Since the data is stored in a single Availability Zone, it is 20 percent cheaper than Infrequent Access.

Therefore, S3 One Zone-IA is a good choice for customers who need frequently accessed data but don't need S3 Standard's availability or resilience. You can use this storage class to store secondary backups of on-premises data or data that can be easily re-created. You can also use S3 Cross-Region Replication to cost-effectively store data that is replicated from another AWS Region.

Glacier

AWS supports three types of Glacier for different access patterns:

Amazon S3 Glacier Instant Retrieval

- S3 Glacier Instant Retrieval offers the same performance as the S3 Standard retrieval in milliseconds.

---

[3] https://aws.amazon.com/about-aws/whats-new/2018/04/announcing-s3-one-zone-infrequent-access-a-new-amazon-s3-storage-class/

Amazon S3 Glacier Flexible Retrieval (Formerly S3 Glacier)

- In Glacier Flexible Retrieval, the retrieval time can be configured from minutes to hours, with free bulk retrieval.

- As a backup and disaster recovery solution, it is most suitable for situations where large amounts of data occasionally need to be retrieved quickly and cost-effectively.

Amazon S3 Glacier Deep Archive

- S3 Glacier Deep Archive retrieves data within 12 hours.

- This is one of the lowest-cost storage classes, designed for long-term data storage lasting 10 to 12 years.

- This is an excellent alternative to magnetic tape libraries.

Amazon S3 Glacier is the lowest-cost storage class in S3 and supports long-term retention and digital preservation for data that's accessed once or twice a year.[4]

The class is useful for customers in highly regulated industries such as finance, healthcare, and government. It is necessary for these industries to retain data sets for 10-12 years or longer in order to comply with regulatory requirements.

The class is designed to make objects 11 nines (99.999999999 percent) durable across multiple Availability Zones.

As the name suggests, you expect that your data will be frozen, which means it will be maintained for a longer period of time. It means object retrieval validity is very long.

---

[4] https://aws.amazon.com/s3/storage-classes/glacier/

Reduced Redundancy

Reduced Redundancy Storage (RRS) is a legacy storage class. It is the oldest storage class (besides Standard) and was originally announced back in 2010.

At the time, it was cheaper than Standard because it contained less physical redundancy (fewer device failures were required to lose the object completely).

However, something paradoxical happened, and Standard's cost significantly decreased. As a result, Standard's cost was reduced significantly in most regions below the cost of RRS. Consequently, RRS is no longer cost-effective and is not recommended.

I hope you now understand the storage class. If you have any questions, I recommend you go through this section again.

Summary

The chapter started with a basic understanding of the Amazon S3 service. It's AWS storage built to store and retrieve any amount of data from anywhere. You can store any data, such as images and videos and it's designed to deliver 99.999999999 percent durability and 99.999 percent availability.

Furthermore, the chapter explored how to manage data for cost optimization, access control, and compliance using S3 storage classes. I strongly urge you to review if you need clarification.

Note that it's good practice to terminate all the resources that you created in your AWS account so that you do not get charged. The S3 bucket doesn't cost anything, but if you uploaded data and keep it there, you will be charged for storage costs. In order to avoid being charged, you must delete all the objects from the S3 bucket or delete the S3 bucket altogether.

CHAPTER 5

Virtual Private Cloud (VPC)

This chapter covers the VPC, which is the networking section of cloud computing. It dives deeply into the topics like VPCs (Virtual Private Clouds), route tables, a NAT gateway, an Internet gateway, subnets, security groups, and NACL (Network Access Control List). You'll also run through a demo in AWS to create a VPC and public and private subnets.

What Is a VPC?

VPC stands for Virtual Private Cloud. It is the networking aspect of cloud computing and it may be a little difficult to relate it to your day-to-day life.

I will try to make it as simple as possible. Since this is a very important section and a building block for the rest of the topics in this chapter, I recommend that you pay special attention.

Figure 5-1 shows an example. Suppose there is a residential building, and it has many flats. There are hundreds of people living in these flats. Say that I own flat number A10 and you own flat number B20. We can also say that flat B20 is your private section of the building where you keep your stuff, and you have complete control over it. You can add security features such as a lock, camera surveillance, and so on. In the same way, other people have private areas that they own.

© Pravin Mishra 2023
P. Mishra, *Cloud Computing with AWS*, https://doi.org/10.1007/978-1-4842-9172-6_5

Let's connect this example to AWS and VPC and replace the building with AWS and the flats with VPCs.

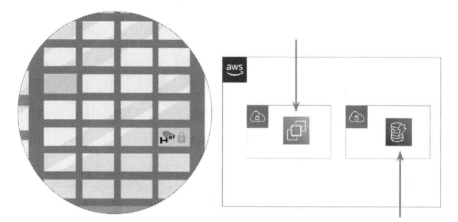

Figure 5-1. *Apartment and AWS account*

In this AWS account, you create and manage all types of resources like EC2, RDS, and so on. These resources in your VPC are just like your stuff in your flat, and the AWS VPC is like your private area in AWS in which you can place your resources and services. Just like an apartment has different levels of security, you can also put a level of security over these resources. In other words, you can say that there are ways for you to either grant people access to your database or your cloud resources or you can also prevent them from doing so.

Now, let's look at the definition of AWS VPC. A virtual private cloud (VPC) is a virtual network dedicated to your AWS account. It is logically isolated from other virtual networks in the AWS Cloud, where you can launch your AWS resources, such as Amazon EC2 instances.[1]

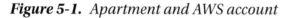

[1] https://aws.amazon.com/vpc/

A VPC is nothing but a virtual data center on Amazon Web Services. It is private because it's only for you and you have complete control over it. It is a completely isolated logical network that you can use the way you want. When you create a VPC, you basically create a logically isolated network.

If I create a VPC in my account and you create a VPC in your account, these are two isolated networks, as shown in Figure 5-2.

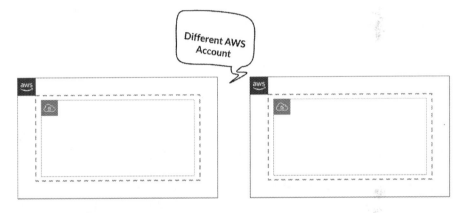

Figure 5-2. *AWS different accounts*

Two or more VPCs with different IP addresses within the same account will be isolated. You can think of the IP address as the address of your flat. The IP address is called the CIDR (Classless Inter-Domain Routing).

Networks need unique identifiers to communicate over the Internet, and they use the Internet protocol (IP) to accomplish that.

In order to create a VPC, you specify the IP range for the VPC in the form of a CIDR block; for example, 10.0.0.0/16.

As of now, you understand that a Virtual Private Cloud is a network within the AWS account that you own. A network can also have subnetworks, which are also known as subnets (see Figure 5-3). I cover subnets in the next section.

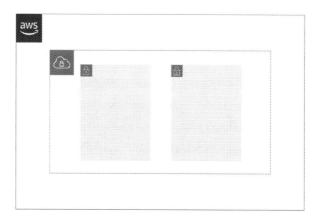

Figure 5-3. *AWS VPC subnet*

Subnets, Internet Gateways, Route Tables, and NAT Gateways

This section looks at subnets, Internet gateways, and route tables.

As discussed in the previous section, VPC is a network in your AWS account. You can also create subnetworks inside your VPC. These subnetworks are also known as subnets.

From the previous example, you own a flat in the apartment and this flat is your private section. You have a bedroom, a living room, and a kitchen in this flat. Essentially, these are different subsections of this flat (see Figure 5-4) used for various purposes.

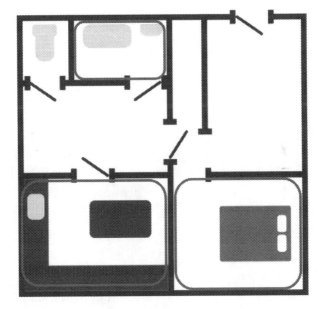

Figure 5-4. *Three subsections in the flat*

Similarly, in AWS VPC, you create a subnetwork like a public subnet and a private subnet (see Figure 5-5). When you create a subnet, you specify the CIDR block for the subnet, which is a subset of the VPC CIDR block. If the CIDR of your VPC is 10.0.0.0/16, you can use 10.0.0.0/24 and 10.0.1.0/24 as the CIDR of your subnet.

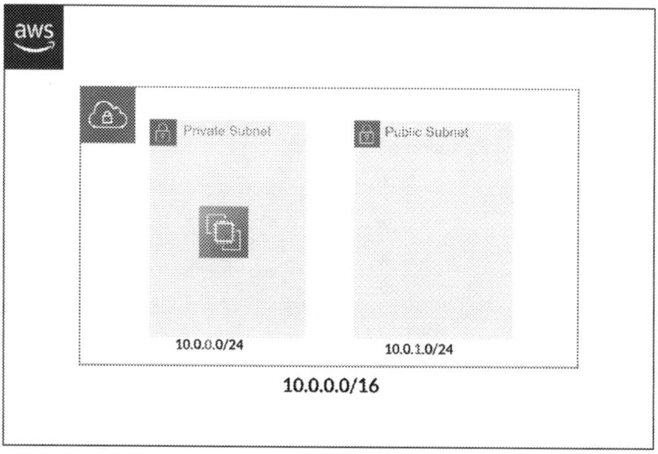

Figure 5-5. *Public and private subnets*

You can launch AWS resources into a specific subnet, such as EC2 instances. One important point to remember is that each subnet must reside entirely within one Availability Zone (AZ) and cannot span across zones. You will see why this is so during the hands-on lab.

There are two types of subnets: public and private. This can relate it to the flat. If you have a guest room with direct access from outside, it is like a public subnet. While your bedroom is completely private for you.

Public Subnet

A public subnet interacts with the Internet and can be accessed through the Internet. Any resources created in your public subnet, for example, web servers, are accessible through the Internet. Since public subnets interact with the Internet, we will deploy our load balancer or Internet-facing applications in the public subnet. I cover this in detail in Chapter 6.

Private Subnet

A private subnet cannot be reached from the Internet. You can create the
AWS resources that are used only inside the VPC for internal purposes.

Now let's put it all together. You have a region in your AWS account and
there will be a VPC in that region. The VPC will have what's called a CIDR
range, which is a range of IP addresses allowed within your VPC. The VPC
can also go across two Availability Zones: AZ1 and AZ2. Availability Zone
AZ1 contains a public subnet and a private subnet. Similarly, Availability
Zone AZ2 contains a public subnet and a private subnet. Hence, you have
two Availability Zones (see Figure 5-6), one VPC, and four subnets in this
example.

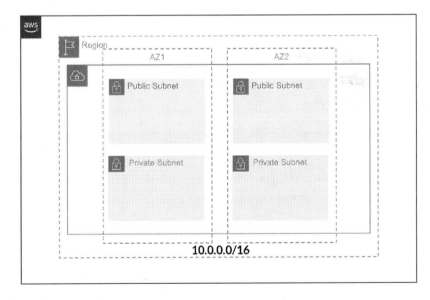

Figure 5-6. *AWS Availability Zones*

Now you must be thinking, what is the difference between a public
subnet and a private subnet? Well, there is no difference in their
architectures. The process of creating them is exactly the same—what you
configure inside them determines whether a subnet is public or private.

You need to make two changes to a subnet to make it public—add an Internet gateway and add a route table.

Internet Gateway

First, you need to add an Internet gateway.

This is an AWS managed component that is attached to your VPC. It acts as a gateway between your VPC and the Internet, basically the outside world. Let's add an Internet gateway here.

Figure 5-7 shows an Internet gateway attached to the VPC, which will establish a connection from the Internet.

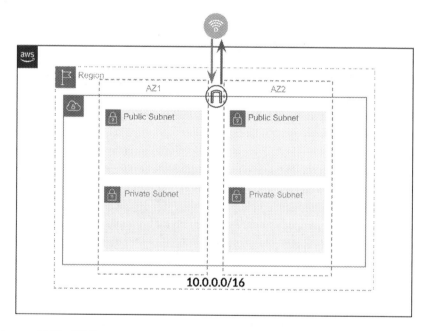

Figure 5-7. *S3 Internet gateway*

The public subnet does not yet have access to the Internet.

Route Table

There is another component called a router inside VPC, and it determines where the incoming traffic is directed.

This process is known as *routing*. The router uses something called route tables to control network traffic. Each subnet inside VPC must be associated with a route table.

Whenever you create a subnet, it will come with a default route, which is a local route. The route table has a destination field and a target field. The destination field contains the destination address that you are trying to reach, and the target specifies the route to that destination. That means any request in the VPC IP address is local.

Destination	Target
0.0.0.0/0	igw-id

To create a public subnet, you need to add the Internet as the destination address, which is 0.0.0.0/0, and the target must be the Internet gateway. This new route in the route table in Figure 5-8 has a destination of 0.0.0.0/0.

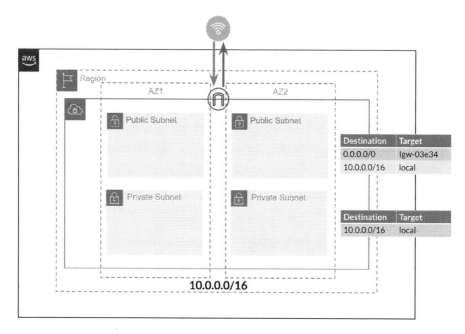

Figure 5-8. *Route table*

It means that any IP address not known within the route table sends it to this target, and in this case, this target is the Internet gateway. This part is simply the ID of the Internet gateway.

Any traffic other than the VPC network will go to the Internet gateway and hence, which means the subnet is a public subnet. These two subnets are public subnets, and the rest two are private subnets.

NAT Gateway

If you have an instance in a private subnet, it will not be accessible through the Internet. However, you might want to give it access to the Internet in order to download files or get the operating system updates.

In this case, you can use what is known as a NAT gateway. A NAT gateway is managed by AWS or a NAT instance, as it can also be self-managed. That way, you can access the Internet in your private subnet.

A NAT gateway is essentially a highly available AWS managed service that enables your instances in private subnets to connect to the Internet (see Figure 5-9).

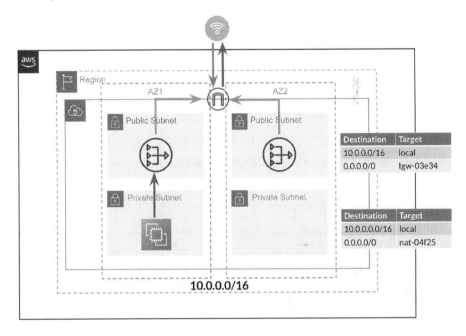

Figure 5-9. *NAT gateway*

You set up a NAT gateway inside your public subnet and add a route from the private subnets for the NAT gateway and from the NAT gateway to the Internet gateway. This will allow your private subnets to get Internet connectivity.

That's all for this topic. I hope you now understand the VPC and its elements. If you have any questions, I recommend that you go through this section again. This is a very important concept to understand.

In the following section, we will explore security groups and NACLs.

Security Groups and NACLs

This section explains why you need a security group and an NACL (Network Access Control List), what they are, and the differences between them. Let's start with why you need security groups and NACLs.

Security groups and NACLs act as virtual firewalls. They set rules for traffic to and from the resources of a VPC, following inbound and outbound rules. Inbound and outbound represent the direction of traffic between networks.

Keep in mind that the traffic direction is defined with respect to a reference network. This reference network is your computer.

Inbound Traffic

Inbound traffic refers to the information coming in to a network. The reference network is your internal network; it could be your computer. As you can see in Figure 5-10, data is flowing from the Internet to your computer, so it's called *inbound* traffic.

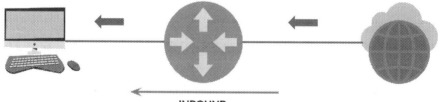

INBOUND

Figure 5-10. *Inbound traffic*

Outbound Traffic

Outbound traffic refers to information going out of the network. In Figure 5-11, you see that the data is flowing out from the reference network, which is your computer. The data traffic flow is from your computer to the Internet. So it's called outbound traffic.

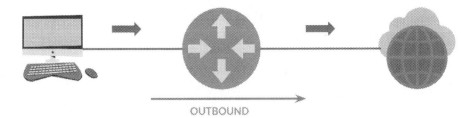

Figure 5-11. Outbound traffic

Now let's return to the topic of security groups and NACLs. Let's begin with security groups.

What Is an AWS Security Group?

A security group is an AWS firewall solution for filtering the incoming and outgoing traffic from an EC2 instance.

A security group acts as a virtual firewall for EC2 instances to control the inbound and outbound traffic based on some defined rules. It ensures instance-level security. Inbound and outbound rules work independently. For example, an inbound rule may only permit traffic from a specific IP address to access the instance, while an outbound rule may allow all traffic to exit.

It is important to understand that security groups operate at the instance level within a VPC.

It is possible to apply a security group to one or more instances as well. Similarly, an instance can be associated with one or more security groups.

What Is an NACL?

NACL stands for Network Access Control List, and it controls the traffic to or from a subnet according to some defined rules.

It adds an additional layer of security at the subnet layer. For example, inbound rules may deny incoming traffic from certain IP addresses, while outbound rules may allow all traffic to leave the subnet.

Considering the fact that NACLs operate at the subnet level of a VPC, you can apply an NACL to one or more subnets. However, every subnet must be attached to a single NACL only.

What Is the Difference Between a Security Group and NACL?

Security Group	NACL
Operates at the instance level.	Operates at the subnet level.
Supports only allow rules.	Supports allow and deny rules.
Is stateful: Returned traffic is always allowed, regardless of rules. There is no way to add an outbound rule, so all allowed traffic returns by default. It maintains a state of allowed traffic. That's why it is called stateful.	Is stateless: Return traffic is not allowed by default; there should be explicitly allowed rules to allow it.
A security group can only be associated with an instance if it's specified when launching the instance or later associated with it.	Automatically applies to all instances in the subnets that it's associated with (therefore, it provides an additional layer of defense if the security group rules are too permissive).

NACLs and security groups operate on different layers in a VPC. Is it better to use NACLs or security groups to ensure your network's security?

Layers of security are what make up an in-depth defense, and security groups and NACLs make up two of these layers. Therefore, the best solution is to implement both to lock down your network.

That's all for this topic. The next section explains how to create a VPC, a public subnet, and a private subnet.

Create a VPC, Public, and Private Subnet

In this demo, you will create a VPC in your AWS account. You will also look at the parameters and options that AWS offers to create a VPC. You will also create an Internet gateway and configure public and private subnets. By the end of this lab, you will know how to create VPCs and make private and public subnets.

Start by going to the AWS Console:

1. First, you need to select the region. I chose Mumbai, as I wanted to create a VPC in the Asia Pacific Mumbai Region. Choose the region that's appropriate to your location.

2. Go to the VPC dashboard and search for VPC in the search bar. Click VPC to open the dashboard.

   You already have a VPC in your account. This is the default VPC that AWS creates. This VPC has a routing table and an Internet gateway in all the regions. You can use the default VPC for demo purposes, but it is always recommended that you create your own VPC for the Development, Test, and Production environments for the most suitable configuration. If you go to any region, you will find one VPC and some route tables, as well as an Internet gateway associated with that region.

3. Create your own VPC. Click VPCs and then click Create VPC.

4. Name the VPC Patckup. The next option is to select either IPv4 or IPv6 addresses for the VPC. Use IPv4 and provide 10.0.0.0/16 as the private IP range for this VPC.

5. Next is tenancy, which specifies where your infrastructure is provisioned. If you select the default tenancy, your EC2 instances will be on shared hardware with other AWS users. If you want a VPC where all EC2 instances are on dedicated hardware, you can create a dedicated VPC.

6. The next option is tags. As you can see, AWS created a Name tag for you. You don't need any more tags, so click Create VPC.

   You have now your own VPC in the region. Go back to the VPC page. You can see that there are now two VPCs in this region.

7. You will now create an Internet gateway and attach it to your VPC. To do that, click Internet Gateway. As you can see, you already have an Internet gateway for the default VPC.

8. Click Create Internet Gateway and name it Patckup-igw. Now, click Create an Internet Gateway.

9. Next, attach this Internet gateway to your VPC. You can do that directly by clicking Attach to VPC in the top green bar or by clicking the Actions button.

10. Click Attach to VPC and select your VPC. If you are using the AWS CLI, you can click the scroll bar and attach it to your VPC. But as this lab is not using the AWS-CLI, you can click and attach this Internet gateway directly.

You now have a VPC with an Internet gateway.
But you still cannot create an infrastructure in
the VPC. For that, you need subnets. Let's create
subnets next.

11. Click Subnets. Based on which region you are in, you
     will see three to four subnets. These are the default
     public subnets attached to the default VPC.

12. To create a subnet, click Create Subnets. First, you
     need to choose the VPC; choose the Patckup VPC
     that you created. Call this subnet PublicSubnet1.
     Select ap-south-1a AZ and give an IP range of
     10.0.0.0/24 for the subnet. You can skip the tags for
     now; click Create Subnet.

     You can now see the subnet in the list. You will
     create three more subnets.

13. Select the Patckup VPC, call this one PublicSubnet2,
     select ap-south-1b, and give an IP range of
     10.0.1.0/24. Click Create Subnet again and repeat
     the process. This time, name it PrivateSubnet1, AZ
     ap-south-1a, and an IP range of 10.0.2.0/24. Name
     the final subnet PrivateSubnet2, AZ ap-south-1b,
     and an IP range of 10.0.3.0/24.

     Note that you cannot have overlapping IP ranges in
     subnets.

     Now you have four subnets across two Availability
     Zones in the Mumbai region. What is the difference
     between the private and public subnets? You created
     them using the same method; their names are just
     different. As of now, all four of these subnets are

private. The difference between private and public subnets is that the route tables of the public subnets have an Internet gateway entry. If you see the details of the route tables in your subnets, you only have one entry, `10.0.0.0/16`, that is local. This simply means that any requests going to routes within this range are to be routed within the VPC.

14. Now you'll create a public route table for these subnets. Click the route table. There are two route tables in this account. One is attached to the default VPC of the region and the other is attached to the new VPC you created. If you see the default route table of the default VPC, in the Routes section, you can see that there is an entry to the Internet gateway. This means that all the default subnets of the default VPC have this route, which makes them public subnets. If you see the route table of your VPC, you only have the local route, which makes your subnets private.

    Now click Create Route Table and give it the name `patckup-rt-public`. Next, select your VPC and click Create Route Table. You now have another "private" route table.

    You need to add the Internet gateway path to the table. Click Edit Routes and then click Add Route. Select `0.0.0.0/0` as the destination, choose the Internet Gateway as the target, and select `patckup-igw`. Then click Save Changes. You now have a new public route table in your VPC.

15.   Now you need to associate your route table to
       the public subnets. You can do that by clicking
       Actions Edit Subnet Associations and selecting
       PublicSubnet1 and PublicSubnet2. Then click Save
       Associations.

Go to the Subnets page and look at your subnets. You will see that
the public subnets are part of the new route table, which has the Internet
gateway entry. You can also do that by clicking the Edit Route Table
Association button to change the route tables for a subnet.

You set up a VPC with two public and two private subnets that you
will be using throughout this book. Creating and keeping VPCs, Internet
gateways, and route tables is completely free, so you do not need to
delete them.

I hope you understood all that you did in this demo. That's all for
this topic.

Summary

VPCs (Virtual Private Clouds) are virtual networks dedicated to your AWS
account. They are logically isolated from other virtual networks in the
AWS Cloud. They give you complete control over the virtual networking
environment, including selecting IP ranges, creating subnets, and
configuring route tables and gateways. Within your VPC, you can launch
Amazon EC2, RDS, and so on.

When you create a VPC, you need to give a name and a range of IP
addresses called CIDR (Classless Inter-Domain Routing)—for example,
10.0.0.0/16.

Some facts about VPC:

- A virtual private cloud spans across all the Availability Zones (AZs) in the region.

- You have complete control over your network and can decide who has access to the AWS resources inside your VPC.

- You can select your own IP address ranges and create subnets, route tables, and network gateways.

- A default VPC gets created inside each region in your account.

- In each region, a default VPC is created with a subnet in each AZ.

That's all about VPCs. Note that it's good practice to terminate all the resources that you created in your AWS account so that you do not get charged. However, resources created in this chapter will not cost you anything.

See you in the next chapter.

CHAPTER 6

Elastic Compute Cloud (EC2)

This chapter covers the compute services in AWS. You will learn about virtual machines, Elastic Cloud Compute (EC2), Amazon EC2 features, the naming conventions for EC2 instances, and the different types of EC2 instances. You will also learn how to create an EC2 instance.

Compute Services in AWS

Compute is another one of the core offerings in cloud computing, and there are various cost-effective and flexible compute services available in AWS for different requirements. This section explains what compute is and discusses the different compute services available in AWS.

Consider this example. Imagine you have your dream job as an architect at a space technology company, where your job is to work with the data science team and process the data to make some sense of it. The research team has collected huge amounts of image data that might lead to the discovery of water on Mars! It is the job of your team to process that image data and come up with the findings. But when you start processing this data, you realize that you don't have any free servers to do the work.

What does it mean to not have free servers? Well, you need powerful computers to process the huge amount of data and, in this case, you also need processing power to process that data. This processing power is known as compute. For any program or application that you want to run, you need memory to open the program and CPU to process the commands that you give the program. Hence, the combination of memory and CPU is what is referred to as *compute*. It can also include other resources like networking, storage, and so on, depending on the type of application you are running.

Cloud computing makes it very easy to get compute power whenever you want, configure it based on your requirements, and pay only for what you use.

AWS has various compute services for different requirements, but it is important to understand which compute resource best suits your workload and which compute options are available in AWS.

First of all, let's look at what AWS Compute is.

AWS offers an on-demand computing service for running cloud-based applications. These are useful for applications that can be deployed on a remote server and accessed over the Internet.

AWS provides computing resources like instances and containers. Instances are nothing but virtual machines.

AWS also provides serverless computing to run applications and you do not need infrastructure setup or configuration when you go for a serverless compute option.

AWS Compute resources are available on-demand and can be created with just a few clicks of a mouse. You only pay for the resources you use and only for as long as you're using them.

AWS Compute resources are broadly classified into three categories:

- Instances, which are virtual machines
- Containers
- Serverless computing

In this chapter, we discuss them all. This will help you decide which is the best compute service for your requirements.

If you want to learn more about AWS Compute, check the link[1] provided in the Resources section. The document has different examples and scenarios of where you might use different compute services.

Now that you know what compute is and know about the compute services that are available in AWS, let's move on to virtual machines.

Virtual Machines

This book has mentioned the term virtual machines several times already. I hope you already have an idea about what these are. Before diving deeper into the things, let's look at virtual machines in detail.

A virtual machine is a virtual environment that works like a computer within a computer. Sounds complex, right? Let's break it down.

A virtual machine (VM) acts just like any other physical device, such as your computer or smartphone. It is equipped with a CPU, memory, disks for storing your files, and a network to connect to the Internet.

Your laptop and smartphone seem real because they are physical. VMs can be thought of as virtual computers within a physical computer.

Say you have a laptop and it has Windows operating system on it. But you feel like learning Linux. For that, you need the Linux operating system. Do you have to buy a new laptop and install the Linux Operating System? No, you can simply use the virtualization technique to virtualize your existing laptop and install the Linux Operating System on it. Basically, you can use both operating systems on the same laptop.

How do you use virtualization techniques to create a virtual machine? Let's look at this animation. Your physical computer is shown in Figure 6-1. This could be your own computer, a remote server, or a server located in a data center owned by a cloud provider.

---

[1] https://aws.amazon.com/products/compute/

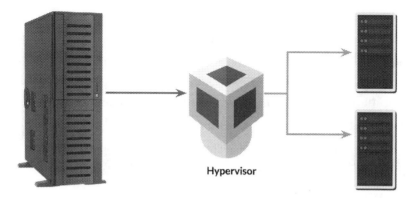

Figure 6-1. *Virtualization*

You use software called a hypervisor, which is also known as virtual machine manager. In this case, you can use the Oracle VM VirtualBox.

Hypervisors create virtual versions of computers that contain the desired amounts of processors, memory, and storage. The virtual machine always borrows CPU, memory, and disk space from the physical host computer. That means a part of your computer's CPU, RAM, and storage will now work as a stand-alone computer.

To understand it better, assume you have a physical computer with 8 GB RAM, two CPUs, and a 40 GB hard disk. You can use a virtualization tool to create two or more virtual machines and distribute this CPU, memory, and hard disk between these two virtual machines. You could have two virtual machines called VM1 and VM2. They have 4 GB RAM, one vCPU, and a 20 GB hard disk each, and more importantly, they run two different operating systems (see Figure 6-2).

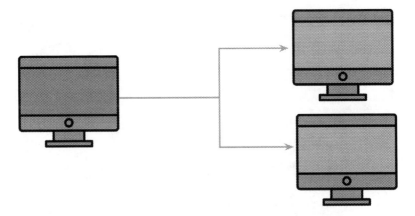

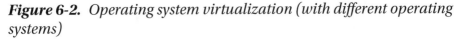

Figure 6-2. *Operating system virtualization (with different operating systems)*

A virtual machine acts like an actual computer, and it has a different operating system. Despite using the same hardware, virtual machines operate in a completely independent manner. There is no interaction between the software inside the virtual machine and the host or other virtual machine on the same physical computer.

As a result, virtual machines run as separate computers with their own operating systems. The virtual machines remain completely independent from another virtual machine and the physical host machine.

A virtual machine is highly portable since it is independent of other virtual machines. That means you can instantly move a virtual machine from one hypervisor to another. Virtual machines are flexible and portable. They offer many benefits, as discussed in the following sections.

Cost Savings

You can run multiple virtual machines on a single physical host. This can drastically reduce your physical infrastructure costs, as you will have to buy fewer physical computers.

Agility and Speed

It is relatively simple and quick to spin up a virtual machine. A virtual machine can be provisioned much faster and easier than a physical machine. In this way, virtualization speeds up the process of running dev-test scenarios, so that the entire process can be completed a lot faster.

Less Downtime

A virtual machine is portable and easy to move. As a result, they make excellent backup solutions in case of an unexpected downtime on the host machine.

Scalability

Virtual machines make it easier to scale your application as creating a virtual machine is easier than setting up a physical machine.

You can simply add multiple virtual servers and distribute the workload among them. This is how you can improve the performance and availability of your application.

These are all benefits of virtual machines. In the next section, you will learn about AWS EC2 (Elastic Cloud Compute).

Amazon Elastic Compute Cloud (EC2)

This section starts with the most common compute service that AWS has to offer. This is the Elastic Compute Cloud, commonly known as EC2. It provides a scalable computing option in the Amazon Cloud. But what is compute capacity?

Well! You have already learned that it is nothing but virtual machines and EC2 is a compute service in AWS.

EC2 is scalable. That means you can increase or decrease the size of a virtual machine based on your requirements. If that doesn't work, you can create additional virtual machines as well.

By using Amazon EC2, you can avoid setting up the hardware to run your applications and can develop and deploy applications faster. Another benefit of using an EC2 is that you do not need to invest in hardware. You can have virtual machines of desired capacity that can be accessed using your normal computers.

EC2 is an IaaS (Infrastructure as a Service). Because you rent a virtual machine from AWS, AWS will take care of purchasing and maintenance of hardware. You can get the desired capacity without having to worry about the hardware. This is intended to make web-scale cloud computing more accessible to developers.

To understand this, let's go back to the times when cloud computing wasn't there. To host an application, you had to set up a data center or rent a physical server. That's entirely possible for big organizations but think about mid-size companies, start-ups, or even individual developers like you and me. They cannot afford to get the data centers and hardware. After cloud computing, it became significantly easier for developers to get virtual machines. All thanks to cloud computing.

You can use Amazon EC2 to launch as many or as few virtual machines as you need.[2]

There is no limitation. If you want one virtual machine, you can get one, if you need 1,000 virtual machines, you can get 1,000 virtual machines.

Amazon EC2 makes it easier to scale up or down the virtual machines to handle unexpected loads. You don't need to forecast traffic.

You can scale up and scale down virtual machines based on traffic and the popularity of your applications. Amazon EC2 has an autoscaling

---

[2] https://aws.amazon.com/ec2/

feature that you will learn about later. You can configure autoscaling to increase or decrease the number of virtual machines based on the load on your application.

It lets you run on Amazon's proven computing environment and gives you complete control of your computing resources.

As you know by now, EC2 virtual machines are located in the Amazon data center. SINCE security is very important for your applications, AWS gives you complete control of these servers so that you can secure your application as you need. There are other ways to secure those servers that are covered in later chapters.

Recently, Amazon web services have also started supporting macOS operating system-based virtual machines.

These are some of the major benefits of Amazon EC2. In the next section, you will learn about the different components of EC2.

Amazon EC2 Components

Now that you've learned about Elastic Compute Cloud (EC2) and its benefits. you will learn about the elements of Amazon EC2.

Instances

So when you launch a virtual machine in Amazon, you say that you launched an EC2 *instance*. Going forward, instead of calling it an EC2 virtual machine, this book refers to it as an EC2 instance.

AMI (Amazon Machine Image)

Another important element in Amazon EC2 is AMI (Amazon Machine Image). This is basically a template that contains an operating system and additional software needed to launch EC2 instances.

Let's make it simple. An EC2 instance is a virtual machine, right? A virtual machine is similar to your laptop.

Let's assume you bought a new laptop. You need to install the operating system and some general software, such as drivers, browsers, media players, and so on. Without these operating systems and software, your laptop is just an expensive box.

The same is the case with an EC2 instance. It is also like your computer, and that's why it requires an operating system and additional software in order to use it. In AWS, you can do this by using AMI. All you need to do is attach an AMI to your instance and it will load the operating system and the supporting software on your instance.

Key Pairs[3]

Once you launch an EC2 instance, you need to access it so that you can install your application or do some configuration. To access your EC2 instance, you need some kind of credentials; those credentials are nothing but a key pair.

A key pair consists of a public key and a private key. It is a set of security credentials that you use to prove your identity when connecting to an Amazon EC2 instance.

In the process of launching an instance, AWS will ask you to specify a key pair. You can use an existing one or create a new one.

When you create a key pair on AWS, you can easily download the private key, while AWS keeps the public key. As a consequence, when you run an EC2 instance, Amazon stores the public key automatically on each instance you launch.

The idea is that you will use the private key that you have created to log in to the EC2 instance of your choice. You will see how this works during the EC2 demo.

---

[3] https://docs.aws.amazon.com/AWSEC2/latest/UserGuide/ec2-key-pairs.html

An important point to note here is that since you use a private key to log in to your EC2 instances, anyone who has this private key can also connect to your instances. Make sure that you store your private key in a secure place.

Security Groups

Another essential element of EC2 is the security group. This is another service that you can use to further secure your instances. Security groups let you control who can access your EC2 instances.

They act as virtual firewalls for your EC2 instances and control the inbound and outbound traffic.

Inbound means you can configure who can connect to your EC2 instance from the outside, and outbound means what your EC2 instance can connect with.

EC2 Tags

Another element of EC2 are tags. A tag is a label for your AWS resources. It can be assigned by you or by AWS. Tags have keys and values.

When you create an EC2 instance, you can tag your virtual machines with different names. They can be the environment, the cost center, the owners, or the application name. These tags help you identify your servers when you have thousands of servers running in your account.

Each tag key must be unique for each resource, and each tag key can have only one value.[4]

You can use tags to organize the resources in your account and to track your AWS costs by using cost allocation tags.

---

[4]https://docs.aws.amazon.com/AWSEC2/latest/UserGuide/Using_Tags.html

Let's look at cost allocation tags. Some organizations have cost centers, and when you run multiple applications in one AWS account, you can tag EC2 instances with the cost center key and value, which will help you track the cost, per the cost center.

So far, these are the different terms and features you need to know and understand regarding Amazon EC2.

In the next section, you learn about the EC2 instance naming conventions.

EC2 Instance Naming Conventions

Recall that EC2 instances are comprised of various elements, like Amazon machine images, security groups, key pairs, and tags. There is one more important feature of the EC2 instance that you need to understand. It is the *type* of EC2 instance. But before that, you need to understand the EC2 instance naming conventions. This will teach you how to read the names of EC2 instances. In this section, you first learn the EC2 instance naming conventions. You will not find a clear explanation about this over the Internet, not even in the AWS documentation, so be sure that you understand this section, as it will help you a lot during your journey with AWS Cloud.

An AWS instance name looks something like M6g.2xlarge. As you can see, the name contains characters and numbers. The complete name doesn't really have a meaning. Let's break it down and try to make sense of it. One thing is clear, if you put everything together, this is an instance type. If you look at any instance type, it will look something like this.

The name of this instance type (see Figure 6-3) is made up of four components:

- Instance family
- Instance generation

- Additional capability

- Instance size

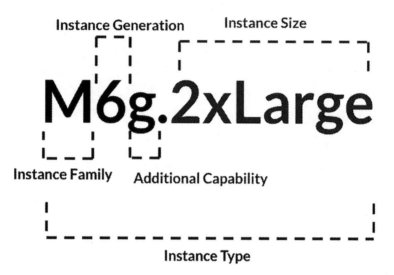

Figure 6-3. *Instance type*

Let's go over these one by one.

An AWS EC2 Instance Family

The first letter of the instance type represents the EC2 instance family. Here, the M represents the instance family (see Figure 6-4).

Figure 6-4. *Instance family*

This AWS EC2 instance belongs to the general-purpose computing instance family type. It is available in four types: general-purpose, compute-optimized, memory-optimized, and storage-optimized. The next lesson covers them in detail. (There are also sub-classifications within these four instance families, but they are not essential at this level, so we will skip them.)

An AWS EC2 Instance Generation

Next, the number 6 in M6g represents the generation (see Figure 6-5) of the AWS EC2 instance.

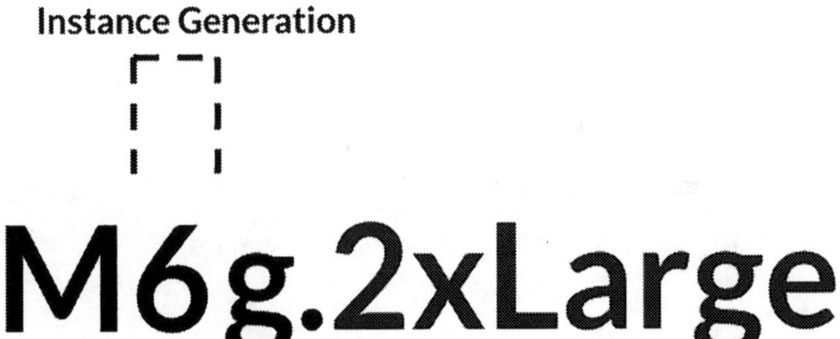

Instance Generation

M6g.2xLarge

Figure 6-5. Instance generation

The latest or the most current generation of AWS EC2 instances is always better. It is also cheaper than the previous generations. That's why AWS always recommends using the newest generation instance type.

You can relate this to a car; the company always launches new car models with new features and it recommends the latest models to its customers.

AWS EC2 Additional Capability

Then you have g in the same, which represents the additional capability (see Figure 6-6) of the EC2 instance.

Figure 6-6. *Additional capabilities*

Table 6-1 lists all these capabilities.

Table 6-1. *EC2 Additional Capabilities*

Property	Representation
AMD	a
Graviton2	g
Local NVMe SSD	d
High networking (100Gbps)	n
Extra capacity	e

AMD and Graviton2 are the two processors inside these EC2 instances. If the processor is also in your requirements, you can select a processor-based EC2 instance as well. AWS also offers Local NVMe SSD storage, which is directly attached to EC2 to get better network performance. Hence, high networking and extra capacity are two capabilities of this instance type.

The final and most important component of this instance type is the instance size.

AWS EC2 Instance Size

The 2xlarge part of M6g.2xlarge represents the instance size (see Figure 6-7). Let's look at what the 2xlarge means.

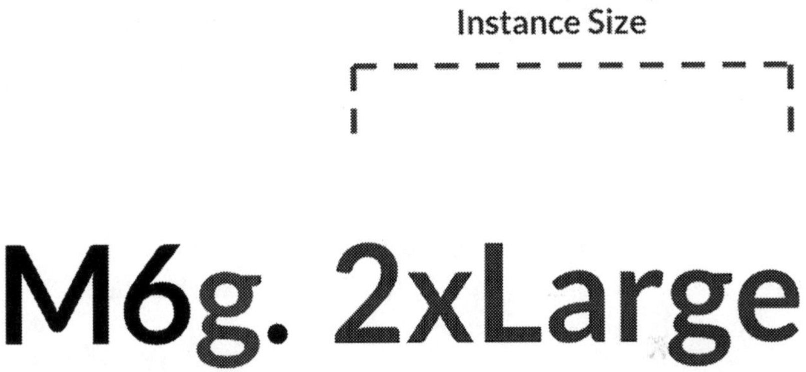

Instance Size

M6g. 2xLarge

Figure 6-7. *Instance size*

The 2xlarge denotes the T-shirt size representation of the AWS EC2 instance. It represents the amount of CPU, memory, storage, and network performance of an EC2 instance.

This instance size (2xLarge) has twice the amount of CPU, memory, and storage resources as compared to the base size (xlarge).

Let's look at how this works with instance sizing.

Instance Sizing

Each instance size (2xlarge) has twice the amount of CPU and memory as the previous size (xlarge) (see Figure 6-8). Two m6g.xlarge equal one m6g.2xlarge. Similarly, two m6g.2xlarge equal one m5g.4xlarge.

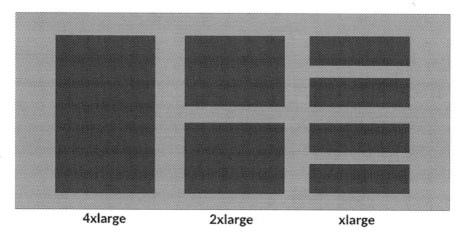

4xlarge   **2xlarge**   **xlarge**

Figure 6-8. *Instance sizing*

Let's look at this concept from a capacity perspective. If you go to the
AWS documentation and navigate to the m6a instance type, you will see the
image shown in Figure 6-9.

Viewing 404 of 404 available instances					
Q m6g					✕ ‹ 1 ›
Instance name ▲	**On-Demand hourly rate** ▽	**vCPU** ▽	**Memory** ▽	**Storage** ▽	**Network performance** ▽
m6g.medium	$0.0385	1	4 GiB	EBS Only	Up to 10 Gigabit
m6g.large	$0.077	2	8 GiB	EBS Only	Up to 10 Gigabit
m6g.xlarge	$0.154	4	16 GiB	EBS Only	Up to 10 Gigabit
m6g.2xlarge	$0.308	8	32 GiB	EBS Only	Up to 10 Gigabit
m6g.4xlarge	$0.616	16	64 GiB	EBS Only	Up to 10 Gigabit
m6g.8xlarge	$1.232	32	128 GiB	EBS Only	10 Gigabit
m6g.12xlarge	$1.848	48	192 GiB	EBS Only	12 Gigabit
m6g.16xlarge	$2.464	64	256 GiB	EBS Only	25 Gigabit

Figure 6-9. *Available instances*

As you can see, xlarge has twice the amount of CPU and memory compared to large. The on-demand hourly cost is also twice as much.

How do you decide if you should use one 2xlarge instance or two xlarge instances, for example? For that, let's look at the price and capacity of each instance. As you can see, there is no difference between them. Whether you select two xlarge or one 2xlarge, you will end up getting the same capacity at the same cost.

It is always better to use a smaller instance sizes instead of bigger ones unless you have specific needs. There are far too many instance classifications of AWS EC2; you will learn about the essential ones in the next section.

Although this is not well documented anywhere, AWS EC2 uses excellent naming conventions. I hope this section helped you understand this.

In the next section, you learn about the different EC2 instance types.

Instance Types

You learned about the instance type naming conventions and about EC2 instance size, family, generation, and the additional capabilities. All these will help you when determining the EC2 instance type for your application. This section digs a little deeper and explains the different EC2 instance types. Once you successfully complete this section, you will be able to decide which instance type best suits your requirements.

Let's start with a quick recap of what the EC2 instance type is. It is a combination of CPU, memory, storage, and networking capacity. Having different combinations helps when choosing the appropriate mix for your applications.

When you launch the EC2 instance, the instance type is one of the mandatory elements you need to determine. Let's look at why this is important with an example.

When you need to buy a laptop, you first define your requirements. Based on those requirements, you select a configuration for your laptop like memory, storage, graphics, and so on.

The same goes for an EC2 instance. When you launch an EC2 instance in Amazon, you need to provide CPU, memory, storage, and networking configurations. To make this easy, AWS has instance types with different instance sizes in terms of CPU, memory, storage, and networking.

Each instance type has multiple size options for different workloads. You learned about instance size in the last section. You should launch instance types that best fit your applications.

Let's look at what is meant by "best fit" here. Each application is designed differently, and they each require a specific hardware configuration. Some need more memory, others need more CPU, and so on. You should use the appropriate compute capacity for your applications.

It is easy to select the best configuration for your applications in AWS, as Amazon instance types are grouped into families to meet different use cases.

This section looks at these four basic and essential EC2 instance types:

- General-purpose instances

- Compute-optimized instances

- Memory-optimized instances

- Storage-optimized instances

Let's start with the general-purpose instance type.

General-Purpose Instances

This instance has a good balance of compute, memory, and networking resources that makes it well suited for a variety of workloads. As its name suggests, this is the most basic AWS EC2 instance type.

Use general-purpose instances when you are not sure whether the application needs more CPU or memory. They come with a balance of memory, compute, and networking,. If you find out later that your application is more memory-optimized or compute-optimized, you can go for specific types of instances.

General-purpose instances are best suited for web servers, caching fleets, and distributed data store applications, as these applications require a good balance of memory, CPU, and networking.

They are also suitable for development, test, and demo environment applications.

Compute-Optimized Instances

Compute-optimized instances are ideal for compute-bound and high-performance applications that benefit from high-performance processors.

This instance type is optimized for CPU in comparison to other compute power, like memory, storage, and networking.

Therefore, the instance type that has more powerful CPUs comes inside this category.

For applications that require the most compute power, this is the best option. In addition to batch processing and media transcoding, compute-optimized instances can also be used for high-performance web servers, high-performance computing (HPC), scientific modeling, game servers, advertising servers, machine learning inferences, and many other applications that require high levels of computing power.

Memory-Optimized Instances

Memory-optimized instances can deliver fast performance for workloads that require a huge amount of memory to process large data sets.

These instances are optimized on memory. When you look at instance types in the memory-optimized category and memory-optimized family, they have more memory than storage, CPU, and networking. In other words, memory-optimized instance types are optimized for memory over other features.

An application such as an open-source database, an in-memory cache, or a Big Data analytics solution that involves real-time analysis of large data sets are best uses for memory-optimized instances.

Storage-Optimized Instances[5]

Storage-optimized instances are designed for workloads that require high, sequential read and write access to massive data sets on local storage.

This instance type can deliver tens of thousands of random input/output (I/O) operations per second (IOPS), which can be accessed by applications with extremely low latency.

This instance type is optimized at the network side of the EC2 instance. It supports more read and write actions to the disk. When your application does a lot of reading and writing to the disk, database, or network, you should use a storage optimized instance type. With this instance type, input-output intensive or business-critical workloads can be processed as many transactions as possible per second (TPS).

Transactions per second (TPS) refers to the number of transactions the network can process in a second. If an EC2 instance can complete ten transactions to and from storage without delay, you say that the instance can process a max of ten transactions per second.

---

[5] https://docs.aws.amazon.com/AWSEC2/latest/UserGuide/storage-optimized-instances.html

An application that has medium-size data sets that need high compute performance and high network throughput is a good use of a storage-optimized instance. As an example, there are relational databases such as MySQL, MariaDB, PostgreSQL, as well as NoSQL databases such as KeyDB, ScyllaDB, and Cassandra.

A storage-optimized instance is also an excellent choice for workloads that need access to relatively large amounts of data on local storage very quickly, such as search engines and analytics projects.

To sum up, the most important point here is to understand these four main classifications and their common use cases. When you're selecting an instance type for your application, ask yourself these questions:

- Does your application perform memory heavy work?

- Does your application perform compute heavy work?

- Does your application need high IO work?

- Will generic work do the trick?

Once you have an understanding of the main classification, the sub-classification will come naturally. For example, with a memory-optimized instance, you may need higher RAM or higher optimized memory.

Once you know the instance type, you should always choose the smaller size instance to run experimentation. Based on the experiment and the tests, decide on the actual instance size. As a rule of thumb, always choose a smaller instance size, because it will save you money.

Amazon EC2 Purchase Types

This section explains the different EC2 instance purchasing options. Amazon EC2 instances can be purchased in five ways: on-demand, reserved instances, spot instances, savings plans, and dedicated hosts. Using the best purchasing option, you can optimize your costs based on your requirements.

You will get a 90 percent discount on spot instances and a 75 percent discount on reserved instances compared to on-demand instances.

As you see, there is a significant cost difference between the different instance purchasing options. A proper understanding of instance purchasing options can you save a significant amount of money.

On-Demand Instances

With Amazon EC2 on-demand instances, you can purchase compute capacity by the hour or second (a minimum 60 seconds), with no long-term commitment, and you can manage their lifecycles at any time.

There are three crucial concepts that you need to understand.

Paying for Compute Capacity by the Hour or Second

This means that you only pay for the capacity you use.

If you use one EC2 instance for one hour, you will pay for one EC2 instance for one hour. If you use two EC2 instances for three days, you will pay for two EC2 instances for three days. This is a pay-per-use pricing model, and you only pay when you use it.

No Long-Term Commitments

Another benefit of on-demand purchasing is that you do not need to commit to using it. Suppose you need an EC2 instance for two hours. You use it for two hours. You can stop, start, or terminate an EC2 instance any time and you no longer need to pay.

No Upfront Payment, But High Cost

Again, you don't need to pay in advance. Suppose you use an instance for two hours. AWS will charge for two hours, which will come in your monthly bill.

Use Cases for On-Demand Instances

Let's look at some use cases. On-demand instances are generally used for short-term, spiky, or unpredictable workloads, and they are also suitable for the application development and testing phase. When you don't know your needs, they will keep changing over time. In this case, you should use on-demand instances.

One important point here: the on-demand instance is the costliest instance type in AWS.

Reserved Instances

As its name suggests, you can reserve these instances. With the reserved instance purchasing option, you book an EC2 instance for one or three years, and you get a 75 percent discount compared to on-demand instances. Let's break that down.

Reservation Periods

With the reserve instance purchasing options, you commit to using EC2 instances for either one year or three years. As you are willing to book EC2 instances for a longer period, AWS gives you a significant discount.

75 Percent Discount Compared to On-Demand Instances

The longer you commit, the better the discount you get. Your discount on a three-year commitment will be larger than a one-year commitment. Apart from the long-term commitment, a payment factor also decides how much discount you get. You can pay in three ways: no upfront, partial upfront, or all upfront.

- **All Upfront:** Selecting All Upfront means you pay for your EC2 instances right now. Because you pay a one-year EC2 cost once at a time, AWS gives you an even bigger discount.

- **Partial Upfront:** If you select Partial Upfront, you pay some upfront and the remaining monthly. Your discount will be relatively less.

- **No Upfront:** With No Upfront, you pay monthly and you commit to using it for one year.

When you reserve for one year and make All Upfront payments, you get a 75 percent discount, whereas for Partial Upfront, you get a 60 percent discount, and for No Upfront, you get a 50 percent discount.

As far as the difference between No Upfront and on-demand, you still get a discount when committing for either one year or three years, but the discount will be less.

There is another factor you need to consider while purchasing reserved instances, and that's the instance type.

Reserve-Specific Instance Types

As you are booking an EC2 instance, you have to reserve a specific instance type. So, for example, you have to say you want a T2 micro or a m5.large.

You also need to even commit specific instance types in reserve instances, and you will only get a discount in that particular instance type.

Additionally, reserved instances are allocated to specific Availability Zones. In this way, the instance type provides a capacity reservation, giving you additional assurance that this instance type is always available for you in a particular Availability Zone.

But there is a problem: This type of benefit also makes you inflexible, and you will be stuck with one instance type and Availability Zone.

That's where AWS introduced three flavors of reserved instances: Standard, Convertible, and Schedule Reserve instance types.

Standard Reserve Instance Types

In comparison to on-demand instances, standard reserved instances (RI) provide you with an extremely significant discount (up to 72 percent) if you purchase them for two or three years.

If you want to change the Availability Zone, instance size, or networking type of your standard reserved instances, you can do so at any time.

Convertible Reserved Instance Types

It is a good idea to purchase convertible reserved instances if you need extra flexibility, such as the ability to switch instance families, operating systems (OS), or tenancy levels at any time.

Convertible reserved instances provide a discount (up to 66 percent) compared to on-demand instances. They can be purchased on one-year and three-year terms.

For example, if you purchase the T2.micro instance type, you can change it to an r5d.xlarge.

This will give you less of a discount, because you can change the EC2 instance type.

Schedule Reserve Instance Types

AWS scheduled reserved instances let you reserve capacity scheduled to recur daily, weekly, or monthly, with a specified start time and a one-year term. After you complete your purchase, the instances are available to launch during the time windows that you specified.[6]

For example, if you know you need to launch the EC2 instance within a specific time window every day or weekly, you reserve it and get a discount.

Spot Instance Type

Next are spot instances. Spot instances are great because they provide you with the highest discount in AWS. You get 90 percent discount compared to on-demand instances!

Lost Any Time

But the particularity of the spot instances is that you can lose them at any point in time if the price you're willing to pay for them is less than the current spot price. What this means is that the spot price changes over time, and you're saying what you're willing to pay the maximum amount for these spot instances, so you can lose them.

Spot Instance Type User Case

These are the most cost-efficient instances in AWS, but if you use them, you need to use them for workloads that will be resilient to failure. For example, batch jobs, data analysis once at a time, and image processing. If you want to transform images, but somehow don't transform one, that's fine, as you can retry later.

---

[6] https://docs.aws.amazon.com/AWSEC2/latest/UserGuide/ec2-scheduled-instances.html

For any distributed workloads, this is the cloud so the servers can work together in a distributed fashion. If one of these servers fails, the other ones will know how to react to that failure and work together without the one server that has been terminated.

For example, if you have a workload that has a flexible start and end time, a spot instance could be great. But spot instances are really not great at running critical jobs or databases.

The Savings Plan

Before you choose a savings plan, analyze which EC2 purchasing option is best for you. Of course, reserve an instance if you know that you will use it for one or three years. I have seen customers save a million dollars with the reserve instance purchasing option.

To summarize, you are committing to a specific instance type for a period with a reserved instance.

For example, you could reserve a `m5.large` instance for 12 months. For some reason, if you no longer require the `m5.large` instance, you can give credit to another `m5` instance running the same operating system.

To make this flexible, AWS introduced Convertible RIs (reserve instances) RIs, which allow you to change the RI credit to another similar instance type or a different operating system.

As you know, you can save up to 72 percent on the reserve instance purchasing options. But you have to do significant management for purchases and exchanges.

That's why AWS introduced savings plans. In a savings plan, you simply commit to a minimum hourly spend on compute usage over a 12- or 36-month term. Every AWS Compute service has an hourly rate and a savings plan rate.

Significant Savings

Savings plans help you reduce AWS Compute costs by up to 66 percent. The best thing is that it applies to all compute resources regardless of the AWS region, instance type, or size.

Ideally, you no longer need to get involved in complex reserve instance management. Once you have committed, compute resources are in the Savings Plan. That's all.

Flexible Plans

AWS offers three types of savings plans:

- Compute savings plans

- EC2 instance savings plans

- Amazon SageMaker savings plans

Let's look at these one by one.

Compute Savings Plan

First is the Compute savings plan. It helps you reduce compute costs by up to 66 percent. It automatically applies to all instance types regardless of instance family, region, or operating system. It also covers instances launched by other AWS services, such as Elastic MapReduce, Elastic Container Service, and Elastic Kubernetes Service.

Instance Savings Plan

Next is the EC2 instance savings plan. It offers the most significant savings, up to 72 percent. This plan applies to a specific EC2 instance type within a particular region. This savings plan enables you to switch to different instance sizes within the same instance type, such as from m5.large to m5.xlarge, and it is like the Convertible RI. You can change operating systems.

You can easily sign up for a one- or three-year term savings plan in AWS Cost Explorer. You can manage your plans by taking advantage of recommendations, performance reporting, and budget alerts.

Amazon SageMaker Savings Plan

The Amazon SageMaker savings plan is a flexible pricing model for Amazon SageMaker.

You can select a reserve instance or a savings plan. Savings plans offer a more flexible and easier-to-manage alternative to optimizing AWS Compute costs.

Dedicated Hosts

The last EC2 purchase option is the dedicated host. AWS Dedicated Hosts are physically dedicated servers with Amazon EC2 instance capacity, which are fully dedicated to your needs. There are additional benefits that can be derived from Amazon EC2 Dedicated Hosts, such as better visibility, greater flexibility, and complete control over the placement of instances.

In order to meet your compliance and regulatory requirements, AWS Dedicated Hosts make it easier for you to deploy your instances in a way that meets these requirements.

Reservations are also available for the dedicated host. Reservations for the dedicated host can be purchased and assigned to the host, and you will benefit from a low rate over the term compared to on-demand charges. You can save up to 70 percent on your on-demand charges over the term with reservations.

Create an EC2 Instance

In this section, you learn how to launch an EC2 instance via the AWS Console. You also learn about the different steps and features AWS offers while launching the EC2 instances. By the end of this chapter, you will be able to launch EC2 instances through the Management Console, so pay special attention and then try it yourself.

1. Go to the AWS Management Console. Type **EC2** in the search bar and click the EC2 search result to go directly into the EC2 dashboard. As you can see, you have no instances in your account. If you click Instances, it will take you to the Instance page. This page contains a list of all instances in this region. Since you don't have any instances, the list is empty. Let's launch your first EC2 instance.

2. First make sure you choose a region that is close to you or your customers. Since I am in India, I select the Mumbai region.

3. Click Launch Instances. First, you have to choose an AMI (Amazon Machine Image). Here, you have a list of AMIs to choose from—Amazon Linux2, macOS, Red Hat, and many more. If you look at the dashboard on your left, you will see other options.

   Go to My AMIs, where you will see a list of your own custom-made AMIs. (As of now, you do not have any, so you won't see any AMIs listed here.)

   The next option is AWS Marketplace, where you have thousands of AMIs created by third-party vendors. Then you have community AMIs, which are developed by AWS and its users. They are free for everyone to use. Note that you should always be careful when using AMIs created by people other than AWS or trusted AWS vendors. There could be security holes in them.

For the purpose of this demo, you will create a Linux EC2 instance with Amazon Linux 2 AMI. This AMI is free tier eligible, which means that you can launch the instance without spending any money. So select Amazon Linux 2, which will take you to Step 2, to choose an instance type.

4. As you can see, you have many instance types available. Scroll down and you will see a long list of instances. You can filter these instances based on their families and generations.

    There are varieties of instances based on different requirements; the list includes instances with RAM optimized, CPU optimized, GPU optimized, and so on. In this demo, you will use `t2.micro` because you do not have any special requirements and you also want to stay in the free tier. And as you can see, `T2.micro` is the only instance available for free. In some regions, you will see `T3.micro` as well. If you are just practicing, make sure that you choose the free tier eligible instance type to avoid any code.

    You could now review and launch this instance immediately just by clicking here. But before doing so, go to Configure Instance Details, which will open up a whole lot of options. Let's explore some of the important parameters one by one.

The first option is the Number of Instances. If you need more than one instance, you can change this and create multiple EC2 instances with the same configuration. You can also launch an EC2 instance in Launch into Auto Scaling Group by clicking the Launch into Auto Scaling Group link. For now, stick to one instance. This is covered in the next chapter.

5. Next, you have the network option to choose your VPCs. Choose the patckup VPC that you created in the previous lab. Select the subnet where you want to launch the instance. Since you want the instance to be accessible from the Internet, you should choose a public subnet. The next option asks you if you want AWS to assign a public IP to this Instance. Leave this enabled for now.

6. Now you need to specify a key pair. Since you don't have any existing key pairs for your account, you need to create one. Choose to create a new key pair and add a key pair name. For this example, name the key pair pakctup and then click the download key pair. You will see that a .PEM file is downloaded. It is important to keep this file safe, as you will need it to access your EC2 instance. Also, remember that it cannot be downloaded again.

7. The next important parameter is the role. This role is used to give permissions as to who can access this EC2 Instance. Select the role you created in your first lab. If you want to create a new role, you can navigate to IAM by clicking the Create New IAM Role link and then create a role.

8. Click Next to go to the next page, Add Storage. As you can see, you already have one EBS volume selected; this is the root volume that holds the operating system and other software for this instance.

    Add new storage to your instance. Click Add a New Volume and specify the parameters of your volume. Under the Device column, you can see the /dev/sdb path. This is where your volume will be attached. Leave it set as the default for now and move on. In the Snapshot option, you can choose to create a new EBS from a snapshot that you created before. Since you have no such requirements, you can leave it empty for now.

    Next is the Volume Size. Change the volume to 10 GBs. The next column is the Volume Type. You have SSDs, HDDs, and magnetic storage to choose from. If you look at the volume type for root volume, you will see that you have fewer options there. This is because only SSDs can be a root volume for an EC2 instance. You do not have the HDD option for the root volume. Coming back to this new volume, leave this as GP2, which is the general-purpose SSD.

    The next option is IOPS. As you can see, you have no option to change this. Go back and change your volume type. If you choose io1, io2, or gp3, you can provide IOPS. This is because IOPS are fixed for gp2 volumes at three IOPS per GB. If you select gp2 again, you can see the IOPS are 100, which is more than three IOPS per GB. Since your volume size is 10 GB, three times 10 means you should only have

30 IOPS. This is because you have a minimum of 100 IOPS for gp2. If you change the volume size to say 100 GBs, you can see that you have 300 IOPS now. Let's change the size back to 10 and choose the gp2 volume type.

The next option is Throughput, which will tell you the throughput of your volume. I cover throughput in the EBS screen. You can change this for only one volume type, the gp3 volume type.

The next option is the Delete on Termination checkbox. This is where you specify what to do with the EBS volume after the EC2 instance is terminated. If you have Delete on Termination checked, the volume will be deleted when your instance is terminated. Remember that if you want your data to remain even after termination on instance, be sure to uncheck this. For this demo, let's leave it as the default, which means that when EC2 is terminated, the root volume will also be deleted.

9. The next page is Add Tags. Skip this for now and move on to the next page, which is Configure Security Group.

10. On the Configure Security Group page, the first option is to create a new security group or use an existing one. Since you have not created a security group in your account, you'll create one here. You can change the security group name and description as desired.

11.   The next and the most important option is to
      configure the security group rules. As you can see,
      AWS has added a default SSH (Secure Shell) security
      group. This group allows you to SSH into your EC2
      instance. But why do you still have a warning? That's
      because if you see the Source column, this SSH rule
      is open to all IP addresses. This is an issue. Change
      this value to something like 123.123.123.123.
      The warning should disappear. Since you have no
      mission-critical systems here, change it back to
      0.0.0.0/0. It is not the best practice to allow SSH
      from any IP in the world, so if you have production
      EC2 instances, make sure to change this value to
      your own IP address range.

      Now you'll add a new rule to allow HTTP
      connections to your instance. As you can see,
      choosing HTTP fixed the protocols to TCP and
      the port to 80, which is the default HTTP protocol
      and port. You want everyone to be able to make
      HTTP connections to this instance, so you leave the
      Source set to the default. The last column is to add a
      description to the rule. Don't add a description here.

12.   Now that you have configured the security group of
      the EC2 instance, you're ready to move on to Review
      and Launch. You can see all the parameters for your
      EC2 instance from there.

13.   Click Launch.

Clicking Launch Instance will take you to the final page. If you click the
view instance, you will see that AWS is creating an EC2 instance for you.
The instance state is pending, which means that the instance is "creating."

The whole advantage of the cloud is that you can launch 100 instances like this in just a few clicks. Cloud computing is very flexible and provides you with quick access to computing power whenever you need it.

As you can see, the instance is running now; if you click the checkbox, you will find all the instance details—the public IP security groups, health checks, and so on. Whenever you need any details about EC2 instances, this is where you find them.

If you click the volumes option from the left dashboard, you can also see the two EBS volumes that you created—an 8 GB root volume and a 10 GB extra volume that you created separately.

You have successfully created an EC2 instance. Once you play around it, I recommend you terminate it. Otherwise, you will get charged for it.

Summary

That's all for this chapter. See you in the next one.

CHAPTER 7

High-Level Architecture

This chapter covers the Amazon elastic load balancer and autoscaling. You will learn about the following topics:

- Autoscaling

- EC2 autoscaling and policies

- Launch Configuration and Launch Template

- Load balancers

- Elastic load balancers

- AWS Elastic Load Balancer

You will also go through architecture using ELB and autoscaling.

Autoscaling

This section answers the following questions:

- What is autoscaling?

- What is autoscaling in AWS?

- What are the benefits of using the scaling service?

© Pravin Mishra 2023
P. Mishra, *Cloud Computing with AWS*, https://doi.org/10.1007/978-1-4842-9172-6_7

Before you get started, you need to understand how scaling works in a traditional data center. Scaling is reactive and manual in traditional data centers.

Reactive scaling means that servers are manually brought up and down based on the changes in workload. As the workload increases, you add more servers. When the workload decreases, you'll remove the servers.

Let's look at this with an example. Suppose there are application servers that are accessed by the users. As the users of this application will increase over time, load on the server will also increase. If the number of users keeps rising, there will be a time when your server will reach its full capacity (see Figure 7-1). There will not be enough memory and CPU to serve the new users.

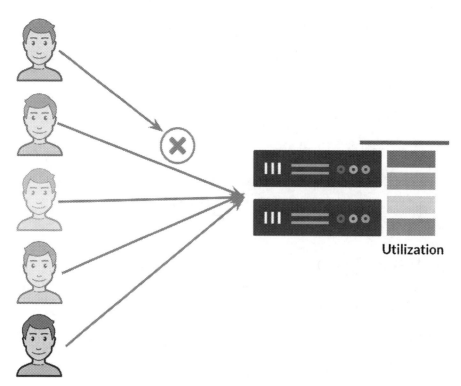

Figure 7-1. *Load on the server*

The administrators need to monitor server capacity. They can monitor it manually (see Figure 7-2) or with the help of a tool. When they see that the application server has reached its full capacity, they will add a new server and configure the application on the new server again.

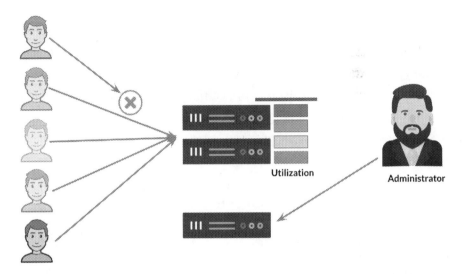

Utilization

Administrator

Figure 7-2. *Manual scaling*

This process can take some time based on the availability of servers or the availability of server engineers to add the server.

Sometimes, scaling means buying new servers. To do this, you have to get approval from management, and it can take several months for the servers to arrive.

As you can see, this is a time-consuming process and is not sustainable. Another issue with this process is that once the load on the server goes down, you have to remove the extra server. Otherwise, it will be running idle.

Cloud computing solves all these problems, as it is a lot easier to add and remove compute resources depending upon the load on the application. This happens automatically through autoscaling.

Autoscaling is a feature of cloud computing that automatically adds and removes compute resources depending on actual use and demand. This feature is available only in a cloud environment.

Autoscaling provides flexibility and elasticity to your compute demands. Hence, it is sometimes referred to as elasticity as well. Elasticity means adding or removing compute resources based on use and demand.

Autoscaling ensures a seamless increase in resources when the demand spikes and a seamless decrease when the demand drops. Therefore, it ensures a consistent application performance at a lower cost.

Autoscaling is so efficient that it will only add resources when demand goes up, and immediately remove them when it goes down again. This way, you do not need to keep running the additional resources all the time to match the demand during peak hours.

Autoscaling is a general term in cloud computing. Next, let's look at what autoscaling is specifically in AWS.

What Is AWS Autoscaling?

AWS Autoscaling monitors your applications and automatically adjusts capacity to maintain steady, predictable performance at the lowest possible cost.[1]

The key points are that it monitors your application, and based on need, it adds or removes additional capacity to maintain application performance at the lowest possible cost.

How exactly does it monitor your application? AWS Autoscaling uses an AWS service called CloudWatch to monitor the application demand, and it raises alarms to scale up or down the resources depending on your application's needs.

---

[1] https://aws.amazon.com/autoscaling/

CloudWatch is discussed in detail in Chapter 10. For now, CloudWatch is a monitoring service, and it monitors application metrics like CPU usage, memory, network, and many more. You can set a threshold value, and the service will trigger an alarm when it reaches that threshold. For example, if CPU utilization goes beyond 80 percent, it will add a server and remove it if it goes below 30 percent.

Autoscaling uses CloudWatch to monitor the application and, based on the requirements, it either adds or removes servers to meet the demand.

Let's look at some benefits of AWS Autoscaling:

1. **You can automate the process to scale up or down quickly.**

   With the help of the AWS Autoscaling group, you can automate adding and removing EC2 instances to meet the actual demand. This is one of the most important achievements of the cloud. As mentioned earlier, it brings agility to adding resources and removing resources to meet the customer demand. Hence, it removes all the reactive work of traditional data centers.

2. **It's optimized for cost.**

   Another significant benefit is cost optimization, and this is again a big win in the cloud. You do not need to run extra resources to meet the peak demand. Autoscaling ensures that you pay for only what is required to serve your customers. You no longer need to pay for unused resources.

3. **Application performance is maintained during peak hours.**

   Last and most important is application performance, because it helps you add and remove resources to meet the demand. The application always performs better. Your customers will not face any latency and slowness in the application.

The next section continues this discussion about autoscaling groups.

EC2 Autoscaling Group[2]

So far, you have learned that autoscaling adds and removes EC2 instances. Now let's look at how this works. In order to scale Amazon EC2 instances, you must create an autoscaling group. This is where autoscaling adds and removes EC2 instances.

This means that the EC2 Autoscaling Group ensures that you have enough Amazon EC2 instances available to handle the load on your application. This is done with the EC2 Autoscaling Group Configuration. There are three configurations—Minimum Size, Desired Capacity, and Maximum Size.

Based on these configurations, autoscaling will adjust the number of instances within the minimum and the maximum number of EC2 instances. The desired capacity configuration will determine the size of the autoscaling group.

By definition, autoscaling groups are groups of Amazon EC2 instances that are grouped logically for automatic scaling and management. An autoscaling group also enables you to use Amazon EC2 Autoscaling features such as health check replacements and scaling policies.[3]

---

[2] https://docs.aws.amazon.com/autoscaling/ec2/userguide/auto-scaling-groups.html

[3] https://docs.aws.amazon.com/autoscaling/ec2/userguide/ec2-auto-scaling-health-checks.html

Autoscaling maintains the number of instances by performing periodic health checks on the instances. If any instance becomes unhealthy, the autoscaling group will terminate the unhealthy instance and launch another instance to replace it.[4]

Now, let's look at the autoscaling group size configuration, as it's crucial to understand it from the cloud practitioner certification and interview perspective.

Minimum Size[5]

Minimum Size defines how many instances must run in an autoscaling group. In this case, you have one. The minimum size ensures that you always have a fixed number of instances running. The autoscaling group will never terminate instances below this number.

Desired Capacity[6]

Desired Capacity determines how many EC2 instances you want to run ideally.

In this case, you have two, so autoscaling will try to maintain two EC2 instances all the time. The desired capacity is resizeable between the minimum and maximum size limits. It must be greater than or equal to the minimum size of the group and less than or equal to the maximum size of the group.

---

[4] https://docs.aws.amazon.com/autoscaling/ec2/userguide/ec2-auto-scaling-health-checks.html

[5] https://docs.aws.amazon.com/autoscaling/ec2/userguide/asg-capacity-limits.html

[6] https://docs.aws.amazon.com/autoscaling/ec2/userguide/asg-capacity-limits.html

Maximum Size[7]

Maximum Size refers to the number of EC2 instances allowed to run. This is the maximum number of instances running in the autoscaling group. Autoscaling groups will never create more than the maximum number of instances specified.

To summarize, the Amazon EC2 Autoscaling Group maintains the number of instances and scales automatically. That's all I wanted to cover in this section.

The next section covers autoscaling policies.

EC2 Autoscaling Policies

So far, you have learned that autoscaling needs an autoscaling group to maintain and scale EC2 instances. Right? This pretty much depends on the autoscaling group configuration, which are Minimum Size, Maximum Size, and Desired Capacity.

You also learned in the last section that the desired capacity should change based on the load and traffic on your application. How does this number change? How does the number of instances scale up and down?

Scaling starts with an event or scaling action. It instructs the autoscaling group to either launch or terminate the Amazon EC2 instances. That's where autoscaling policies come into existence.[8]

There are different types of autoscaling policies that are designed for various purposes. Let's look at these.

As a note, this is a very important topic for the exam and from an interview point of view, so I recommend paying special attention and taking notes. I also added an additional learning link in the resources section.

---

[7] https://docs.aws.amazon.com/autoscaling/ec2/userguide/asg-capacity-limits.html

[8] https://docs.aws.amazon.com/autoscaling/ec2/userguide/as-scaling-simple-step.html

Manual Scaling[9]

The first autoscaling policy is Manual Scaling. It is the most basic way to scale your resources. Here, you change your autoscaling group's maximum, minimum, or desired capacity. Amazon EC2 Autoscaling manages the process of creating or terminating instances according to these updates.

If you know when more traffic is likely to flow to your application, you can manually change the size of an existing autoscaling group. You can either update the desired capacity of the autoscaling group or update the instances that are attached to the autoscaling group.

Manual Scaling can be useful when you need to maintain a fixed number of instances. The next is dynamic scaling.

Dynamic Scaling[10]

In dynamic scaling, you define how to scale the capacity of the autoscaling group in response to changing demand.

This means you can increase the number of instances during the peak demand, also known as scaling out, and decrease the instances during low demand, also known as scaling in.

Let's look at this with an example. Say that you have a web application that currently runs on two EC2 instances. Your goal is to maintain the CPU utilization of these instances at around 50 percent, regardless of application loads. It means you need to add an EC2 instance whenever CPU utilization crosses 50 percent. But you don't know when it will reach 50 percent. Don't worry! You can configure your autoscaling group to scale dynamically to meet this need by creating a target tracking, step, or simple scaling policy.

Let's look at these dynamic scaling policies.

---

[9] https://docs.aws.amazon.com/autoscaling/ec2/userguide/as-manual-scaling.html

[10] https://docs.aws.amazon.com/autoscaling/ec2/userguide/as-scale-based-on-demand.html

Simple/Step Scaling[11]

Step and simple scaling allow you to choose the scaling metrics and thresholds for the CloudWatch alarms that initiate scaling.

You will learn more about CloudWatch in Chapter 10. You define how your autoscaling group should be scaled when a threshold reaches a specified number of times.

As an example, whenever the average CPU utilization of all EC2 instances goes over 50 percent for five minutes, you want to add one EC2 instance to the autoscaling group. Alternatively, whenever the CPU utilization is less than 30 percent for 10 minutes, you want to remove one EC2 instance from the autoscaling group.

This is simple or step scaling, because you define the trigger point to take action and define how many instances to add or remove.

Target Tracking Scaling[12]

You select a scaling metric and set a target value in the target tracking scaling policies. That's it. It is a very easy way of defining a dynamic scaling policy.

Amazon EC2 Autoscaling will create and manage the CloudWatch alarms that trigger the scaling policy and calculate the scaling adjustment based on the metrics and target values. The scaling policy adds or removes EC2 instances to keep the metric at or close to the specified target value.

As an example, you can set up a target tracking scaling policy to maintain the autoscaling group's average aggregate CPU utilization at 50 percent. The ASG will scale automatically to ensure that it stays around that target of 50 percent. Next is scheduled scaling.

---

[11] https://docs.aws.amazon.com/autoscaling/application/userguide/application-auto-scaling-step-scaling-policies.html
[12] https://docs.aws.amazon.com/autoscaling/ec2/userguide/as-scaling-target-tracking.html

Scheduled Scaling

Scheduled scaling helps you set up your scaling schedule according to predictable load changes.

For example, say that every week, the traffic to your web application starts to increase on Wednesday, remains high on Thursday, and starts to decrease on Friday. You can configure a schedule for Amazon EC2 Autoscaling to increase capacity on Wednesday and decrease capacity on Friday.[13]

This is very useful when you know that changes are going to happen ahead of time and you can anticipate scaling based on user patterns.

The next is predictive scaling.

Predictive Scaling

Predictive scaling helps you scale faster by launching capacity in advance of the forecasted load.

The difference is that dynamic scaling is reactive, and it scales when the demand arises. On the other hand, predictive scaling scales the capacity based on both real-time metrics and historical data.

For example, consider an application that has high usage during business hours and low usage overnight. Predictive scaling can add capacity before the first inflow of traffic at the start of each business day. It helps your application maintain high availability and performance when going from a lower utilization period to a higher utilization period. You don't have to wait for dynamic scaling to react to changing traffic. You also don't have to spend time reviewing your application's load patterns and trying to schedule the right amount of capacity using scheduled scaling.[14]

---

[13] https://docs.aws.amazon.com/autoscaling/ec2/userguide/ec2-auto-scaling-scheduled-scaling.html

[14] https://docs.aws.amazon.com/autoscaling/ec2/userguide/ec2-auto-scaling-predictive-scaling.html

Predictive scaling predicts traffic ahead of time based on machine learning. It looks at the past traffic patterns and forecasts what will happen to traffic in the future. It will then automatically provide the correct number of EC2 instances in advance to match that predicted period.

It is beneficial when you have recurring on-and-off workload patterns or applications that take a long time to initialize and cause noticeable latency.

Now, let's go back and look at how the autoscaling policy completes the autoscaling process. As you know, autoscaling depends on various factors, such as events, metrics, and thresholds. Based on your requirements, you configure an autoscaling policy. This policy instructs autoscaling to add and remove EC2 instances.

The next section covers the process of launching configurations and templates.

Use Launch Configuration and Launch Template

So far, you have learned that autoscaling increases and decreases the number of EC2 instances to meet demand. As you know, when you launch the EC2 instance, you need to provide a configuration. You need to predefine this configuration for autoscaling as well. That is what you do with Launch Configuration and Launch Template.

Launch Configuration and Launch Template both define the characteristics of the EC2 instances that you want to launch when demand arises.

AWS introduced Launch Configuration in 2014; it is used with EC2 autoscaling groups. On the other hand, Launch Template was introduced recently and it does a similar task as Launch Configuration. Since Launch Template is the newer service, it has some extra features and capabilities to make the job a little easier.

Let's start with a Launch Configuration then you will learn about Launch Template.

Launch Configuration

Launch Configuration is an EC2 instance configuration template in which you define configurations of your EC2 instance that you want autoscaling to launch when the demand arises.

Launch Configuration is the configuration template for Amazon EC2 instances that autoscaling will use to create new EC2 instances.

When you launch an EC2 instance, either from the Management Console or by using the AWS CLI (command-line interface), you provide different EC2 instance configurations like AMI ID, the instance type, size, the configuration of the storage that instances use, and the key pair used to connect to that instance. You also define the networking configuration and security groups. They determine the IP address and port from which the instance will be accessible. You can define user data, which is a set of commands or scripts that run while an instance is launched. You can also define the IAM roles, which will be attached to the instance and give permission to access other AWS services.

Essentially, this includes everything that you usually define while launching an instance. You can define and save all the settings in the Launch Configuration, which will act as a template for autoscaling when launching new instances.

Launch Configuration is not editable. You define it once, and that configuration is locked. If you want to adjust Launch Configuration, you need to create a new configuration.

There are some challenges with Launch Configuration that have been improved in Launch Template.

Launch Template

Launch Template serves basically the same purpose as Launch Configuration.

It provides EC2 configuration, which is used by the EC2 autoscaling group as part of the process of launching EC2 instances.

Moreover, EC2 instances or fleets of EC2 instances can also be launched directly from the AWS Management Console or from the AWS CLI.

Since Launch Template is the newer service, it includes several additional features. Let's look at them one by one:

- It lets you create multiple versions of Launch Template through different configurations.

- You can specify multiple instance types, even instance types based on instance type attributes, such as memory, CPU, storage, and so on.

- It has the capability to use both on-demand and spot instances, which further leads to huge savings.

- It also covers T2/T3 unlimited features.

- Placement groups, capacity reservations, elastic graphics, and dedicated host features are available in Launch Template, but these features are missing in Launch Configuration.

- It allows EBS Volume tagging and elastic interfaces.

AWS recommends using Launch Template instead of Launch Configuration, as it offers more architectural benefits.

Let's look at where Launch Configuration and Launch Template fit into the autoscaling process. If you remember from the previous section, autoscaling depends on various factors like events, metrics, and thresholds. Based on your requirements, you configured an autoscaling policy. This policy instructs autoscaling to add and remove EC2 instances. Autoscaling needs the instance

Launch Configuration to launch the EC2 instance, right? So to launch EC2 instances, you have to provide multiple launch configurations. You use the Launch Configuration and Launch Template to provide EC2 configuration to the autoscaling group. Every time autoscaling launches an EC2 instance, it refers to the Launch Configuration, which you configure with autoscaling.

That's all for this topic about Launch Configuration and Launch Template. The next section covers the Load Balancer.

Load Balancer

You just learned how EC2 autoscaling automatically scales up and down your EC2 Instances based on demand. In this section, you learn the general concept of load-balancing, as it's the foundation for the next topic, the Elastic Load Balancer.

Let's assume you enter a five-star hotel to check in (see Figure 7-3).

Figure 7-3. *Hotel reception check-in*

There are four receptionists checking bookings, checking customers in, and checking customers out. Most of the customers are standing in a few lines, which results in an uneven distribution of customers per line. Other receptionists are standing around doing nothing but waiting for customers. Customers are walking in and they have no idea where to go. It would be helpful to have a host at the entrance.

Customers walking in need to know which queue has the fewest people and which receptionist is the most efficient.

The customers are greeted by a host at the door. They will direct customers to the appropriate line in the hotel for check-in and check-out. The host keeps an eye on the receptionists and counts the number of people in each line. Any new customer will be directed to the receptionist with the shortest line, which is the least backed up. Consequently, there will be even waiting for lines among receptionists, allowing customers to be served as efficiently as possible.

Now think about AWS autoscaling groups (see Figure 7-4). You have multiple EC2 instances running the same application. When a request comes in, how does the request know which EC2 instance will handle it?

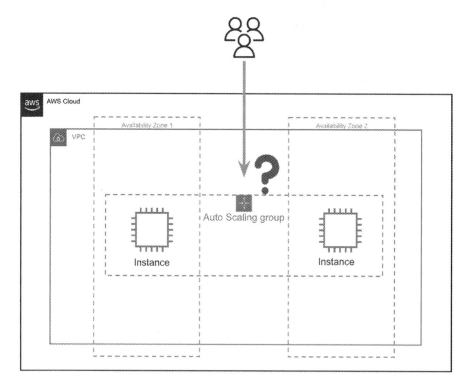

Figure 7-4. *Autoscaling group*

How can you ensure an even distribution of workload across EC2 instances? You need a way to route requests equally to different instances to process these requests. That's where a load balancer comes into the picture. It is a networking solution that distributes traffic across multiple servers to improve application performance. It is a piece of software you can install, manage, update and scale.

A load balancer can be installed for two or more EC2 instances. But the problem is the scalability. Let's look at this. You have one load balancer sitting in front of two instances of Amazon EC2, and your number of EC2 instances will increase based on load. Especially if you have autoscaling, there is no limitation on the EC2 instances. It can scale from nothing to 100 or even more EC2 instances. How can one load balancer handle all requests (see Figure 7-5)? The answer is that it also needs to be scaled.

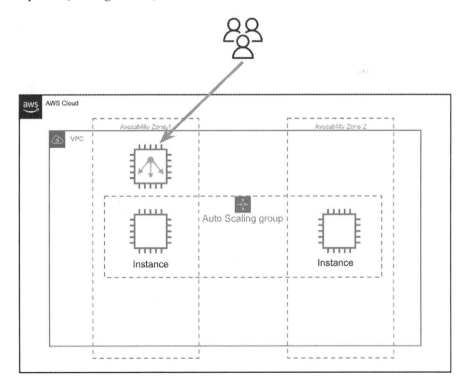

Figure 7-5. *Load balancer*

That's where AWS provides another service, called the Elastic Load Balancer. The next section explains this service in detail.

Elastic Load Balancer

This section explains the Elastic Load Balancer (ELB), which is another AWS service. It works very closely with autoscaling to distribute traffic equally to EC2 instances.

An Elastic Load Balancer (see Figure 7-6) is an AWS service that is used to distribute the load. It's designed to address the undifferentiated heavy lifting of load balancing.

In the previous section, you learned about a load balancer that is responsible for the distribution of incoming traffic between available EC2 instances. ELB scales automatically as traffic to your servers changes. If the traffic grows, ELB enables the load balancer to handle the additional load by distributing it.

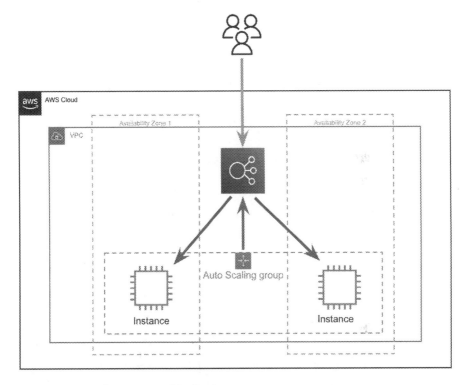

Figure 7-6. *Elastic Load Balancer*

Whenever your EC2 Autoscaling Group scales up and adds a new EC2 instance, the autoscaling service sends a notification to the Elastic Load Balancer that a new instance is ready to handle the traffic. Similarly, when the EC2 Autoscaling Group scales in (it initiates the process to terminate an instance), it sends a notification to Elastic Load Balancer. It's ELB's job to stop sending the traffic to the selected instance. After that, it waits for the existing requests to complete. Once all the existing requests get fulfilled, autoscaling terminates the instances without disturbing the existing customers.

The Elastic Load Balancer automatically routes the incoming application traffic across different instances.

It acts as an interface to the incoming traffic, so any traffic coming to your application first meets with the load balancer and is then sent to an available instance. It also monitors the health of the running EC2 instances, as it sends the traffic requests to the healthy instances only.

As of now, you have learned how Elastic Load Balancer routes external traffic to your EC2 Instances. Not only that, but it is also used for internal traffic rerouting.

Let's look at an example using Gmail. Suppose a lot of users are using their Gmail. They open the inbox, and then the page acts as a web server. A user compiles the message and clicks the Send button. If you talk about what's happening in the Gmail server, an app server is processing your emails, including storing them to a database, sending them to the respective user, and so on. If more and more users start using Gmail, the number of web servers will also increase. Hence, EC2 Autoscaling will have to increase the number of app servers. It should be acknowledged to every web server that a new app server is available to accept the traffic. Imagine you have potentially hundreds of server instances on both tiers. You can solve the app server traffic chaos with an internal ELB as well. ELB will direct traffic to the app server that has the least outstanding requests. The web server doesn't know and doesn't care how many app server instances are running. ELB handles directing the traffic to the available app servers. This is known as true decoupled architecture. In this architecture, all the computing components remain completely autonomous and unaware of each other, doing the instructed task independently.

Elastic Load Balancer is the service you can use in front of a web server to distribute the incoming traffic; it is also called a public load balancer. You can also use Elastic Load Balancer behind the web server to equally distribute traffic to the web server, and since this is working internally, it is called an internal private load balancer. Next, we discuss the different types of elastic load balancers.

AWS Elastic Load Balancer (ELB)

This section explains the different types of ELBs. AWS offers four load balancers (see Table 7-1):

- Application Load Balancers

- Network Load Balancers

- Classic Load Balancers

- Gateway Load Balancers

Let's look at them one by one.[15]

Table 7-1. *Different AWS Load Balancers*

Feature	Application Load Balancer	Network Load Balancer	Gateway Load Balancer	Classic Load Balancer
Load Balancer type	Layer 7	Layer 4	Layer 3 Gateway + Layer 4 Load Balancing	Layer 4/7
Target type	IP, Instance, Lambda	IP, Instance, Application Load Balancer	IP, Instance	Deprecating Soon
Protocol listeners	HTTP, HTTPS, gRPC	TCP, UDP, TLS	IP	TCP, SSL/TLS, HTTP, HTTPS

These load balancers work with different OSI models. The OSI Reference Model is an acronym for Open System Interconnection Reference Model. It describes how information is exchanged from one

---

[15] https://aws.amazon.com/elasticloadbalancing/features/

computer to another using a network. This is achieved by dividing the data communication into seven layers and giving control over sending data from one layer to another.

As the name suggests, application load balancers work on the OSI model's seventh layer, the Application layer. The Network Load Balancer works at layer 4, which is the Network layer. The classic load balancer has been around for a long time and is the oldest and first Elastic Load Balancer service. It is designed to work at the Application and Network layers. The Gateway Load Balancer is the newest service in the Elastic Load Balancer family, and it works at Layers 3 and 4.

The next is the Protocol Listener, which means the different protocols where these load balancers can listen. HTTP and HTTPS are the only protocols supported by the Application Load Balancer. The Network Load Balancer handles TCP and UDP protocols. The Gateway Load Balancer only listens on IP. As mentioned earlier, a Classic Load Balancer can work at the Application and Network layers. Therefore, it supports application and network layer protocols, including TCP, SSL/TLS, HTTP, and HTTPS.

The most common use case for the Application Load Balancer is for web apps. A web app built on the microservices framework can use ALB as the load balancer before incoming traffic reaches your EC2 instances or the containers hosted for a service.

Network Load Balancers (NLBs) cover the remaining scenarios that ALBs don't. For example, the apps that depend on a protocol apart from HTTP—the time-sensitive apps, the real-time data flow apps, and the apps dependent on streaming audio, video, currency quotes, and so on—will benefit from using NLB.

The Gateway Load Balancer works at layer 3. It simplifies the deployment, scaling, and management of third-party virtual appliances.

The Classic Load Balancer can be used in almost all use cases of the Application Load Balancer and the Network Load Balancer. But since the Application Load Balancer and the Network Load Balancer are the newest and are designed for a specific purpose, you should use them to get the most out of this process. AWS retired the Classic Load Balancer on August 15, 2022, so it's no longer recommended for use.

Next is the target type, which means where the load balancer can direct traffic. It could be an AWS Lambda function, an EC2 instance, or a fixed IP address, among others. You can simply relate this with the use case. The Application Load Balancer supports IP, EC2 instance, and Lambda. The Network Load Balancer supports IP, EC2 instances, and the Application Load Balancer. It can send traffic to ALB as well. The Gateway Load Balancer supports IP and EC2 instances. The Classic Load Balancer also supports IP and EC2 instances.

For this course, you only need to remember these four types of load balancers, types, protocols, and use cases. In the next section, you will run through a hands-on lab on ELB and autoscaling.

Using ELB and Autoscaling Together

In the previous lab in Chapter 6, you launched the EC2 instance, which you created from the AWS Console. In this lab, you create EC2 instances using an AWS Autoscaling Group. You learn how to configure the autoscaling groups. The program will automatically deploy the HTTPD service to all instances in the autoscaling group and see the resulting HTTPD application access via the Application Load Balancer.

Go to the AWS Console and type **EC2** into the search bar.

Create a Launch Template

1. Click EC2 to go directly to the EC2 dashboard. From the left dashboard, find and click Launch Templates. They specify the configuration of EC2 instances. Take a look.

203

2. Click Create Launch Template. Add a launch template called `packtup-LT`. Then add "Launch Template for Autoscaling Demo" as the description. You can add tags by clicking the drop-down button. If you want to copy, modify, or create a new template from an existing Launch Template, you can do so by clicking the Next drop-down.

3. The next option you have is to choose the AMI. Type **Amazon Linux 2** in the search bar and select the first AMI. As you can see, this AMI is free tier eligible, which means you don't have to pay anything for this.

4. The next option is to choose the instance type. You can see multiple instance types if you scroll down. Since you don't have any special instance requirements and you also want to stay in the free tier, choose the `t2.micro` instance.

5. Next, you have to choose the key pair. You will need it when you SSH into the instance. Also, you must specify a key pair. Since you will not SSH to the instance in this lab, leave this as the default. If you want to try SSH and run commands yourself, you can choose an existing key pair like this or create a new key pair by clicking this link.

6. Next, you have to specify the network settings for your EC2 instances. You do not need to select subnets here, so leave this as the default for now.

7. Next, you have to configure the security group. Note that this security group will ultimately be attached to the EC2 instances that you create from this Launch Template.

You can either create a new security group or select one that already exists. I have the security group from the previous lab. I can choose this, this lab demonstrates the process of creating a security group. Click Create Security Group and add the security group's name and description. Choose the correct VPC.

Next, you will add rules. Click Add Security Group Rule and then add the security group rules. Select HTTP in the type column. In this source, select Anywhere. I have not added the SSH rule since you will not be doing that in this lab. If you plan to try SSH, you need to select a key pair and add the SSH rule. You have now configured the security group for your Launch Template.

8. Next, you could add the EBS volume configuration. Skip this for this lab. You could also add tags to the Launch Template by clicking here, but you have no such requirements, so you can skip this as well.

9. Click the Advanced options. You do not need to change any options here. Move on and scroll to the bottom of the page. You will see the User Data option here. You can enter the commands that you want to run when your instance starts. In the previous lab, you installed HTTPD manually. In this lab, you will add your commands in this text box here, and AWS will automatically run them when your instance starts up.

10. Add the following commands. This command updates the default packages in your instance:

11. This command will install HTTPD on your instance:

```
yum update
yum install httpd -y
```

12. This command will start the HTTPD service on the EC2 instances:

```
systemctl start httpd
```

13. This command will show you a custom HTML page:

```
echo "<h1>Instance $(curl
http://169.254.169.254/latest/meta-data/
local-ipv4)</h1>" > /var/www/html/index.html
```

14. Click the Create Launch template. You have successfully created a Launch Template. Click to view Launch Templates. You can see your Launch Template in the list.

Create an Autoscaling Group

This section moves on to the Autoscaling Group dashboard:

1. Click AutoScaling Groups from the left dashboard and click Create AutoScaling Group. Enter the name packtup-ASG and choose the Launch Template you just created. Note that you can go to the Create Launch Template page from this link as well. Click Next. Choose the patckup VPC and select PublicSubnet1 and PublicSubnet2. Select any two default subnets from the list if you don't have your own VPC in your account.

2. Click Next. You could add a load balancer to your
    autoscaling group directly from this page, but you
    will do that later from the Load Balancer dashboard.
    Skip this for now and click Next.

    There are three important and useful options.

    a. Desired Capacity. This value specifies the desired
       number of instances that you want to have.
       Change this to 3.

    b. Minimum Capacity. This value specifies the
       minimum number of instances you want the
       autoscaling group to have. So, if you have min
       capacity of 2, AWS will always ensure that you
       have two instances at a minimum. Change this
       value to 2.

    c. Max Capacity. This value specifies the maximum
       number of instances that you want the
       autoscaling group to have when it scales up. If
       you have a max capacity of 4, change this value to
       four instances.

3. You can add the TargetTracking Scaling policy by
    selecting the option. But for this example, you will
    add simple scaling policies to your autoscaling
    group later. Click Next. You can add notifications on
    this page. For example, you can create an SNS topic
    that sends you an email every time the autoscaling
    group scales up or down. You have no such
    requirements; click Next. You can also add tags here,
    but let's skip this as well. Click Next.

4. Review your autoscaling group and then click Create AutoScaling Group.

    You can see the autoscaling group listed with the desired capacity of 3, min capacity of 2, and a max capacity of 4. The status shows the updating capacity. Since you have the desired capacity of 3 and currently this autoscaling group has no instances, it will try to create three EC2 instances for you.

    You can view this by selecting your autoscaling group and clicking the Activity tab. You will see three successful instance launches, and in the Cause column, you can see that the autoscaling group service is trying to increase the capacity from 0 to 3.

Create a Scaling Policy

Before you go to the EC2 dashboard and look at your instances, you need to add scaling policies to the autoscaling group. Click the Automatic Scaling tab next to the Activity tab. You will see that you have no policies added to your autoscaling group.

1. Choose Simple Scaling from the Policy Type and use the name Add 1 instance when CPU Utilization > 80. The autoscaling group needs CloudWatch alarms to track the CPU utilization. You need to create the alarm.

2. On the CW-Alarms page, click Select Metric. Click EC2 for EC2 metrics. You need the overall autoscaling group metrics and not the per-instance metrics for this alarm. Select By AutoScaling Group and find CPU utilization under the Metric Name.

3. Select the CPU Utilization Row and click Select
    Metric. You can see the CPU Utilization graph on
    your left. You want your autoscaling group to scale
    up when the CPU utilization is over 80 percent.
    Scroll down and, in the Conditions box, select
    Greater and enter the value 80. This means that your
    alarm will trigger when the CPU utilization value is
    more than 80. You don't need to change the other
    parameters for the alarm.

4. Click Next. You could add notifications and actions
    on this page, but let's skip this for now. You will
    add an alarm action to the AutoScaling Group
    page. Click Next, enter the name and description,
    and create the alarm. Back on the AutoScaling
    Group page, refresh the alarm option and find your
    ScaleUP alarm in the list. Select the alarm. In the
    action, choose to add one capacity unit. This will
    add one instance to your ASG every time this alarm
    triggers. You have created your simple scaling policy
    to scale up the autoscaling group.

5. Now you'll create another policy to scale down.
    Click Create Dynamic Scaling Policy, select simple
    scaling, and call it Remove 1 instance when CPU
    Utilization < 30. You also have to create a new
    alarm, so click the Create Alarm link. Click Select
    Metric, EC2 metrics, By Auto Scaling Group, and
    the CPU Utilization metric. This time you want
    your alarm to trigger when CPU utilization is below
    30 percent. In the Alarm Condition box, select
    Lower and add the value 30. Click Next. Skip the
    notifications, add a name and description, and

create the alarm. Refresh the AutoScaling Group page, select the alarm, and choose to remove one capacity unit. Then create the policy.

You can see these policies in action. You just added a policy to scale down when CPU utilization is below 30 percent. Since you do not have any workloads on your EC2, the average CPU utilization will be below 30 percent, triggering this alarm. Go to the Activity tab of your autoscaling group, where you will soon notice that AWS decreased the desired capacity from 3 to 2 and is now terminating the instance.

In the Cause section, you will see that this is because you just created the policy. Even after your ASG has scaled down, if you see it in the CloudWatch tab that the scale down alarm is still in the trigger state. This is because you still have no processes running on your EC2 instances and the CPU utilization is low.

Ideally, AWS will decrease another instance from your ASG. But since you specified the min capacity as two, AWS will not scale down your instance. AWS changes your desired capacity as per the scaling policies, but it never changes the min and max capacity values. If you edit the autoscaling group and change this min capacity value to one, very soon you will see another instance terminated.

Don't do that. Instead, keep your two instances running. Go to the Instances page on the left dashboard. You can see that you have two instances in the running state and one instance in the terminated state. Select any of the running instances and copy their public IP addresses. Paste the IP address of the instance in the browser. You will find that even though you did not manually run any commands in the instance, it has HTTPD installed and running.

Create an Application Load Balancer

Now you'll learn how to create an Application Load Balancer and view this web page from the Load Balancer's URL. Click Load Balancers from the left dashboard. You can see that you have no load balancers in your account.

1. Click Create Load Balancer. Select Application Load Balancer. Enter the name TheCloudAdvisory-ALB.

2. The next option is to choose whether you want an Internet-facing or internal load balancer. Internal load balancers are only accessible locally within the VPC. Since you want to see your website via the ALB, from anywhere in the world, you need to select the Internet-facing option.

3. In the Network box, choose the VPC and the public subnets. In the security group section, create a new security group. Add the name and description, select the same VPC as the EC2 instances, and add an HTTP rule to allow HTTP connections from anywhere. Create the Security Group. Back in the Load Balancer page, refresh the Security Group options and choose the one you just created.

4. ALBs require something called the *target group*. This refers to a group of EC2 instances or other resources where ALB forwards its requests. Create a new target group by clicking this link.

5. Enter the name of the target group and leave the
    other values as the defaults. Click Next. Choose your
    instances and add them as pending. Click Create
    Target Group.

6. Back in the ALB Creation page, refresh the
    Target Group option and choose the one you just
    created. Click Create the Load Balancer. You have
    successfully created your ALB.

    Click View Load Balancers. Your load balancer is
    now visible in the console. Select the load balancer.
    You can copy the DNS value and paste it into your
    browser. You can see the web page and the IP
    address of the instance that's serving your request.
    Since the load balancer randomly forwards your
    requests to the EC2 instances, you will see that the
    IP address changes every time you reload the page.

    Take a look at the security groups of your
    application. As of now, your website is accessible
    from the IP address of the instance as well as the
    ALB DNS. This is not desirable. You do not want
    your application to be accessible via IP addresses
    anymore. Select the security group of the EC2
    instance and click in the Inbound Rules tab. Then
    click Edit Inbound Rules. In the source, the column
    removes the current value and finds the security
    group of ALB. Select the security group. This is not
    possible. You cannot edit IP rules like this. Delete
    the rule and create a new HTTP rule to allow
    connections from ALB. Click Add Rule, select HTTP,
    and select the security group of ALB as the source.
    Click Save Rules.

Your website is no longer accessible from the IP address of your EC2 instances but you can still use the ALB URL to access your website. This is how you deploy web applications in the real world.

You have successfully deployed a highly available and scalable architecture using an autoscaling group and ALB. Go ahead and delete your infrastructure.

To do that, go to the Autoscaling Group console and delete the autoscaling group by clicking Actions. Go to the Load Balancer page and delete the load balancer. Delete the target group on the Target Group page. On the Security Groups page, delete all the security groups except the default security group for your VPCs. That's all for this topic; see you in the next chapter.

Summary

This chapter discussed autoscaling and the AWS Elastic Load Balancer. You learned that autoscaling is a feature of cloud computing that automatically adds and removes compute resources depending on actual use and demand. This feature is available only in a cloud environment. You also learned that EC2 Autoscaling Group is a collection of EC2 instances that are grouped to perform scaling policies and health checks of instances. If any instance is unhealthy, the autoscaling group terminates it.

You also looked at various autoscaling policies and their functions. These are Manual Scaling, Dynamic Scaling, Simple/Step Scaling, Target Tracking Scaling, Schedule Scaling, and Predictive Scaling. You saw that autoscaling depends on various factors like events, metrics, and thresholds. You also configured an autoscaling policy based on your requirements. This policy instructs autoscaling to add and remove EC2 instances.

You also learned that Launch Configuration is the configuration template of EC2 instances that autoscaling uses to launch new EC2 instances. Launch Template is the improved version of the Launch Configuration, with some extra features. You saw how a load balancer helps distribute traffic to EC2 instances. The AWS Elastic Load Balancer automatically routes the incoming application traffic across different instances. It acts as an interface for incoming traffic, so any traffic coming to your application first meets with the load balancer and is then sent to an available instance. You also looked at different types of AWS Elastic Load Balancers and looked at a scenario where you use autoscaling and Elastic Load Balancer together.

That's all for this chapter; let's meet in the next one!

CHAPTER 8

Databases

This chapter covers databases for different types of data. You learn about relational and NoSQL databases. You also learn about on-premise vs cloud database hosting. Relational databases include the Amazon Relational Database Service and Amazon DynamoDB.

The demo topic in this chapter has you creating an Amazon RDS database and an RDS subnet group.

Data Types

As you know, this chapter is all about databases, but before you get into it, it's important to understand the types of data. You'll decide on an appropriate database based on the nature of your data. Therefore, it is very important to understand data and its type. Let's begin with data source types.

There are three types of data sources: structured, unstructured, and semi-structured.

Structured Data

Structured data has predefined data types and is stored in a specific format. The following phone book example is a good way to think about predefined data types and their specific format (see Figure 8-1).

© Pravin Mishra 2023
P. Mishra, *Cloud Computing with AWS*, https://doi.org/10.1007/978-1-4842-9172-6_8

SL. No	First Name	Last Name	Phone No
1	Ram	Kumar	+91 9832453289
2	Shyam	Kumar	+91 9678675645

Figure 8-1. Phone book information

In the table in Figure 8-1, you can see that the top row has different names that define what kind of data is present in the different columns. For example, the serial number (SL. No.) represents the number of data sets you have, the First Name column lists the first name of every entry in the data, and so on. This is a format and if you want to add more personal detail to this data, you have to create a new column for it.

Say that you wanted to add address information (see Figure 8-2).

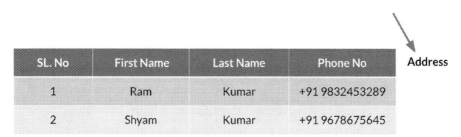

Address

SL. No	First Name	Last Name	Phone No
1	Ram	Kumar	+91 9832453289
2	Shyam	Kumar	+91 9678675645

Figure 8-2. Phone Book - 1

In that case, you need to add an additional header named Address and only then could you add addresses to this data. Basically, this is a specific format.

Now let's look at the data types. As you can see, there are numbers in the Serial Number and the Phone Number columns, whereas and the First Name and Last Name columns have alphabetical characters. As per the defined columns, you are expected to enter numbers in the Serial Number and Phone Number columns, and characters in the First Name and Last Name columns (see Figure 8-3).

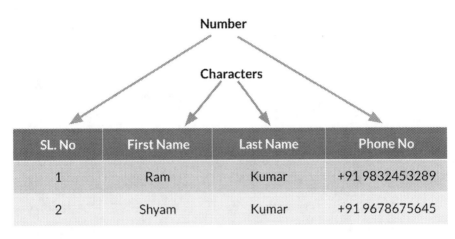

Figure 8-3. *Phone Book - 3*

This table defines the kind of data you can enter into the different columns. Structured data is stored as a series of data values, in defined tables, and managed by a database engine such as MySQL. This data is highly structured, that's why it is very easy to analyze and can be used in highly complex queries.

The next data type is unstructured data.

Unstructured Data

Unstructured data has an internal structure but does not contain a predefined data model. Consider a video, for example; it is also data but the way it is stored is different from structured data.

This type of data is usually in the form of files that are stored in a storage such as Dropbox. Dropbox is like a storage unit where you can store text files, photos, videos, and so on (see Figure 8-4).

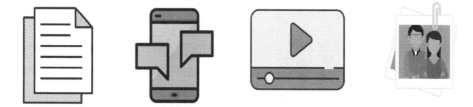

Figure 8-4. *File, photos, videos, and images are unstructured data*

Unstructured data as a whole is irrelevant information. As an example of unstructured data, you can think about text messages, videos, photos, and other images.

There is no order to these files, and they are not well organized. They can only be placed into a filesystem or object store. If you want to get meaningful information out of this data, you need to process it. You need special tools to query and process the unstructured data.

The last data type is semi-structured data.

Semi-Structured Data

It is possible for semi-structured data to be classified as a form of structured data. The only difference is that semi-structured data is flexible and can be updated without changing the schema for every single record in a table.

Figure 8-5 shows an example of semi-structured data. There are two sets of data, and they look the same. If you notice, the second data has one additional line of information; address.

```
{
    "Sl. No.": 1,
    "First Name": "Ram",
    "Last Name": "Kumar",
    "phone": +91 9832453289
},
{

    "Sl. No.": 2,
    "First Name": "Shyam",
    "Last Name": "Kumar",
    "phone": +91 9678675645,
    "Address": "New Delhi"
}
```

Figure 8-5. *Semi-structured data*

Semi-structured data allows users to capture data in any structure as the data evolves and changes over time.

Semi-structured data is stored in JSON files that are loaded into a database engine such as MongoDB. This data is highly flexible because the structure is not strict and can be changed as needed within the table. You can also analyze semi-structured data.

Relational Databases

In the last section, you learned about three types of data types: structured, unstructured, and semi-structured data. As the nature of this data is different, it will be stored differently. This section explains where and how this data will be stored. By the end of this section, you will understand why you store structured data in a relational database.

Let's start with an example. People often use an Excel sheet to store data because it is easier to organize and manage data in Excel than in any other tool. This type of data is known as structured data, as discussed in the last section.

Excel sheets are fine for personal data. But if you think about big businesses, that's a different world altogether. They deal with huge amounts of data, which is very challenging to store and manage. When data grows, it often leads to data inconsistency and redundancy.

Suppose you have a spreadsheet that stores student course registration data, as shown in Figure 8-6.

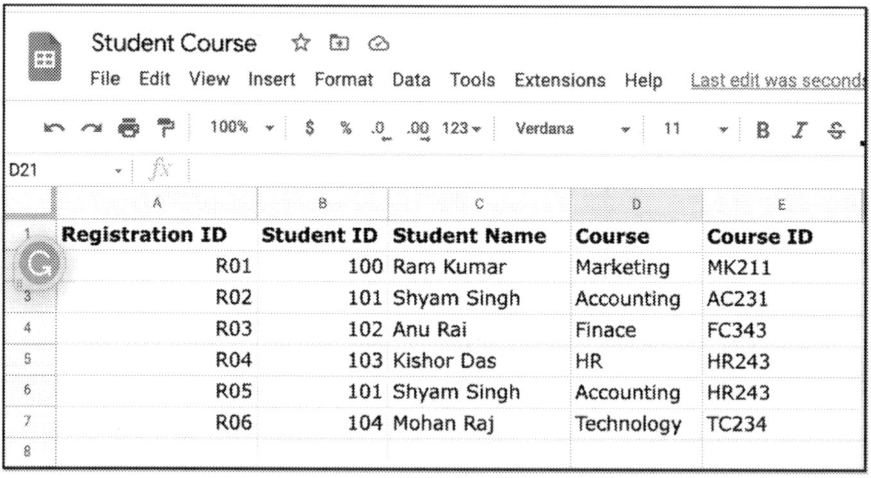

Registration ID	Student ID	Student Name	Course	Course ID
R01	100	Ram Kumar	Marketing	MK211
R02	101	Shyam Singh	Accounting	AC231
R03	102	Anu Rai	Finace	FC343
R04	103	Kishor Das	HR	HR243
R05	101	Shyam Singh	Accounting	HR243
R06	104	Mohan Raj	Technology	TC234

Figure 8-6. *Student course data*

Take a look at Shyam Singh with student ID number 101; he is stored more than once. This is called data redundancy.

Say Shyam Singh changes his last name; in that case, his last name must be changed everywhere in the data. Otherwise, it could lead to data inconsistency.

For small data systems, these issues can be easy to solve. But when the data system is huge, it is difficult to manage the data. In order to avoid these problems, you use database technology. This is an organized collection of data so that it can be easily accessed and managed.

Say you want to send an email to Kishor Das. There is another sheet that holds details like email ID, phone number, and so on (see Figure 8-7).

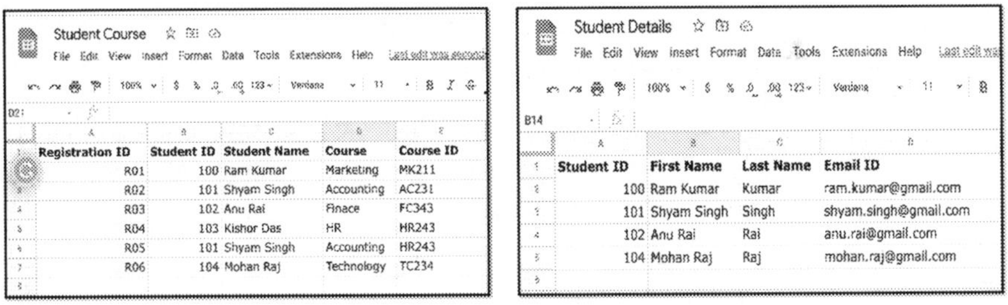

Figure 8-7. *Student course and student details sheets*

From the first sheet, you know that Kishore is in HR, but you cannot find Kishor Das in the Student Details sheet. This means the data is inconsistent.

You can solve this problem with some rules like "A student can't register for a course without registration." This way you will have all the sheets populated for each student.

The point here is that the two Excel sheets have a relationship and follow certain rules to organize data. This is known as *relation data,* which brings you to the concept of relational databases.

An organized collection of data is referred to as a database. Databases are organized collections because the data sets are described and linked to each other.

Data is organized into relations (tables) in a relational database. Every table has a set of *fields* that define the type of data structure (schema) that is stored in the table. A *record* in a table is a set of fields that are arranged in a particular way. You can think of a record as a row (or a tuple) and a field as a column.

221

As shown in Table 8-1, this table contains student information, where each row represents a student record, and each column represents a student field. A field or combination of fields that determine the uniqueness of a record is called the primary key (or key). For example, student ID is unique for each student. This is usually the unique identifier of each record.

Table 8-1. *Student Information*

Student ID	First Name	Last Name	Email ID
100	Ram	Kumar	ram.kumar@gmail.com
101	Shyam	Singh	shyam.singh@gmail.com
102	Anu	Rai	anu.rai@gmail.com
104	Mohan	Raj	mohan.raj@gmail.com

Structures are used so that data can be identified and accessed in relationship to other data in a database. Each student has a unique ID that can be used to find the record of the same student in the Student Registration table.

As you see in Table 8-2, this data has a certain structure, known as a *schema*.

Table 8-2. *Student Information Details*

Student Details
Student ID
First Name
Last Name
Email ID

Relational databases store structured data. They allow you to rapidly collect, update, and query data using a structured data model.

Tables provide an easy way to store and manage data by storing it in columns and rows. AWS offers database solutions for relational databases. That is covered in the introduction to RDS section. In the next section, you learn about NoSQL databases.

NoSQL Databases

In this section, you learn about NoSQL databases.

Let's start with a quick review of the previous section. You learned that the data in a relational database is organized in a way that the values in one table can define or change the values in another table. In other words, a relationship exists between the different tables of data.

Let's look at the same example of the relational database that stores student course registration details.

Table 8-3 contains various details of students, and Table 8-4 defines the courses that the students registered for.

Table 8-3. *Student Registration*

Student ID	First Name	Last Name	Email ID
100	Ram Kumar	Kumar	ram.kumar@gmail.com
101	Shyam Singh	Singh	shyam.singh@gmail.com
102	Anu Rai	Rai	anu.rai@gmail.com
104	Mohan Raj	Raj	mohan.raj@gmail.com

Table 8-4. *Student Courses*

Registration ID	Student ID	Course	Course ID
R01	100	Marketing	MK211
R02	101	Accounting	AC231
R03	102	Finance	FC343
R04	103	Accounting	HR243
R05	101	Technology	HR243
R06	104	Accounting	TC234

In a relational database, you can run a single SQL query that returns a result showing all of the students who registered for Accounting, even though the data is in two different tables. This is the superpower of relational databases.

Now, let's talk about *non-relational* databases. This type of database stores data differently due to the nature of data. You store semi-structured data in a non-relational database.

Consider the same student course registration database example. If you have to store student course registration data in a non-relational database, all the information about a student, including the associated course, would be stored in a single item within the database table:

```
{
      "Studentregistration": {
            "student_id": 101,
            "email": "ram.kumar@gmail.com",
            "first_name": "Ram",
            "last_name": "Kumar",
            "course": {
                  "registration_id": "R01",
```

```
            "student_id": "101",
            "course": "Marketing",
            "course_id": "MK211"
        }
    }
}
```

Let's deep dive and learn how data is stored in a non-relational database. Let's say, after one year, the college decided to add the 12th standard grade to the Student Registration table in the database. How would each database type need to change?

In the case of relational databases, you need to update the schema to add the grades of students. This means adding a new column for the grade. Once you add the new column, it will be empty. This can cause problems, because as a rule, relational databases require you to enter values in every column if that column is set to true for the database. You need to create a process to add the grade for every record in the table. Once this process is completed, you can begin to add new records for grade. Any guesses on what you need to do in a non-relational database?

All you need to do is create new items with the new attribute. You might go back and look at the existing records, but you are not required to do anything with them. This is one of the advantages that non-relational databases have over relational databases. Non-relational schemas do not require you to define new attributes of data before you use them. In a relational database, you have to update the schema before you can add new fields of data.

When it comes to storing and dealing with semi-structured or unstructured data, the choice is often a non-relational database.

In the next section, you learn about on-premise vs cloud database hosting.

On-Premise vs Cloud Database Hosting

In this section, you learn how to manage databases in the on-premises scenario and the different database options available in the AWS cloud.

Let's start with on-premise databases. They operate on hardware that your organization owns and maintains. These systems are handled by a team of database administrators (DBAs), who are responsible for the entire setup and working with the database. In the case of on-premise, the company deploys several servers and networking devices to handle the system's peak load.

Once they get the server from the infrastructure team, they install the operating system and prepare an OS patching schedule. The next is a database software installation, and again, they need to plan and do database patches. Once the database is ready, it can be used by the application. These databases need to be managed, updated, upgraded, and optimized over time.

The next considerable effort goes into database backup and high-availability setup and configuration for the business-critical applications. In the case of high-availability configuration, the DBAs need to follow the same steps for another DB server that will act as a standby for failover scenarios.

On top of that, you are also responsible for scaling your database server now and then. That's a lot of work. See Table 8-5.

Table 8-5. *Database Team*
Responsibilities in Data Centers

Scaling
High Availability
Database Backup
DB s/w Patches
DB s/w Install
OS Patches
OS Installation
Server
Networking

When it comes to the cloud, you have two options. The first option
is like an on-premises database, where you rent a virtual machine (IaaS)
that comes with networking and a server that is managed and taken care
of by AWS. However, you have to manage the rest of the tasks. Again, it
requires effort and a team of DBAs to take care of OS patches, DB software
installation and patching, DB backup, high availability, scaling and so on.
See Table 8-6.

Table 8-6. *Database Installation on an EC2 Instance*

Scaling
High Availability
Database Backup
DB s/w Patches
DB s/w Install
OS Patches
OS Installation ✔
Server ✔
Networking ✔

The second option is to use Amazon RDS. Amazon RDS is an AWS managed database, where you get the database out of the box in a few clicks. See Table 8-7.

Table 8-7. *Amazon RDS Managed Tasks*

Scaling ✔
High Availability ✔
Database Backup ✔
DB s/w Patches ✔
DB s/w Install ✔
OS Patches ✔
OS Installation ✔
Server ✔
Networking ✔

That's all for this section. In the next section, you learn about the Amazon Relational Database Service.

Amazon Relational Database Service

In this section, you learn about the Amazon Relational Database Service, commonly known as Amazon RDS.

Amazon RDS Overview

The Amazon Relational Database Service (Amazon RDS[1]) is a collection of managed services that makes it simple to set up, operate, and scale databases in the cloud.

As you know, managing a database in either an on-premise or EC2 instance is not an easy task. Amazon RDS is designed to minimize the effort involved in managing relational databases, such as setting up hardware, configuring databases, patching them, taking backups, and so on.

All you need to do is select the database that you want to launch and you will have a database in just a few clicks.

Let's look at this with an example. Suppose you have a team of four people (see Figure 8-8).

---

[1] https://aws.amazon.com/rds/

Figure 8-8. *Team of four*

You want to launch an application that will be backed by a MySQL database. You installed MySQL on the EC2 instance. Since you know that it requires a lot of work to set up the OS, the database, do backups, and do patching, it is likely that the development work might fall behind, and that could further delay the application launch. Only two people can focus on development (see Figure 8-9).

| Coding | Coding | Backup | OS/DB Update |

Figure 8-9. *The team with different roles*

Imagine this same example again, but this time, using Amazon RDS. As RDS is a managed service, it will take care of all database-related work for you, and your developers can focus on application development (see Figure 8-10).

Coding   Coding   Coding   Coding

Figure 8-10. *Team working as developers*

RDS is designed to help you reduce the database management costs. It is a managed service that automates the provisioning of databases. AWS will do the patching of the operating system. You will have continuous backups and restore options with a point-in-time restore. You will also have monitoring dashboards to see if your database is doing well. You can scale the reads by creating a read replica and improving the read performance.

You will have a way to set up multi-AZ to make sure that your application has a plan for disaster recovery in case an entire Availability Zone goes down. Finally, you can also set up maintenance windows for upgrades and scale vertically or horizontally. The only thing that you cannot do with an RDS database is SSH into your RDS database instance.

Let's look at some features and elements of Amazon RDS.

RDS Availability[2]

The Amazon RDS multi-AZ deployment provides higher availability and durability. This means that Amazon RDS creates multiple instances of the database in different Availability Zones in order to provide a more reliable service to users. If there is a failure of infrastructure, Amazon RDS automatically switches to standby in another Availability Zone. The database will resume operations once the failover is complete. Your database connection endpoint does not need to be updated since Amazon RDS uses a DNS service to identify the new master instance. That's a very good feature.

RDS Instance Type

In order to build your first Amazon RDS database, you have to make a few important decisions. To begin, you need to choose your database instance type, which determines how much CPU and memory your database will have. It's somewhat similar to an AWS EC2 instance.

RDS Database Engine

After that, you need to decide what kind of database engine you want to use. A variety of databases are available, including PostgreSQL, MySQL, MariaDB, Oracle Database, SQL Server, and Amazon Aurora.

Aurora is a cloud-based relational database that is compatible with MySQL and PostgreSQL. AWS designed and developed this database to meet the demands of enterprise-class databases.

Each database engine has its own unique characteristics and features. Select one based on your application and business requirements.

---

[2] https://aws.amazon.com/rds/ha/

RDS Pricing

One of the biggest benefits of Amazon RDS is that you pay as you go. The Amazon RDS billing process consists of two parts.

Instance Cost

The first thing you have to pay for is the instance hosting the databases. In terms of pricing, there are two options: on-demand and reserved.

With on-demand instances, you can pay by the hour for compute capacity. It's perfect for short-term or unpredictable databases.

The reserved instance pricing model is great when you have a good understanding of your database's resource usage. Unlike on-demand, this type of instance allows you to secure a one- or three-year term and receive a substantial discount.

Storage Cost

In addition, you must pay for the storage and I/O your database consumes. Storage is charged per gigabyte per month, while I/O is charged per million requests.

I hope you now have a good understanding of Amazon RDS. Read this section again if you have any doubts. You will now learn about the AWS NoSQL offering called Amazon DynamoDB.

Amazon DynamoDB

In this section, you are going to learn about the AWS NoSQL database offering called DynamoDB.

233

DynamoDB Overview

This is a fully managed no-SQL database service that provides fast and predictable performance with seamless scalability.[3]

DynamoDB is one of the best options to store NoSQL, semi-structured data. As this is a fully managed database, you don't have to deal with hardware provisioning, setup, configuration, replication, software patches, or cluster scaling when you use DynamoDB.

As another benefit of DynamoDB, it automatically encrypts data at rest, which reduces the complexity and operational load of managing encryption keys. You don't have to worry if it doesn't make sense. The only thing you need to remember is that encryption is enabled by default. I cover encryption in detail in the AWS management chapter.

In DynamoDB, you create a table for storing and retrieving your data. This is important to understand. When you create an Amazon RDS instance, you create a database inside it. Inside the database, you create a table. But in the case of DynamoDB, you create the table directly inside it. So when you go to the DynamoDB dashboard, you will create a table.

A DynamoDB table can scale horizontally. It distributes the data across different backend servers to make sure that you can scale whenever required and get excellent performance.

Let's look at how to store data inside DynamoDB. A DynamoDB table is made up of three components: tables, items, and attributes. First, you have the table itself and that's where all of your data is stored. A table is a collection of items, and each item is a collection of attributes. Items are like rows in a relational database, for instance, the student with student ID 101 is an item. Each item has a series of attributes associated with it; it is the data that you see in these fields, such as the `LastName`, `FirstName`, and `Email`.

---

[3] `https://docs.aws.amazon.com/amazondynamodb/latest/developerguide/Introduction.html`

```
{

     "student_id": 101,
     "email": "ram.kumar@gmail.com",
     "first_name": "Ram",
     "last_name": "Kumar"

}

{

     "student_id": 102,
     "email": "shyam.singh@gmail.com",
     "first_name": "Shyam",
     "last_name": "Singh",
     "course": {
            "registration_id": "R01",
            "student_id": "102",
            "course": "Marketing",
            "course_id": "MK211"
     }

}
```

In DynamoDB, primary keys uniquely identify items in a table, and secondary indexes enhance query flexibility. DynamoDB streams can be used to capture events related to data modification.

The performance of DynamoDB tables depends on their throughput capacity. Adding or reducing throughput can be done without any downtime or degradation of performance for your tables. The AWS Management Console provides performance metrics and resource utilization information.

DynamoDB offers on-demand backup capability, so you can create full backups of your tables for long-term storage, archiving, and regulatory compliance. In addition, Amazon DynamoDB tables can be backed up on-demand and restored at a point-in-time. Using point-in-time recovery, you can protect your tables from accidental write and delete operations. You can restore a table to any point in time within the last 35 days using point-in-time recovery.

Additionally, this lets you automatically delete expired items from tables, which helps you reduce storage usage and costs associated with storing data that is no longer relevant.

Let's now take a look at some use cases for DynamoDB. As a result of its flexible data model and reliable performance, it is an excellent choice for mobile web-based applications, gaming applications, EdTech applications, and IoT applications. DynamoDB can also be used for other applications.

I hope you now understand Amazon DynamoDB, its features, and its applications.

Create Your First Amazon RDS Database

In this section, you create a MySQL RDS instance and connect to it from your computer. You also learn about the other resources and configurations that are needed to spin up an RDS MySQL instance.

Go to the AWS Console. Type **RDS** in the search bar and click the RDS option; this will take you to the RDS dashboard.

Create a Subnet Group

The first thing you need to do when creating RDS instances is to create a subnet group. A subnet group is simply a logical grouping of subnets where you provision the RDS instance.

Go to the Subnet Groups page by clicking Subnet on the left panel.

1. Click Create DB Subnet Group. Assign a name to the subnet group. You need to add a description here, as it is a required field. I added "Subnet group for MySQL DB."

2. Next, select a VPC. I have only one, so I will choose this one.

3. Next, you need to select the Availability Zone. Select the Availability Zones where you want the RDS instances to be deployed. For me, I have subnets in ap-south-1a and ap-south-1b. If you have subnets in another Availability Zone, you can select ap-south-1c as well.

4. Next, select the subnets in these Availability Zones. I have a public subnet and a private subnet in each of the Availability Zones. Usually, you would want to create RDS instances in private subnets, so select your private subnets.

5. RDS instances are usually created in private subnets and accessed from within VPCs. In production applications, you do not want your databases to be accessible over the Internet. But, if you want your on-premises servers or personal computers to be able to reach the RDS instance, you need to create RDS in the public subnets. I choose my public subnets here. Click Create when you're ready.

You should now have successfully created a subnet group for your database. Next, you'll create the RDS database.

Create an RDS Database

1. Click Databases. Before you click the Create Database button, note the Restore from S3 button next to it. When you take backups of your RDS DBs, they are stored in AWS S3. By clicking this button, you can create a new instance from one of your backups in S3.

2. Moving back to creating the database, click Create Database.

3. The first option you can see is the standard create or easy create. If you choose the Easy Create option, AWS will use default values for creating your DB. I have selected Easy Create. Now the only options I have are the database types and some other options. If you scroll down and open the View Default Settings for Easy Create drop-down, you can see that AWS has hardcoded some values for you.

4. Don't want to create your DB like this. Move back to standard creation and choose the parameters yourself. Click Standard Create at the top. Choose the MySQL Engine type.

   Next, you can choose the MySQL version. I choose the latest version available for me right now, which is MySQL 8.0.28.

5. The next option you have is to choose the template as per your use case. If you choose production, AWS will choose some default options for simplicity. Like when I have a Production template selected and I scroll down to Availability & Durability.

6. The default option is to create a standby instance. When I change the template to dev and scroll down again, the default value is not to create a standby DB. Selecting a template will simply set some default values for you. Stick to the free tier and select the free tier template.

7. The next option you have is the DB identifier. This is the name of your DB instance. You should note that this is not the name of the database but the name of the RDS instance. Change this to `TheCloudAdvisory-MYSQL-DB`.

8. Next, you have to create the master username and password for the RDS instance. Change the username to `RDSMASTER` and type a password here. You can have AWS auto-generate passwords for this username if you want.

9. The next option you have is to select the instance class for your DB. If you selected the free tier template, you cannot change the instance types. There is only one option, `t2.micro`. If you select the dev or prod templates, you will get all the instance options.

10. Next, you have to select the storage type for your RDS instance. The current option you have is the general-purpose SSD gp2. You can change this value to io1 for more complex workloads. For now, stick to the gp2 SSD type. You can also enable autoscaling for your RDS storage. If this checkbox is selected, you can add the maximum storage you want your RDS instance to scale up to. The default value for this field is 1000 GB. If you database storage gets filled up, AWS will automatically scale the storage to up to 1000 GBs.

11. The next option is Availability and Durability. You saw earlier that you had this option when you selected the dev and production templates. However, this option is not supported in free tier.

12. Next, you have the option to select the connectivity for your RDS instance. You can select the VPC in which you created your subnet group and then select the subnet group in the next option. You have the next option if you want your RDS instance to be accessible outside the VPC. Although you created the subnet group with public subnets, AWS gives you another option to not allow public access to your DB. Since you will be accessing this DB from your personal computers, select Yes.

13. Next, you have to specify the security group for your RDS. Choose to create a new SG and give it the name rds-MySQL-sg.

14. You can see the default port for MySQL Database here. Leave this as it is.

15. The next option is Database Authentication. You have three options here—for this example, choose Password Authentication. If you want more security and control over RDS access, you can choose the other options.

16. You can see the additional options for RDS by clicking this drop-down. The first option is the database name. If you remember from earlier, you had the option to add the database identifier, which was the name of the RDS database instance. Here, you can ask AWS to create a database like users, employees, and so on, inside `TheCloudAdvisory-MYSQL-DB`. If you leave this value empty, AWS will not create a DB and you will have to do that using MySQL commands when you connect to this instance. Create a `users` database for this example. Leave the other values at the defaults.

17. Next, you have the automatic backup option. You can choose how frequently you want to take backups of your DB and even specify the time window for the backups.

18. The next option is Enhanced Monitoring. This is a popular question on the AWS exams. The difference between normal CloudWatch monitoring and enhanced monitoring is that, in the case of normal monitoring, RDS gathers the metrics from the hypervisor for a DB instance. Enhanced monitoring gathers its metrics from an agent on the instance. If you want OS-level metrics, you need to enable enhanced monitoring.

19. For this use case, do not select the enhanced monitoring option. You can choose the log exports. You can have AWS send logs to CloudWatch logs by selecting the options.

20. The next option allows AWS to do minor version upgrades on your DB and to select the time window for these upgrades. Leave these values at the defaults.

21. The final option to enable delete protection. This simple option will prevent you from deleting your RDS instance. Select this option now, and you will see how it works later in this chapter. Click Create Database. On the Databases page, you can see your MySQL database being created.

22. As you can see, the RDS instance has been created. Click the instance to see the connection details.

    In the Connectivity & Security tab, you can see the endpoint and the port of this RDS instance. These values are needed to access the RDS instance. Before you move ahead and connect to the RDS instance from your computer, you need to make sure that the security group allows inbound connections. Find the security group and click its ID. If you see the inbound rules, you will notice you already have an inbound rule from an IP address to allow RDs connections. This is the IP address of your computer from which you created the RDS instance. As a default feature, when you create a publicly accessible RDS, AWS adds this rule to allow connections from your PC. If you want the RDS to be accessible from other IP addresses or if your IP address changes, you have to create a similar rule for other IP addresses.

You now have an RDS instance that should only be accessible from the IP address of your computer.

Connect to this instance using MySQL Workbench. You can download MySQL Workbench for your PC using this link: https://dev.mysql.com/downloads/workbench/.

23. Open MySQL Workbench. Click the Database option in the taskbar and select the Connect to Database option. Add the hostname as the endpoint specified in the RDS console and add the 3306 port. Add the RDSMASTER username and the password. Click Connect.

24. You should have successfully connected to the RDS instance and be logged in as the master of the RDS instance.

25. Take a look at the databases in your RDS instance. To do so, enter the Show Databases command and click Run.

26. Your Users database should be listed among the other default RDS databases. Select the Users database by running this command:

```
use Users;
```

27. You should now be using the Users database in your
     RDS. Create a sample table and add some data.

28. Create the table by running this command:

```
create table user_data(
    user_id INT NOT NULL AUTO_INCREMENT,
    firstname VARCHAR(100) NOT NULL,
    Lastname VARCHAR(100) NOT NULL,
    PRIMARY KEY ( user_id )
);
```

29. Enter some data in the table by running these
     commands:

```
INSERT INTO user_data (firstname, lastname) VALUES
("Ram", "Kumar");
INSERT INTO user_data (firstname, lastname) VALUES
("Shyam", "Kumar");
```

30. Finally, take a look at the data in your users_data
     table by running this command:

```
select * from user_data;
```

     You should see that you have successfully run
     MySQL commands in the RDS instance.

31. Delete the RDS database. There is one last thing I
     wanted to demonstrate. Go to your database in the
     RDS console. Click Actions and then click Delete.
     You will not be able to delete the database. The issue
     is that you selected the Enable Deletion Protection
     parameter when you were creating the database. To
     finally delete the DB, click Modify and scroll down

to uncheck the Delete Protection option. Click
Continue and choose the Apply Immediately option.
Then click Modify.

32. Finally, you can now click Actions and delete the
     instance. AWS has chosen to create a snapshot
     of your RDS instance. I strongly recommend that
     you do not take a snapshot here, as you will not be
     needing the data you used in this tutorial. Uncheck
     the Create Final Snapshots option and check the
     Acknowledgement button. Enter **Delete Me** and
     delete the RDS instance.

With this, you come to the end of the chapter. You looked at all the
parameters you have when creating the RDS subnet groups and databases.
You created your own RDS database, connected to it, and finally did some
CRUD operations in the database.

Summary

This chapter provided you with an overview of database types. You looked
at two important databases: Amazon RDS and DynamoDB. You also
created your first Amazon RDS database.

You learned about three data types: structured, unstructured, and
semi-structured. As the nature of this data is different, it will be stored
differently. You came to know that storing small data can be managed
through Excel sheets and tables. But when it comes to huge amounts
of data, you need databases. You learned that relational databases
store structured data. When it comes to storing and dealing with semi-
structured or unstructured data, the choice is often a non-relational
database.

You learned how to manage on-premises and cloud databases. You should now understand that managing databases on-premises is a difficult task as compared to managing databases in the cloud. Also, you learned that Amazon RDS is designed to minimize the effort involved in managing relational database tasks, such as hardware provisioning, database setup, patching, backups, and so on. Also, you learned about Amazon DynamoDB, an excellent feature offered by AWS. It is one of the best options for storing semi-structured, NoSQL data. Since DynamoDB is a fully managed database, you don't need to manage hardware provisioning, setup, configuration, replication, patches, or cluster scalability.

I hope you have understood everything in this chapter pretty well. If you have doubts about anything, I recommend that you read the chapter again. Let's meet in the next chapter.

CHAPTER 9

Advanced AWS Services

This chapter focuses on advanced AWS services that are essential for you to know as a cloud learner. Upon completion of this chapter, you will have complete understanding of Elastic Block Storage (EBS) and its functioning. Similarly, you learn about the Elastic File System (EFS), a cloud-based file storage service, and its functioning. You also review the features and use cases of AWS networking, such as DNS and Route 53. Finally, you look at AWS Direct Connect and its applications in networking, such as AWS Snowball, a petabyte-scale data transport service that uses secure devices to transfer large amounts of data, and the AWS Storage Gateway, a hybrid cloud storage service.

EBS Overview

This section explains one of the storage options for EC2 instances, the Elastic Block Storage (EBS). The section starts with the definition and basics of EBS followed by its use cases and types.

Amazon EBS is like a hard drive in the cloud; it provides persistent block storage for Amazon EC2 instances. EBS storage is referred to as EBS volumes in AWS terminology. Therefore, this chapter refers to it as an EBS volume from now on.

© Pravin Mishra 2023
P. Mishra, *Cloud Computing with AWS*, https://doi.org/10.1007/978-1-4842-9172-6_9

You can attach EBS volumes to your EC2 instances and create a file system on top of these volumes, run a database or server on top of them, or use them in any other way a block storage would be used.

Block storage is a technology that chops data into blocks and stores them as separate pieces. Each data block is given a unique identifier, which allows a storage system to place the smaller pieces of data wherever is most convenient.

A block storage volume works similarly to a hard drive, and you can store any files in it or even install a whole operating system.

An EBS volume is a network-attached drive. That means that the EBS volume is not actually physically attached to your EC2 instance. It is attached via a network inside AWS. Since it is attached via a network link, an EBS volume can easily be attached or detached for EC2 instances.

This means that you can move your EBS volume from one running instance to another and the change will happen within a matter of seconds.

You can think of EBS as a computer "hard disk" that can be attached to any EC2 instance, detached from an instance and immediately reattached to a different instance via the "network."

You might wonder why this is called Elastic Block Storage. When you provision an EBS volume, you have to define its size and IOPS. IOPS simply means input-output operations per second. You have to tell AWS that you want an EBS volume of say, 100 GB that can do 1000 IOPS, that is, 1000 input-output operations per second.

But just because you defined that your EBS is 100 GB does not mean that you are stuck with a 100 GB drive. You can change the size or the IOPS capacity of EBS volumes at any time. This is the *elasticity* that EBS provides and this is why EBS is an "elastic block storage" and not just a block storage. Let's look at some of its features.

EBS Features

An important point to note about EBS is that it can be attached to only one EC2 instance at a time. You cannot have two EC2 instances connected to a single EBS volume. However, AWS recently released a feature where IOPS SSD EBS volume can be attached to multiple instances. We don't go into that detail in this book.

Essentially, EBS is a network drive that can be moved from one instance to another. But this process has a limitation. EBS volumes are restricted to one Availability Zone. This means that, although the EBS volumes can be quickly moved from one instance to another, they cannot be moved across Availability Zones.

For example, an EBS volume in the Availability Zone ap-south-1a cannot be attached to an EC2 instance in ap-south-1b. It can only be moved between instances in ap-south-1a.

If you do want to move an EBS volume from one Availability Zone to another, you have to take a snapshot of it. You learn about snapshots in a bonus section later in this chapter.

Types of EBS Volumes

Let's move forward and look at the different types of EBS volumes.

As an example, one of the important criteria while buying a new laptop is storage. When you talk about computer storage, this means hard drives. Your computer hard drives could be of different types, like SSD, HDD, and so on. Similarly, EBS volumes are also classified into the following types:

- General-purpose SSD gp2 and gp3

- Provisioned IOPS SSD io1 and io2

- Throughput-optimized St1 (HDD)

- Cold HDD sc1 (HDD)

One thing to note here is that only the SSDs can be used as the system boot volume. Boot volume is the volume that contains the operating system. So, AWS only allows the fast SSDs as a boot volume.

That's all you need to know about EBS and EBS volume types.

EFS Overview

In this section, you learn about one of the storage options of EC2 instances, the Elastic File System, also known as EFS. This section starts with the basics and a short description of EFS followed by its use cases.

Before looking at what EFS is, you should know what a file system is. A file system defines how files are named, stored, read, and used in any storage device. File systems are installed on every storage device, whether it is a disk drive or a CD.

Every time you perform an operation on a file on your computer, like editing, deleting, or reading, your operating system's file system handles it. Storage is simply a massive chunk of data without a file system because, without a file system, the operating system will never know where to look for your data.

Imagine a storage room full of documents and pages, all scattered around. You cannot tell which pages are related to which pages and which ones belong in the same folder. It is just randomly scattered data. This is how a storage device would be without file system. In comparison, a library is a real-life example of a file system, where every document is organized. Just like a library has a system, your operating system has a file system that tells the computer where to find your files.

Operating systems have an industry-standard file system that is managed as a part of your OS. However, it is always possible to make your own file system for applications.

Amazon EFS is a cloud-based file storage service. As the name suggests, it is a scalable storage solution that automatically grows and shrinks as you add and remove files.

You do not need to tell AWS to create a file system of 100 GBs or 200 GBs. You simply create an EFS, and it grows and shrinks as you add or delete files. This ensures that your EFS always has the storage as per your needs. It can grow from a small megabyte to a petabyte-scale file system automatically. There is no minimum fee for using EFS; you simply have to pay for the storage you use. So if you use only 500 MB of EFS, you only pay for the 500 MB.

Similar to EBS, EFS is also a "network-attached" service. This means that your file system storage is attached to EC2 instances via a network and not physically. But unlike EBS, which could only be connected to one EC2 instance at a time, you can connect EFS to any number of EC2 instances.

One of the most important features of EFS is that it stores your data across Availability Zones. You can attach EFS with multiple EC2 instances across availability zones. Let's say you have one EFS in the Mumbai region. This EFS can be used by any number of EC2 instances from any Availability Zones in this region. And not just EC2, you can also use EFS with services like ECS, EKS Lambda functions, or even your local computer.

You can simultaneously connect hundreds of EC2 instances, Lambda functions, and your personal computers to EFS.

As of now, EFS is only compatible with Linux-based instances. It is important to note that Windows instances cannot use EFS. AWS has a different file system for Windows instances, called FsX.

You must be wondering why use EFS and not create your own file system?

Although creating a file system on any storage device is possible, EFS is a managed service. This means that it manages the storage infrastructure for you, and as a user, all you have to do is use the file system. You do not have to worry about the underlying storage or any maintenance or patching of your file system. EFS will manage all of this extra work for you.

Any time there is a requirement for a file system storage that can be used across multiple services and local computers, think EFS.

Now let's look at DNS and the DNS service of AWS, the Amazon Route 53. You will start by learning about DNS and Route 53 and then have a look at its features and use cases.

DNS and Amazon Route 53

DNS stands for Domain Name System. It is the phonebook of the Internet. It is a system that lets you connect to websites by matching human-readable domain names like google.com or Facebook.com. Basically, it translates the domain name to IP address and vice versa (IP to domain name).

Let's look at this with an example. When you make a phone call to your friend. You look for his phone number in the contacts app. But because it's hard to remember a phone number, you save phone numbers in the contacts app.

Similar to phone numbers, websites and applications have IP addresses. Have you ever used the IP address of Google.com or Youtube.com to connect to them? No, Because, again, it is hard to remember. So this is simplified with DNS.

DNS is similar to a phone book, which stores the IP of the websites. The DNS servers simply translate domain names to IP addresses. So when you access Youtube.com, the request first goes to a DNS server and then to the IP address of Youtube.com.

Now you understand DNS and how it works. AWS also offers a DNS service called Route 53. Route 53 does a similar task.

Let's look at Route 53 in detail:

- Route 53 is a highly available and scalable DNS service from AWS.

- It is also the only service on AWS that claims 100 percent availability. This means that Route 53 never goes down.

Say you have a web application in your AWS account running on an EC2 instance. If you want to host this website on the YOURNAME.com domain, you can create a DNS record in Route 53 to point the domain to the IP address of EC2. Following are a few more features as well:

- **Domain Registration.** Route 53 is also a domain registrar. This means that it allows you to buy new domain names from the Route 53 console. If you purchased your domain name on another website like GoDaddy, Route 53 also has a feature to transfer domain names from other domain registrars to Route 53.

- **Hosted Zone.** You can create the hosted zones. A hosted zone is a container for records, which include information about how to route traffic for a domain.

- **Health Check.** Route 53 also has the ability to perform health checks of your resources. It uses these health checks to determine the state of your resources and then sends traffic to only healthy resources.

- **Traffic Flow.** Traffic flow gives you another level of automation for how you send your traffic to your resources.

The next section covers AWS VPN and Direct Connect.

AWS VPN and AWS Direct Connect

In this section, you will learn about the different connectivity options from AWS to the on-premises data centers.

Let's look at these with an example. Assume your organization is planning to migrate a business-critical application to an AWS Cloud that has compliance data. Your security team insists that you can move the application to the cloud, but data must remain on-premises and meet all compliance requirements.

You have decided on the Mumbai region and created a VPC inside your AWS account. In order to deploy your application, you created an EC2 instance. Your application also uses other AWS services, like Amazon S3, CloudWatch, and so on.

This is your on-premise data center, where you have a database. Finally, you configured your application that was running on an EC2 instance to an on-premise database.

Your security team realized that this database connects with applications via the public Internet. They explain that it's against security guidelines. This connection must be private and secure.

There are a couple of options you can use in AWS to make this connection private. One of them is using a site-to-site VPN.

This is called a *site-to-site VPN* because you connect one AWS site to another site's data center.

VPN stands for Virtual Private Network. The VPN creates a "tunnel" that you use to access the Internet and bypass your Internet Service Provider (ISP). This process encrypts all the data that you send and uses different security measures to ensure that all the data is secure.

What you do is create a VPN between your AWS account's VPC and your on-premises network (see Figure 9-1).

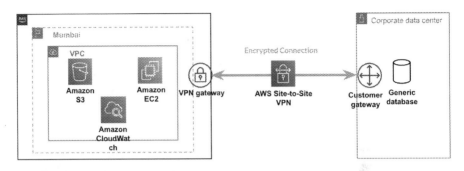

Figure 9-1. *VPN between the AWS account and the*
on-premises network

There are a couple of components that you need to configure. On the
VPC side, you have a virtual private gateway deployed in AWS. You also
have the customer gateway, which is deployed in the corporate data center.
Now that's a device in the corporate data center that you've configured a
certain way, but the actual customer gateway is created within AWS. It's
essentially a configuration element that you create that points your virtual
private gateway to whatever your VPN device is in your corporate data
center. Once you've configured those, you can establish a virtual private
network connection. This is an encrypted connection that's going over the
Internet. You get the protection of encryption, but you're still using the
Internet.

Say you have a security audit again, and they explain that this
connection is encrypted but it is still going through the Internet. As per
security guidelines, this connection must be private.

There is another service, called AWS Direct Connect (see Figure 9-2),
that you can use. It is a private connection between AWS and your data
center or office.

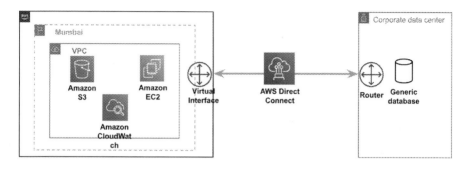

Figure 9-2. *AWS Direct Connect*

AWS Direct Connect is a high-speed, low-latency connection that allows you to access public and private AWS Cloud services from a local (on-premises) infrastructure. As a result, there is no network instability or congestion in the network due to the fact that it is enabled via dedicated lines, which bypass the public Internet.

One end of the cable goes to your router, while the other end goes to an Amazon Direct Connect router. By using this connection, you can connect virtual interfaces directly to Amazon Virtual Private Clouds, which can be created using this connection. In the region that it is associated with, an AWS Direct Connect location gives you access to AWS services.

It uses a private connection between your data center and the AWS direct connect location and, from there, a private connection into AWS.

It is more expensive than having a VPN. The key takeaway is that Direct Connect is a private connection, which means that you get that consistent network experience, whereas a VPN is public, and even though it's encrypted, it's still public.

Compute Fundamentals for AWS
Elastic Container Service

In this section, you learn about one of the compute services of AWS, which is the Elastic Container Service, also known as ECS. You will learn what ECS is, its types, and most importantly, its use cases. Let's get started.

Before you learn about Elastic Container Service, it's important that you know what a container is, because ECS is developed on container technology.

When you develop applications, they work on your computer, but they break as soon as you move these applications to another machine. This can be due to multiple reasons—it may be the different operating system, a different version of dependencies, and so on. How do you resolve this issue?

Containers are the solution to this issue. Application containers are standardized units that hold application code and dependencies, configuration, networking, and sometimes, even a part of the OS. Essentially, all the software required to run your application is inside a container. Containers make it possible for you to run your applications on any machine. You can rest assured that if it works in one system, it will work in all the systems.

Docker is the most widely used software platform that allows its users to create applications and containers. You can install Docker onto your machine and make a container for any application. I don't discuss Docker in detail at this point.

Amazon ECS is a fully managed container orchestration service that makes it easy for you to deploy, manage, and scale containerized applications. It means ECS makes it easier to use and manage Docker containers. When you use ECS, you do not need to install, operate, or scale your containers; ECS takes care of all these tasks for you.

Integrated with the rest of the AWS platform, it offers a secure and easy-to-use interface for running container workloads inside the cloud, which is seamless and highly integrated with the rest of the AWS platform.

To understand ECS, you should know some terms frequently used in ECS:

- **Task Definitions:** These are JSON scripts that hold multiple parameters to run your application. In simple words, task definitions tell ECS how to run a container. For example, you can define exactly how much RAM and CPU a container will need or on which EC2 port your application should start. ECS will then ensure that all your requirements are met.

- **Tasks:** When ECS runs a container based on your task definition, it is known as a task.

- **Task Roles:** Your containers can be running multiple operations on AWS. For example, a container might need to read messages from an SQS queue or interact with S3 or any other AWS service. Therefore, you need to give permission to do your tasks. This is done by using the task role. A task role is an AWS IAM Role that is defined in the task definition. This role is used to provide AWS access to ECS tasks.

Let's learn about how this all looks in ECS. You need an ECS cluster to run your container application. This ECS cluster is made up of two or more EC2 instances, called *container instances*. Then, you have services that span across these available two instances. That's where ECS create tasks or Docker containers.

One of the first things to do when using ECS is to provision and maintain infrastructure. ECS then takes care of starting and stopping containers for you. You can do this in two ways by using ECS launch types: using the EC2 launch type or the Fargate launch type.

EC2 Launch Type

The EC2 launch type in ECS requires you to create EC2 instances manually or use autoscaling groups in order to run your containers on those EC2 instances. As a result, you have to create EC2 instances manually or use autoscaling groups.

Fargate Launch Type

The option is based on pay-as-you-go serverless technology. It is possible to run containers without managing your infrastructure. By using the Fargate launch type, you are not required to create an Amazon EC2 instance. You tell ECS the number of containers to run and how much RAM and CPU a container should have. ECS Fargate ensures that you always have enough resources to launch containers. In the next section, I will discuss about AWS Elastic Beanstalk.

AWS Elastic Beanstalk

In this section, you learn about one of the compute services of AWS, which is Elastic Beanstalk.

AWS is a cloud computing leader, with close to 200 services. That's why you should know about most of the services to deploy applications on AWS and manage them efficiently. You have to first know about multiple AWS services, and how to use them in a cost-effectively manner. This is fine when you have a multiple applications or one big application, but what if you only have a web application? Spending days learning AWS only to deploy a web application is not a very efficient approach. Even after you learn AWS, you have to go through the effort of maintaining your infrastructure on AWS. As a developer, you don't want to worry about infrastructure, scalability, configuring connections, databases, and more. You quickly want to deploy and test applications. This is the problem that Elastic Beanstalk solves.

AWS Elastic Beanstalk is an easy-to-use service for deploying and scaling web applications. It's also known as EB, and this is a platform as a service offered by AWS.

To use Elastic Beanstalk, you need to create an application, upload the application version in the form of a source bundle (for example, a Java `.war` file) to Elastic Beanstalk, and then provide some information about the application that you want to use. As soon as you launch an Elastic Beanstalk environment, it will automatically configure and create the AWS resources you need to run your code. The environment can then be managed and new versions can be deployed after it has been launched.

The Elastic Beanstalk console, APIs, and command-line interfaces, which include the unified AWS CLI, make it easy for you to view information about your application, including metrics, events, and environment status.

As a developer, if you use EB, you can deploy applications without provisioning the underlying infrastructure. AWS will ensure that your infrastructure is ready and highly available. Internally, EB reuses all the components you have seen before like RDS, load balancers, and EC2 to run applications, but you can use EB without any other knowledge of these internal components. It is a free service on its own, but you pay for the underlying infrastructure provisioned by using Beanstalk.

Now you'll see how Elastic Beanstalk works in AWS.

Say you have an AWS account and a VPC within it. You will now create an Elastic Beanstalk Environment.

As you know, Beanstalk will create all the underlying infrastructure, like EC2 instances, load balancers, databases, security groups, and so on. As a developer, you only care about your code. Developers want to make sure that they spend their time writing great code, testing it, and have all that underlying infrastructure managed for them.

In this case, you have a developer who has a `.war` file with their code. (It doesn't need to be a `.war` file. It could be `.zip` or GitHub code as well.) The developer can deploy this `.war` file using the EB management console or EB CLI. Beanstalk will then deploy the application and do the rest of the configuration, like the elastic load balancing, the autoscaling group, the instances, and even a database. That's all. Elastic Beanstalk takes care of application scaling, OS upgrades, patching, logging, metrics, and everything else.

As a developer, you can focus on your application and business features.

Consider these Elastic Beanstalk features:

- A wide range of programming languages is supported, such as Java, .NET, PHP, Node.js, Python, Ruby, Go, and Docker.

- It is integrated with Amazon VPC, and it allows AWS resources to be launched into the VPC, such as EC2 instances

- It integrates with AWS Identity and Access Management and helps you securely control access to your AWS resources.

- CloudFront can also be integrated. After Elastic Beanstalk is created and deployed, CloudFront can distribute the content from S3.

- Elastic Beanstalk also supports running RDS instances in a development or testing environment.

Elastic Beanstalk is an excellent choice to deploy your applications to the AWS Cloud within minutes. You do not need any experience or knowledge of cloud computing to use Elastic Beanstalk. You create EB application environments and specify some parameters, and you are done.

In the next section, you learn about the serverless concept.

Serverless Services

In this section, you learn about the serverless concept and why it is more popular in cloud computing.

In most of the services you have seen so far, the development and deployment process has been the same. You develop your application, allocate infrastructure, and then deploy and run the application on this allocated infrastructure. That is how it should be. You always need an underlying server to run your application's code. So, there has always been a need to provision and maintain your infrastructure. This is where serverless comes in the picture.

Serverless has been the catchword in the cloud computing world, and many applications are following serverless architecture. The term comes from the idea that the infrastructure used to run your applications no longer needs to be provisioned or maintained by you or your team.

Serverless can also be a confusing term because in serverless architectures, servers do exist. It does not mean that your application does not have an underlying server, it's just that there is no need to worry about managing the server. If you are an end user, it might as well not exist because you never have to worry about servers. Hence the term, serverless. But there is a server, and its provisioning and maintenance are entirely taken care of by the provider.

If you put this in AWS terminology, you no longer need to create an EC2 instance and configure and maintain an operating system for your application.

That means you delegate all of that responsibility for managing the underlying server, and it's all taken care of. The server can scale automatically and charge you according to your usage. Serverless services have become extremely popular with many modern cloud applications.

Following are some benefits of serverless services:

- **No server management is necessary.** With serverless, there are no instances to manage. You don't need to provision any hardware. There is no management of operating systems or software. The capacity provisioning and patching are all handled for you automatically.

- **Developers are only charged for the space they use on the server, which reduces costs.** It can also be very inexpensive to run serverless services. You are only charged for what you use. Code only runs when backend functions are needed by the serverless application.

- **Serverless architectures are inherently scalable.** Serverless scales automatically and elastically. It also has built-in high availability. You just deploy the code as a developer, and it automatically scales up as needed. Suppose a function needs to be run in multiple instances. In that case, the servers will start up, run, and terminate as required, often using containers. As a result, a serverless application can handle an unusually high number of requests. But in a traditional structured application with a limited amount of server space, it gets overwhelmed when there is a sudden increase in usage.

In the next section, you learn about AWS Lambda.

AWS Lambda

Lambda is a serverless service that lets you run code without provisioning or managing servers. Unlike EC2 instances, where your application needs to be running continuously, AWS Lambda allows you to write functions that can run on-demand. AWS Lambda functions can be triggered by events within or outside of the AWS account, and they do not have to keep running.

For example, you can write a function to do a file-processing task and it will be triggered when data is uploaded into the S3 service (see Figure 9-3). Every time a file is uploaded to S3, you have a function that will automatically run and process this file. Or, you can have a Lambda function that fetches values from a database for your frontend application.

Amazon S3   AWS Lambda   Amazon RDS

Figure 9-3. *Lambda function example*

There are multiple ways to use Lambda functions. They can be used for anything, from running small individual tasks to replacing entire backend applications.

You should also note that AWS Lambda functions are only meant for short executions. You can only run code in Lambda for a maximum of 15 minutes, which is a reasonable amount of time for most use cases. (Note that this keeps changing all the time, so I recommend checking the AWS documentation for recent updates.) If you have a single process that takes more than 15 minutes to run, you have to deploy it to a server like EC2 instances or container.

The next section looks at some other features of AWS Lambda.

Automatic Scaling

When you use EC2 instances, even though you have an autoscaling group to scale the infrastructure, you still have to create scaling policies manually. You have to tell AWS to add or remove instances based on CloudWatch alarms. In comparison, AWS Lambda can scale automatically.

Consider the same example of the file-processing Lambda that runs every time a file is uploaded to S3. What happens when you upload, let's say, 500 files? You will have 500 Lambda functions running your file processing tasks. This is the power of serverless services. You need not worry about scaling your infrastructure. AWS ensures you always have enough resources to run your code.

Note that AWS has a service quota limit of 1,000 concurrently running Lambdas per region. In this example, you might see some Lambda failures when you upload more than 1,000 files to the S3. This limit has been placed to avoid misuse of your account and prevent any unwanted charges. If your use case requires more than 1,000 Lambda functions running concurrently, you can request this limit be increased from AWS support.

Pay Per User Price

Lambda's next and most lucrative feature is that it is pay-per-use. This means you pay for the time your code runs. There are no charges when your code is not running. Suppose your file-processing Lambda runs for one minute. You only pay the compute cost of one minute. If you have ten Lambdas running for one minute, you pay for ten minutes of compute time, and so on.

RAM

Lambda functions can get resources to up to 10 GBs of RAM. It is also important to note that when you increase the RAM of your Lambda function, your CPU and networking capability of Lambda also improve.

This is a trendy exam topic. How do you increase the CPU and network of Lambda? The answer is that you need to increase the RAM.

Integration

As mentioned, AWS Lambda has a lot of use cases, and it has been integrated with a lot of AWS services. Take a look at some of the main integrations and their use cases:

- **S3**: Like in the example you have seen so far, you can have a Lambda running on different types of events in S3.

- **DynamoDB**: You can create a trigger so that a Lambda will trigger whenever an event happens in your DynamoDB, which is a database service.

- **API Gateway**: Lambda and API gateway integration is one of Lambda's most widely used use cases. The API gateway is an AWS service that is used to create REST APIs in AWS. You can put Lambda behind an API gateway and create a REST API endpoint to call your Lambda function.

- **SNS**: You can have a Lambda function that reacts to notifications in an SNS topic. SNS is further integrated with all kinds of events in the AWS Console, and with this integration, all these events can be used to trigger Lambda functions.

- **SQS**: Lambda can be used to process messages in the SQS queues.

- **CloudWatch Events**: You can also run Lambda functions with CloudWatch events.

Finally, the next section looks at some small examples of Lambda functions.

Lambda Functions

As you can see in Figure 9-4, you have your frontend application running on EC2 instances. Then, you have an API gateway that calls your lambda functions for the backend. This Lambda function has also been integrated with RDS and fetches and stores data in the RDS database. On the other side, you have the frontend application pushing tasks to the SQS queue, which has been integrated with another Lambda for message processing.

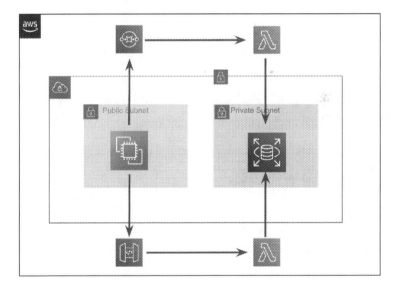

Figure 9-4. *Cloud computing*

You can create a CloudWatch event that triggers at regular intervals. Since you can trigger a Lambda from a CloudWatch event, you can have a Lambda function that runs regularly. This is a popular use case and exam question. How do you run a Lambda to run a command-based job? The answer is by using CloudWatch event triggers.

In the next section, you learn all about Amazon ElastiCache.

Introduction to Amazon ElastiCache and DynamoDB

In this section, you learn about one of the core AWS services, Amazon ElastiCache. This section starts with the basic terms involved in the ElastiCache service.

Caching refers to the process of storing data in an area of memory called a cache. As a result, you can reuse the data that has already been retrieved in the past. The future request for that data is served faster because it doesn't have to be retrieved from the primary location.

A cache is a reserved storage location that collects temporary data. It could be computer memory or an application.

A simple example is storing documents on a computer desktop. You might keep a copy of a frequently accessed document on the desktop, so you do not need to go to the document location each time. Another good example is a bookmark. You bookmark links that you use more often, so there is no need to search for the site each time.

Amazon ElastiCache

In the cloud, ElastiCache is a fully managed, in-memory database caching solution that you can use to optimize real-time performance and support a wide variety of use cases.

There are several benefits to using ElastiCache for caching, which will improve the speed and performance of applications and databases. You put this in front of other databases, so maybe in front of RDS or DynamoDB. Additionally, it can be used as the primary data store for scenarios such as session storage, gaming leaderboards, streaming, and analytics that don't require the reliability of a persistent store.

ElastiCache is the implementation of open-source database engines known as Redis and Memcached.

How ElastiCache Works

You have an application configured and installed on EC2 instance in your AWS account (see Figure 9-5). This application uses an RDS database to stores backed data.

The application is going to write some data to RDS. The application can read data on the RDS database as well. You can put ElastiCache in between your application and the RDS and store session or frequently accessed data on ElastiCache. That data then gets loaded into ElastiCache, which means that the next time the application needs to read the data from the database, it calls the cache. The data is found in the database, and it's retrieved a lot faster than if it were coming from RDS.

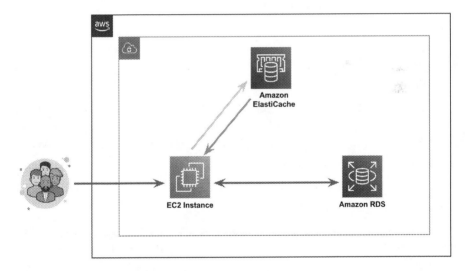

Figure 9-5. *How ElastiCache works*

ElastiCache Use Cases

Accelerates application performance

- As mentioned, ElastiCache is an in-memory data store and cache designed for applications that require sub-millisecond response times.

Eases the backend database load

- Apart from the application, it also helps reduce the load on the database. Once you cache frequent access data to ElastiCache, it will drastically decrease database calls and reduce pressure on your backend database.

Builds low-latency data stores

- This is an excellent solution for a low-latency database, for when you want to store non-durable data sets in memory and support real-time applications with microsecond latency.

In the next section, you learn about Amazon Redshift.

Amazon Redshift

In this section, you learn what a data warehouse is, why you need one, and all about the AWS Data Warehouse service called Redshift. Amazon Redshift is a fast, fully-managed, petabyte-scale data warehouse offering from AWS.

The petabytes scale means Redshift can satisfy the scalability needs of most enterprises. It's not just limited to terabytes but a thousand multiples of it. This level of scalability is difficult to achieve with on-premise implementations.

Redshift is a simple and cost-effective service to analyze data efficiently using business intelligence tools. It's a SQL-based data warehouse, and its primary use case is analytics workloads. Redshift uses EC2 instances. You must choose an instance type and family. It is pay as you go, based on the instances you provision.

Redshift will always keep free copies of your data, and it provides continuous and incremental backups. Anytime you see that the database needs to be a warehouse and to do analytics on it, Redshift is the solution. In the next section, you learn about Amazon CloudFront.

You likely have heard about data warehouses, but maybe are not sure exactly what they are. As the name suggests, they are warehouses of data. They allow you to store large amounts of data from multiple sources, which could be from application log files, transactional systems, relational databases, marketing, sales, finance, customer-facing application, external partner systems, and other sources.

Basically, a data warehouse is a large collection of business data used to help an organization make decisions. How will this data help make a business decision?

The goal of every business is to make better business decisions than the competitors. How do you make a better decision? Either from experience or good data and mathematics.

To do mathematics, you need data. When it comes to big enterprises and organizations, they use business intelligence (BI) tools.

BI tools analyze data and generate reports. Nowadays, most business users depend on reports, dashboards, and analytics tools to extract insights from their data. Data warehouses power these reports, dashboards, and analytics tools by storing data efficiently.

The data warehouse is not a new concept; it has existed since the 1980s. However, it has not been in use due to the huge cost of storing this data on-premises.

Cloud computing revolutionizes this, as storing data in the cloud is easy and cheap. That's where Amazon Redshift comes in.

Amazon CloudFront

In this section, you learn about a content delivery service from AWS, the Amazon CloudFront. CloudFront is a web service from Amazon that enables you to distribute your static and dynamic web content to your users in a faster and more efficient manner, including data such as HTML, CSS, JS, image files, and other web files.

271

Let's assume you have a video-streaming website that's hosted in Mumbai region. You use an EC2 instance for dynamic content and S3 for static content videos. You are serving this content across the world.

When users from India watch your video, they can watch without a buffer, but when your Japanese or European users watch the same content, they will have a buffer and delay. This is because of the distance. Distance is directly proportional to latency.

Latency is mainly caused by distance. If you are watching a video from Japan and the video is actually in Mumbai, that's quite a long distance.

Distance is one of the most significant factors that cause latency, which reduces performance.

CloudFront is a service you can use to cache your content. It delivers your content through a worldwide network of edge locations and data centers, which were discussed in a previous chapter. When a user requests that content be served, it is served with CloudFront. The request is routed to the Edge Location, which has the lowest latency. As a result, the content is delivered with the best performance possible.

Suppose the content is not in that Edge Location. In that case, CloudFront retrieves it from an origin that you've defined, such as a MediaPackage channel, Amazon S3 bucket, or an HTTP server (for example, a web server on EC2) and then stores a copy of it at an Edge Location for future requests.

You can use CloudFront with any website or mobile application that serves static and dynamic content. It is especially useful for large, complex websites with users spread across the globe that are looking to improve their performance. In the next section, you learn about data transfer with AWS Snowball.

Data Transfer with AWS Snowball

In this section, you learn about one of the data migration services from AWS, called AWS Snowball. This section starts with the basics and a short description of AWS Snowball followed by its types and use cases.

AWS offers many data migration services. You can set up a connection between your on-premises network and AWS using Direct Connect or a public Internet over a VPN. But what if you have hundreds of TBs of data that you want to migrate to AWS? Data transfer over the Internet or direct connection will be slow and costly. Even at a speed of 1 Gbps, it would take more than two weeks to copy 100 TB of data to AWS, and you would also pay a high price for the Internet. This is where AWS Snowball comes in.

AWS Snowball is a petabyte-scale data transport service that uses secure devices to transfer large amounts of data in and out of the AWS Cloud. These devices are commonly called AWS Snowball and AWS Snowball Edge.

You can think of Snowball as a portable hard disk. It is just the same with some more features, including security, encryption, and more. You can order a Snowball device from the AWS Console and AWS will ship a physical briefcase-sized device to your location. AWS recently upgraded their Snowball devices and this upgraded version of AWS Snowball is called Snowball Edge.

Snowball versus Snowball Edge Devices

AWS Snowball is an older offering of AWS that's no longer in use. It was simply a storage device, much like a portable hard disk used to migrate data from AWS to your systems or from your servers to AWS.

Snowball Edge is an upgraded and more efficient version of AWS Snowball. It not only has storage capacity for you to migrate your data but also great computational capabilities. Snowball Edge is no longer a simple data migration device. It can also be used as a high power computer to do massive computational jobs and simultaneously transfer your data to AWS.

You might be wondering why you would need computational power in something like a hard disk. You might not need computation in your personal data or personal use, but generally, when you have terabytes of data, you have to do a lot of processing on it to make it useful. For example, you might want to collect information from your data, process it, and gain some real-time insights before moving the information to AWS. When you use a Snowball Edge, your data is not just copied and pasted. You can simultaneously run data processing jobs on the Snowball Edge device itself. You can use Snowball for data migration projects. This is an excellent service when you have a vast amount of data stored locally that you need to move to the AWS Cloud.

In the next section, you learn about the AWS Storage Gateway.

AWS Storage Gateway

In this section, you learn about a hybrid storage option of AWS, the AWS Storage Gateway. This section starts with the basics and a small description of Storage Gateway, followed by its use cases and types.

Imagine that you are using an on-premise environment for your application. As you know, on-premise environments are inefficient and old systems for deploying and running applications.

The cloud is a better option for deploying and hosting your applications. But some of your applications may still need to remain on-premises. For example, you need to maintain user data and your application locally in some countries by law. Or you might want to avoid the costs and effort of moving your application to the cloud. This is why AWS offers a hybrid cloud service and Storage Gateway is one of them.

AWS Storage Gateway is a hybrid cloud storage service that gives you a simple way to integrate your data centers and remote offices with low latency access to cloud storage. You can use the benefits of cloud storage, such as virtually infinite capacity, high scalability, and performance from your on-premise servers without modifying your local applications.

You need to make a lot of changes to your applications when migrating them to the cloud. For example, you have file storage in your local data center. How will you integrate it with AWS S3, an object storage service? The answer is using AWS Storage Gateway. One of the most important features of AWS Storage Gateway is that you can use S3 not only as object storage but also as file and block storage. So there is no need to change your application.

AWS Storage Gateway offers three interfaces: File Gateway, Volume Gateway, and Tape Gateway. AWS Storage Gateway provides a fast and easy path to use cloud storage at your premises while minimizing changes to your current application and storage experience. The service helps reduce your on-premises storage footprint by seamlessly integrating on-premises applications with AWS Storage.

Storage Gateway consists of two parts. One is the gateway that typically runs on a virtual machine (VM) or a hardware appliance in your facilities. The other is the service running in the cloud to which the on-premises gateway connects. The gateway sits in your environment and presents storage protocol interfaces such as NFS/SMB, iSCSI block, or iSCSI virtual tape. This means that your applications can connect to it without you having to rewrite or refactor the applications. The gateway in turn connects these on-premises applications and workloads to AWS Storage services. This enables you to store your data durably and securely in Amazon S3, Amazon S3 Glacier, S3 Glacier Deep Archive, or as Amazon EBS snapshots.

Storage Gateway Use Cases

Consider these common use cases of Storage Gateway:

- **Move backups and archives to AWS Cloud:** When you use the AWS Storage Gateway, you can use the infinite storage of AWS to store and maintain your backups, away from on-premise hardware. Instead of buying hardware and manually using it for backups, you have to move your files from Storage Gateway to AWS.

Services like Glacier and Glacier Deep Archive can be exceptionally cheap and efficient for maintaining backups and archives.

- **Reduce the size of on-premise storage:** This is an obvious benefit of using Storage Gateway. You reduce the size of your local storage when you store data on AWS. For example, when you use a volume gateway in cached mode, only frequently accessed data is stored locally, hence decreasing your local storage requirements.

- **Maintain low latency access to data stored in AWS:** Storage Gateway maintains your frequently accessed files in local devices. So, although your data is stored on AWS, you still have direct and low-latency access to your data. Amazon File Gateway is a good example of using a storage gateway to access data stored on S3 and AWS FSx quickly.

Summary

This chapter covered the advanced services of AWS, which include storage, networking, compute, database, and content delivery.

You learned that an EBS volume can be attached to your EC2 instances to create a file system. A block storage volume works similarly to a hard drive, and you can store any files on it or even install a whole operating system. You also learned that EFS is a cloud-based file storage service, which automatically grows and shrinks as you add and remove files. YOU looked at the example to understand the EFS. You also learned about AWS Snowball and Snowball Edge, which are used to migrate data. Snowball Edge is the upgraded version of AWS Snowball. This is an excellent service when there is a vast amount of data stored locally and you need to move that data to the AWS cloud. You also looked at how AWS Storage Gateway provides a fast and easy path to using cloud storage at your premises while minimizing changes to your current application and storage experience

The chapter looked at advanced networking features such as DNS, which translates the domain name to an IP address. Route 53 allows you to buy new domain names from the Route 53 console. It acts as a health checker of your resources as well. The chapter also explained that AWS Direct Connect is a high-speed, low-latency connection that allows you to access public and private AWS Cloud services from your local (on-premises) infrastructure. You also understood how VPN creates a "tunnel" that you use to access the Internet and bypass your Internet Service Provider (ISP).

You also learned about compute services like ECS, which deeply integrates with the rest of the AWS platform to provide a secure and easy-to-use solution for running container workloads in the cloud.

You also learned about Elastic Beanstalk, its features, and most importantly, its use cases. You came to know the term "serverless," which has been a catchword in the cloud computing world, and many applications are following serverless architecture. You learned about one serverless service which is Lambda. It lets you run code without provisioning or managing servers.

You also learned that ElastiCache is a fully managed in-memory database caching solution from AWS, and it supports a variety of customizable and real-time use cases. And you saw that Amazon Redshift is a fast, fully-managed, petabyte-scale data warehouse offering from AWS.

You finally learned about the content delivery service called Amazon CloudFront. It is a web service that speeds up the distribution of your static and dynamic web content, such as `.html`, `.css`, `.js`, and image files, to your users.

That's all for this chapter; let's meet in the next chapter!

CHAPTER 10

AWS Security and Management Services

This chapter includes a brief description of cloud security and explains how to ensure that your cloud infrastructure is secure from any possible failure.

AWS Security Services Overview

Cloud security is the most crucial topic for all cloud users. Since the cloud is gaining so much popularity in the tech world, it has certainly become a target of cyberattacks. There are many ways to hack the cloud. Attackers can steal sensitive information, prevent computing processes, or even deliver malware to a server to damage the cloud environments. The risk is crucial and in this chapter, you learn how to be prepared to face many security challenges.

The Amazon Web Services cloud computing environment is one of the most secure in the industry today. Millions of big and small customers trust and use the AWS infrastructure and services for their applications, system, and development processes. AWS Cloud security starts with its core infrastructure, which is designed to meet all security requirements. In addition to that, AWS also monitors its own infrastructure 24/7 to ensure customer data is confidential, secure, and always available.

© Pravin Mishra 2023
P. Mishra, *Cloud Computing with AWS*, https://doi.org/10.1007/978-1-4842-9172-6_10

Security in AWS is not the sole responsibility of AWS; instead, it is a shared responsibility between AWS and users. Both parties are responsible for fixing, implementing, and addressing cloud security. AWS is responsible for cloud security under the shared responsibility model, whereas security in the cloud is the responsibility of the customer.

Customers' security responsibilities vary depending on the AWS resources they use. For example, if you use S3 buckets as storage, you should consider all access management, encryption, and storage security standards and rules for AWS S3. As a responsibility, AWS offers many security-related services to its customers, and you can use these services to evaluate security results and take remediation steps.

Important AWS security services are covered in the next couple of sections.

The Shared Responsibility Model

This section explains how security works in the cloud and how the responsibility of securing your application is shared between you and the cloud provider.

Any IT resource has to be secure at every layer and stage of its facilities, compute, storage, networks, and customer applications. If your application is running on the on-premises infrastructure, it is obvious that you are responsible for securing the application.

However, when you move to the cloud, the cloud provider will take care of some part of security; this is called the shared responsibility model. Basically, the security of your resources is divided between you and cloud providers.

Based on AWS, shared responsibility is defined as follows:

Security "of" the cloud is the responsibility of the cloud service provider, while security "in" the cloud is the customer's responsibility.

Security *of* the cloud means that Amazon Web Services, the cloud provider, is responsible for maintaining the security of the underlying infrastructure, including physical data centers and the core infrastructure inside, such as compute, storage, and networking.

On the other hand, security *in* the cloud means, as the customer, it is your responsibility to ensure data and application security.

Now that you have a general idea of AWS's shared responsibility model, the next section takes a closer look at the different responsibilities between AWS and the customer.

AWS Is Responsible for the Security "of" the Cloud

As a global infrastructure provider, Amazon is responsible for the security and reliability of its data centers, networking infrastructure, physical hardware, virtualization technology, and software.

AWS protects their physical data centers with video surveillance, intrusion detection systems, and enforcing their employees to use two-factor authentication at the data center.

Interestingly, AWS physically destroys old storage devices after they've run their lifecycle.

To protect their physical facilities against natural disasters, AWS installs automatic fire detection and suppression systems, redundant power generators, and air conditioners that maintain and prevent their servers from overheating and causing power outages.

Providing high-availability and fast incident detection and response during any incidents happening at the data center is of utmost importance to AWS. This is why they build their data centers as redundantly connected clusters in various geographical regions. AWS can quickly redistribute traffic to an unaffected area if an area is affected by any disaster.

The Customer Is Responsible for Security "in" the Cloud

On the other side of the shared-responsibility model, the customer is responsible for securing activities that occur "in" the cloud or are connected to the cloud. This includes securing the guest operating system (OS), configuring access management, and securing the application data. The customer's responsibilities will vary depending on the service's delivery model the customer selects—whether it's IaaS, PaaS, or SaaS.

Consider the example of an EC2 instance. First and foremost, you have to secure the guest operating system by patching and updating it regularly. In addition to that, you have to take care of the Amazon machine image that you selected, encrypt the EBS volumes, and so on. The customer responsibilities are as follows:

- The guest operating system (security patching and updating)

- Amazon Machine Images (Encrypting the AMI if it's EBS-backed)

- Encrypting the Elastic Block Store volumes

- Configuring security groups

- Creating EC2 key pairs (credentials)

- Creating IAM policies and roles

- Securing applications installed in the EC2 instance

- Enabling encryption in flight through AWS ACM with SSL/TLS

Many of these things might not make sense to you at the moment. Don't worry, the idea is simply to make you aware of the distribution of responsibilities.

AWS Recap

Let's recap what you learned in this section. The AWS shared responsibility model outlines the responsibilities in the cloud for the customer and the cloud service provider. AWS is responsible for their global physical infrastructure, including regions, Availability Zones, Edge Locations, hardware, and software required to provide all their services. The user is responsible for securing their application and resources in the cloud.

In order for AWS to keep their side of the bargain, customers must understand that security in cloud computing is a shared task and they must ensure that they are taking care of their responsibilities, which are necessary to achieve the overall security of their cloud operations.

The next section covers security compliance.

Security Compliance

In this section, you look at the AWS Cloud compliance tools and learn how to leverage them to be fully compliant with your desired industry-standard certification. Let's get started.

Smaller startups and new companies like Netflix and Airbnb have emerged as industry leaders by fully leveraging cloud technology right from the start. However, various banks, financial institutions, healthcare providers, and insurance companies have not arrived there yet. What is the problem in their way?

You could argue that cost is an obstacle. But that's not true. Many of these companies have million dollars of IT budget. Could there be security concerns? Yes and no. Then what is the limitation that prevents these sensitive verticals from migrating their on-premise workloads to the cloud?

Well, this is nothing but compliance. In business, or in the case of a company, the term *compliance* basically refers to making sure that you are following the government's laws, safety regulations, and data protection requirements. If your business is in a certain country, you have to follow country-specific laws. If you are operating in a certain industry like healthcare, you have to follow the healthcare industry guidelines.

When you are moving to the cloud, public cloud providers have worked hard to comply with security and compliance standards. The shared responsibility model includes all possible compliance regulations, so all industry-standard compliance is taken care of by cloud providers.

AWS also has a Compliance Program that is designed to provide great governance and audit capabilities. The AWS Cloud service complies with IT security standards such as SOC 1, SOC 2, SOC 3, PCI DSS, GDPR, CSA, ISO 9001, and more. The following sections look deeper into this issue.

General Data Protection Regulation (GDPR)[1]

AWS is compliant with the new European Union (EU) privacy law regulation, called GDPR. According to the regulation, AWS is both a data controller and a data processor. AWS has implemented solutions to meet data encryption, data processing, data restoration, and data accessibility requirements.

PCI DSS (Payment Card Industry Data Security Standard)

All entities handling card-holder data (CHD) or sensitive authentication data (SAD) must comply with the PCI Security Standards Council's standards. There is a list of AWS services that are PCI-compliant.

You can check other compliance on the AWS documentation page. The link to this document is provided in the resources section under this section.

---

[1] https://aws.amazon.com/premiumsupport/knowledge-center/gdpr-compliance/

AWS Tools and Products for Security Compliance

AWS also has a long list of security, identity, and compliance products. These products make it easier to implement solutions and meet compliance. Some of their services are covered in Chapter 3.

AWS makes compliance easier for the customer, and they take care of a significant number of issues through the shared security responsibility model. Furthermore, AWS provides excellent products and tools to help you better manage your compliances.

Encryption in AWS

As discussed in the previous section, AWS offers services that help prevent unauthorized access to your accounts, data, and workloads. In this section, you learn about data encryption at rest and in transit.

This type of encryption ensures that only authorized parties can access the data. Essentially, encryption transforms human-readable plain text into unintelligible ciphertext, or a form of incomprehensible text. To put it simply, encryption transforms readable data into unreadable text.

Encryption in Transit

Encryption in transit means data is encrypted when it is moving from one network to another.

Whenever you access a website, data is transferred from the application server to your device (laptop or mobile). Basically, the data moves from one location to another, across the Internet or a private network. This movement of data is called data in transit.

Since your data is passing through the Internet, there are chances that the data can be manipulated or stolen. Encryption in transit protects this data while traveling from network to network.

AWS provides encryption in transit for all its public services with HTTPS endpoints. Thus AWS provides end-to-end encryption when communicating with the AWS APIs.

You can also use IPSec with VPN when transferring data from on-premises environments to the AWS Cloud.

Encryption at Rest

As the name suggests, encryption at rest provides security for data that is being stored (data at rest). It means that the data storage is encrypted so if an attacker gets into the storage, they will not be able to read the data.

Now you may be thinking, why do we need to encrypt data at rest? Let's say that before moving to the cloud, you have your own data center where you have the servers and storage, and only a few authorized people operate this data center. You do not need to worry about data at rest.

But when you are on the cloud, encryption at rest is very important, because your data is sitting somewhere inside the AWS data center, and different people from AWS manage this. Although AWS ensures your data is secure, this is your responsibility to make sure your data is encrypted.

Let's learn what data at rest means in the cloud. Let's say you are storing data on an EBS volume, S3, or RDS. This data is stored on a storage device, and the AWS data center people manage it, so there is a chance it can be manipulated.

It's highly recommended that when you store data, it's encrypted. Once your data is encrypted, anyone accessing your data cannot see it, as they need a key to decrypt it

AWS supports encryption at rest for all compute, storage, and database services, including EBS, EFS, S3, and databases. If you enable encryption before storing your data, your data will be encrypted.

In the next section, you learn about the AWS security service called AWS Config.

The AWS Config Service

AWS Config is a service that enables you to assess, audit, and evaluate the configurations of your AWS resources.

Let's assume you are working as a cloud engineer for a big organization with multiple departments. Each department has hundreds of applications running in AWS accounts, and there are thousands of AWS services in use in total. If you have strict security and compliance requirements, how do you make sure your AWS infrastructure is compliant with specific governance guidelines?

How do you ensure that AWS resources configuration meets specific internal and external requirements? Where do you get auditing information that is sent to external auditors for compliance checks? It can be very time-consuming and challenging to answer these questions. You can use the AWS CLI and a custom script to achieve this, more or less. But believe me, it's way harder than you think.

That's where AWS Config service comes in. It's a service you can use to assess and audit the configurations of your AWS resources and check compliance. You need to enable AWS Config and use the AWS Config Rule. Once you have enabled it, AWS Config will continuously validate your AWS resource configurations for desired settings. You can define how you want them to be configured and it will check whether they comply with the defined configuration.

AWS Config has a predefined rule, and you can also create a custom rule based on your organization's requirements. AWS Config Rule will evaluate your resources in case there is a change in configuration or if anything happens that's against the rules.

If a resource violates the conditions of a rule, AWS Config flags that resource as noncompliant.

AWS Config Rules

Consider these sample AWS Config rules:

- S3-bucket-level-public-access-prohibited. In this rule, the Amazon Simple Storage Service (Amazon S3) buckets are checked to see if they can be accessed by the public. If Amazon S3 bucket settings are public, this rule is NON_COMPLIANT.

- Ec2-instance-no-public-ip. If you don't want an EC2 to have a public IP address, you can use this config rule. Most commonly, you will not have a public IP address for your EC2 instance because you are launching it on a private subnet. If an EC2 instance is located in a private subnet, it cannot be directly accessed from the public web. By using this config rule, this can be accomplished.

- Cloudtrail-enabled. You can use this rule to check whether your AWS account has AWS CloudTrail enabled. In the absence of AWS CloudTrail, the rule is NON_COMPLIANT. The next section in this chapter covers CloudTrail.

- Ec2-ebs-encryption-by-default. If your organization requires that every EBS volume be encrypted at rest, you should enable this rule. This will confirm that EBS encryption has been enabled by default. If encryption is not enabled, the rule is NON_COMPLIANT.

Those are just a few examples of some of the default rules that are available in Config. There are many more that you may need to use when you work for an organization. I recommend you explore them.

You learn about AWS CloudTrail in the next section.

AWS CloudTrail

This section discusses the purpose of CloudTrail and explains how it integrates with other AWS services. You can use AWS CloudTrail to track, audit, and monitor all API requests made to your AWS account using this powerful service.

Everything you do in your AWS account from the AWS management console is an API call. When you are starting an EC2 instance, listing an S3 object, or logging into your AWS account, these are all API calls.

Additionally, any programmatic request initiated by a user using an SDK or AWS command-line interface or even by another AWS service is an API call.

The AWS account captures API requests as events. These events are recorded in a log file, which is then stored on S3. There is also an option to configure and send this log to the CloudWatch log. Integrating CloudTrail with S3 and CloudWatch makes it a perfect security analysis tool. It is used by many big organizations for compliance and security reasons.

CloudTrail also records associated metadata with all the events. For example, if a user terminates an EC2 instance from the AWS Management Console, you can see information about that action, like the username, timestamp, the IP address of the user, and so on.

Enabling and Configuring CloudTrail

The first thing is to enable CloudTrail in your AWS account. As CloudTrail is not enabled by default in the account, you do have to enable it. Once it is enabled, it knows what API calls to capture from which region and where to store those logs. When creating the CloudTrail, you need to specify an S3 bucket for your log files. This could be a new or existing bucket. There are additional steps, but we skip them for now.

Once CloudTrail is ready, you can add further configurations like CloudWatch logs, which allow you to deliver your CloudTrail log files to CloudWatch in addition to S3. This will enable you to create CloudWatch monitoring metrics against specific API calls and receive notifications from SNS.

How CloudTrail Works

Let's say you are monitoring any EC2 instance termination event. A developer logged in to an AWS account and browsed the AWS services and resources. The CloudTrial will log each activity and store the log into an S3 bucket and CloudWatch log. As soon as the developer terminates the EC2 instance, it will match the event, and the CloudWatch event will trigger and notify SNS, which will send a notification to you.

This is how you monitor all events in an AWS account and integrate this with other AWS services.

Amazon Trusted Advisor

In this section, you learn about what AWS Trusted Advisor is and how you use it in your AWS account.

AWS Trusted Advisor is an AWS tool that provides recommendations to follow AWS best practices. It basically inspects all your AWS resources present in your AWS account and suggests possible improvements to make your account efficient and safe.

For example:

- It notices that your EC2 instances are over-provisioned, and you are wasting money as a result.

- It checks for automated backups of Amazon RDS DB instances. If you haven't enabled it, AWS Trusted Advisor will recommend you do so.

- It checks security groups for rules that allow unrestricted access to a resource.

- It alerts you if any service limits are approaching.

These recommendations are divided into five categories—optimization of costs, performance, security, fault tolerance, and service limits. Trusted Advisor uses some checks to evaluate your account. It uses these checks to identify ways to improve security and performance, reduce costs, optimize your AWS infrastructure, and monitor service quotas. You can then follow these recommendations to optimize your services and resources.

There are some limitations as to how many recommendations you get in your account, which depend on your AWS Support Plan. Pay special attention to this, as it's important for your certification.

You can perform all checks in the Service Limits category with an AWS Basic or Developer Support plan, but only six in the Security category.

With a Business or Enterprise Support plan, you can access all Trusted Advisor checks using the Trusted Advisor Console and the AWS Support API. You can also use Amazon CloudWatch Events to monitor the status of Trusted Advisor checks. CloudWatch is covered in the next session.

The important fact is that it provides advice. That's why it's called a trusted advisor. It gives you advice and real-time guidance about best practices.

Amazon CloudWatch

In this section, you learn about Amazon CloudWatch and its applications.

CloudWatch[2] is a monitoring and management tool. It provides data and insights related to your resources in AWS, on-premises, and hybrid applications. You can use this single tool to collect and access all your performance and operational data in the form of logs and metrics.

---

[2] https://aws.amazon.com/cloudwatch/

This means you can use CloudWatch to monitor your complete stack, including your applications, infrastructure, and services. You can use alarms, logs, and events data to make informed decisions. If needed, you can also automate actions based on the insights from CloudWatch.

How Amazon CloudWatch Works

CloudWatch is a service provided by Amazon that saves metrics from services such as EC2, RDS, and ECS. You can retrieve data based on those metrics. You can also create and upload your own custom metrics to the CloudWatch repository and retrieve statistics on those metrics.

CloudWatch's console allows you to calculate statistics based on metrics and then present that data graphically in a set of reports.

It is possible to configure alarms that will automatically stop, start, and terminate Amazon EC2 instances upon meeting certain criteria. In addition, you can set alarms that will trigger Amazon EC2 Autoscaling and Amazon Simple Notification Service (Amazon SNS).

CloudWatch Uses Cases

Consider the following use cases for CloudWatch:

- Collects performance metrics for AWS services and on-premises. CloudWatch can be integrated with almost any AWS services, including EC2, Amazon DynamoDB, Amazon S3, Amazon ECS, and AWS Lambda. CloudWatch provides performance metrics for cloud and on-premises services.

- Uses a single platform for observability. CloudWatch allows you to collect, access, and correlate data on a single platform from across all your AWS resources, applications, and services running on AWS and on-premises.

- Improves operational performance and resource optimization. You can set alarms and automate actions based on predefined thresholds and metrics. For example, you can automatically start Amazon EC2 Autoscaling or stop an instance to reduce billing overages. You can also use CloudWatch Events for serverless services to trigger workflows with services like AWS Lambda and Amazon SNS.

- Derives actionable insights from logs. You can derive actionable insights from the collected logs and get operational visibility and insights. You can get answers in seconds, regardless of your log volume or query complexity. Additionally, CloudWatch Dashboards provide complete operational visibility through the publication of log-based metrics, the creation of alarms, and the correlation of logs and metrics.

Here are a few core features of CloudWatch:

- **CloudWatch Metrics**. AWS services provide free metrics for resources such as Amazon EC2, Amazon EBS volumes, and Amazon RDS databases. You can graph this information and make decisions to improve your infrastructure by loading all metrics into CloudWatch.

- **CloudWatch Alarms**. These alarms allow you to monitor metrics and initiate actions. You've seen alarms when you used autoscaling groups and you responded to the amount of load on your EC2 instance.

- **CloudWatch Log**. The Amazon CloudWatch Logs service allows you to collect and store logs from your resources, applications, and services in near real-time.

- **CloudWatch Events**. CloudWatch Events is about responding to state changes in your resources.

AWS Support Plan

In this section, you learn about the AWS Support Plan. AWS Support provides tools and guidance to help AWS customers troubleshoot and improve the use of AWS resources.

For example, if you face some problem with AWS resources, you can contact the AWS support team. They are available 24 hours a day, so you can talk to an AWS expert. The AWS support team provides various levels of guidance and best practice advice for your cloud management and operations.

Before learning more about this, you need to learn about some of the services under the AWS support plan. Based on the plan you choose you will get a different level of support from AWS.

- **AWS Trusted Advisor**. This AWS tool provides you with recommendations on how to implement AWS best practices in your AWS account. It helps increase performance and improve the overall security of your cloud architecture.

- **AWS Personal Health Dashboard**. This is a personalized view of the health status of the AWS services in your account. It also provides an alert when an AWS-initiated activity impacts your resources.

- **A Technical Account Manager (TAM)**. TAM is a technical point of contact from the AWS side, who provides advocacy and guidance to assist you in planning and building solutions in AWS using industry best practices. This person acts as a link between you and subject matter experts and product teams from the AWS side to ensure that your cloud environment operates optimally.

Next, take a look at what AWS Support provides. It offers four support plans. You get different levels of help from AWS depending on the support plan you have.

- **Basic support**. This includes questions and support related to your account, billing, and service limit increment.

- **Developer support**. As the name suggests, you can use this plan for developing, experimenting, and testing in Amazon Web Services.

- **Business support**. For AWS production workloads, business support is recommended.

- **Enterprise support**. The AWS Enterprise Support service is recommended for businesses and mission-critical applications.

The Basic Support Plan

The Basic Support plan is free. In this plan, you get 24-hour customer service and support forums. You only get access to the seven core checks from Trusted Advisor. This is not a lot, but this is what you get from the Basic plan. You also get the Personal Health Dashboard, which was discussed earlier. This dashboard shows information about the health of your AWS services and sends alerts when your resources are going to be impacted.

The Developer Support Plan

You can upgrade your basic plan to the Developer plan. In addition to everything that you get with the Basic plan, you get business hour email access to cloud support engineers. This means you can send emails to the AWS support team by opening support tickets through the support console. You get an unlimited number of cases and one dedicated contact from AWS for your account. The response time may vary based on the severity of your case. For instance, if you are looking for general guidance, you can expect a response within 24 business hours. But if your issue is serious and urgent—for example, if something is not working in your accounts—they will respond to you with a solution within 12 business hours. This plan is good for development and test environment accounts, but as soon as you plan to have a production workload, this plan does not help much. Hence, you may have to switch to the Business Support plan.

The Business Support Plan

If you have a full-fledged business application in AWS, make sure you have the Business Support plan. This plan gives you the full set of checks for Trusted Advisor and its API access. You will have 24*7 phone, email, and chat support with a cloud support engineer. You can have an unlimited number of contacts and can open an unlimited amount of cases. In the Business plan, the response time for general guidance is less than 24 hours. For any system impairment, the time is less than 12 hours. For any production system impairment, it is less than 4 hours. If your production system goes down completely, you get help in less than an hour. If you need instant support for your production workload, you should opt for the Business Support plan.

The Enterprise Support Plan

Finally, if you are a large enterprise and you have mission-critical applications on AWS, you must use the Enterprise plan, which contains everything from the three plans discussed so far, as well as a dedicated technical account manager (a TAM) for your account. You also get AWS billing and account experts who specialize in working with your enterprise accounts. They will quickly and efficiently assist you with your billing and account inquiries. They also work with you to implement billing and account best practices so that you can focus on the things that matter to your business.

Summary

The purpose of this chapter was to provide an overview of AWS's Cloud security and management services. As you know, cloud technologies are booming in the IoT sphere. A lot is happening through the cloud, so it has also become the target for cyberattack. Hackers can steal sensitive data, prevent computing processes, or deliver malware to a server to damage your cloud environments.

This chapter is all about the tools and services in AWS to protect your data in the cloud. It discussed what your responsibilities are as a customer to take care of your applications and data in the cloud. To ensure its users confidentiality, integrity, and availability, Amazon monitors its own infrastructure 24 hours a day, 7 days a week. You also learned how AWS protects their physical data centers with topic surveillance, intrusion detection systems, and the use of two-factor authentication by its employees at the data center. On the other side of the shared-responsibility model, the customer is responsible for securing activities that occur "in" the cloud or are related to the cloud account.

You learned that AWS manages the security compliance standards and business-specific guidelines and rules governed by different countries. You also learned that users can encrypt data both in transit with the AWS APIs and at rest for all compute, storage, and database services, including EBS, EFS, S3, and databases.

You then learned about AWS Config, which enables you to assess, audit, and evaluate the configurations of your AWS resources. It marks the resources as non-compliant if they violate the AWS Config rules.

You also learned about AWS CloudTrail, a powerful service that tracks, audits, and monitors API requests made to AWS accounts. You learned that AWS Trusted Advisor recommends the improvement of resources and services. It basically inspects all your AWS resources present in your AWS account and suggests improvements.

You then learned Amazon CloudWatch, which is a monitoring and management tool. Finally, you learned that AWS Support provides tools and advice to help troubleshoot or improve the use of AWS resources in an account. It supports customers 24/7 by providing four different support plans.

CHAPTER 11

AWS Billing and Pricing

Thus far, you have learned about all the basic concepts of cloud computing, its components, AWS and its services. Now, it's time to look at the pricing principles of AWS and its cost management structure.

Upon successful completion of this chapter:

- You will be able to decide which AWS pricing model is suitable for your AWS account according to your requirements.

- You will be able to apply the knowledge of the AWS Organization in setting up your AWS account structures.

- You will be aware of how to get maximum benefits by using consolidated billing.

- You will implement the AWS cost management and optimization tools when using AWS services.

- You will be able to estimate the total running cost of an ongoing project with the help of the AWS Pricing Calculator.

© Pravin Mishra 2023
P. Mishra, *Cloud Computing with AWS*, https://doi.org/10.1007/978-1-4842-9172-6_11

AWS Pricing Principles

This section explains the different pricing principles in AWS. When you use AWS services or resources, you need to pay for them as a customer. AWS has simplified the payment option through different pricing models for customers. Let's look at these models.

AWS offers four pricing models:

- Pay as You Go

- Pay Less by Using More

- Save When You Reserve

- Free Tier Usage

Pay as You Go

Using this pricing principle, you can rent resources on-demand and pay only for what you use.

There are no upfront charges for services, and you no longer need to pay for them when you stop using them. It is entirely up to you how many machines and for how long you want to run. You have total control over starting, stopping, and delete resources whenever you want. It is best for development and test workloads or if you cannot buy or build your infrastructure. It's important to note that the on-demand infrastructure is expensive, especially if a customer deploys the servers regularly.

Pay Less by Using More

Amazon provides volume discounts. For example, more storage usage means less storage cost.

As AWS grows, it will save money due to economies of scale and will pass some of these benefits to you as well. AWS is famous for making cost reductions every month or every year, which is very good from a customer's point of view.

As their infrastructure grows, they have volume and scale, and therefore, they will share the benefits with customers by providing them with cost discounts.

Save When You Reserve

In this pricing principle, you reserve the capacity for an extensive period (one or three years) and get a discount, ranging between 30 and 72 percent, based on the reserved capacity's price.

This concept applies to services such as EC2, DynamoDB, ElastiCache, RDS, and Redshift.

Free Usage Tier

AWS offers many of its services free for a year or until you reach your quota. For example, in Amazon Simple Storage Service (Amazon S3), you can get up to 5 GB of storage or 750 hours of EC2 instances.

Nevertheless, planning your budget in advance will ensure you effectively leverage free resources.

AWS Organization

This section discusses AWS Organization and its elements.

When you are new to AWS Cloud and just starting out, one of the first questions you will encounter is, how many AWS accounts do you need? It's okay to have one account while you learn AWS. But when it comes to actually using the cloud for your application, you need to think about how many accounts are required and how you will manage these accounts.

As per AWS, a multi-account setup is considered a best practice.

How do you manage these accounts? That is where you use the AWS service called AWS Organization. It allows you to manage multiple AWS accounts.

AWS Organization enables you to centrally add, create, and manage AWS accounts. You can also manage billing, access controls, compliance, security, and shared resources across your AWS accounts. It is easy to set up and is free to all AWS customers.

AWS Organization is also designed to structure your accounts to best fit your organization's needs. It can be aligned with your organization's portfolio, team, or business line.

AWS Organization has four components. The following sections look at them one by one.

Master Account

The first and most important component in AWS Organization is the master account. The master account is also known as the root account, and you can have only one root account. This master account is the AWS account that you use to create your organization.

You can use this account to manage your other AWS accounts. It will act as the central management and governance hub for all your accounts.

Hence, you will use a master account to create new accounts, invite other accounts to join your organization, and remove accounts from your organization.

Member Account

Accounts other than the master account in an organization are member accounts. It means all other accounts you created or invited to be a part of your organization are known as member accounts.

You can add a new account directly to the organization or invite an existing account. If you invite the existing account, the root user needs to accept the invitation.

Organization Unit (OU)

The AWS Organization Unit is my favorite one. It is also known as OU. An OU helps you group AWS accounts within your organization.

For example, suppose you have HR, Sales, and Marketing teams and each team needs an AWS account of their own. You can create three organization units in the AWS Organization and place accounts in the Organization Unit.

Organization units can also contain organization units, allowing you to create hierarchies based on your company's structure. Keep the following points in mind regarding OUs and accounts:

- An account can be added under a single OU.

- One account cannot be added under two different OUs.

- Hierarchy can be five levels deep, including root and AWS accounts created in the lowest OUs.

- You can create multiple OUs within a single organization

- You can create OUs within other OUs.

- Each OU can contain multiple accounts.

- You can move accounts from one OU to another.

- OU names must be unique within a parent OU or root.

Service Control Policy (SCP)

As the name suggests, this is a set of rules that you apply to the AWS organization, account, and organization unit.

Service control policies are a type of organization policy that you attach to the entire organization, OUs, or individual AWS accounts. They define the services and actions that users or a role can perform. This allows you to manage permissions within your organization using SCP. SCPs ensure that your accounts remain compliant with your organization's access control policies.

Figure 11-1 shows what this looks like.

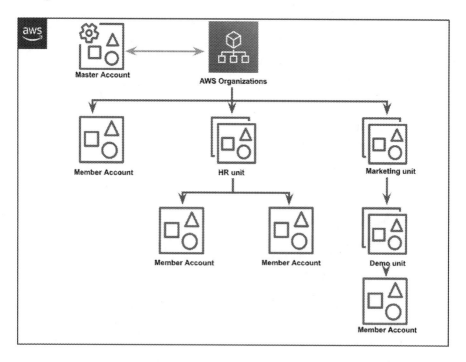

Figure 11-1. *AWS Organization*

Here you have an AWS Cloud. You create an account (let's assume this account is a master account). In this master account, you will have an AWS Organization to manage all member accounts and organization units. In this master account, you can create an account or an Organization Unit. Say you create one account and two Organization Units—one for HR and another for Marketing. Now, HR OU can have two accounts. You can also have an account for Marketing OU, but you can add another OU in Marketing OU, called Demo. Then you can add an account to the Demo OU.

So you see, here, you can organize AWS accounts pretty much to your organization's structure and needs. AWS Organization is priceless for enterprises that need multiple accounts to segregate work and apply unique SCPs to an account. It also provides consolidated billing through the master account to achieve volume discounts.

Additionally, multiple accounts allow for the separation of development, test, and production environments at the account level.

AWS Organization is a must for anyone needing more than a single account and to apply the best practices for managing the services and resources in your AWS environment.

The next section covers consolidated billing.

Consolidated Billing

In the last section, you learned how AWS Organization is priceless for enterprises that need multiple accounts to segregate work. AWS Organization also comes with a feature called consolidated billing.

As the name suggests, consolidated billing means all of the charges for each account are billed against the master account.

This means if you have a hundred accounts, you can get one bill and centrally manage the bill like AWS accounts.

One Bill

A consolidated bill lets you manage all of your accounts in one place, and it allows you to get one bill for all linked accounts.

Easy Tracking

Consolidated billing also gives you an interface to track the charges across multiple accounts and download the combined cost and usage data. It means that you can analyze charges across multiple accounts and download a cost and usage report.

Combined Usage

Consolidated billing has the advantage of allowing all accounts within an organization to share volume pricing discounts and reserved instance discounts. Therefore, you will be charged less for your project, department, or company than if you had individual, standalone accounts.

No Extra Fees

There are no additional fees and consolidated billing doesn't cost you anything. Remember, you have an AWS Organization. You can create multiple accounts in that organization or invite existing AWS accounts into the organization and then get a combined bill for all of the accounts in the management account.

In the next section, you learn about the AWS Cost Management tool.

AWS Cost Management Tool

As you know, AWS offers a wide range of cloud services that you can use in various use cases. If you are a developer or cloud engineer, you are empowered to innovate and move quickly, which means spinning up cloud resources. But all of this comes with a cost, right?

AWS provides several services and tools to help you organize and track AWS costs and usage data. For example, access permission tools (IAM and SCP) enable you to gain greater control, whereas consolidated billing helps you plan budgets and estimate forecasts accurately.

In following sections, you learn about AWS cost estimation and optimization tools.

The Billing and Cost Management Console

Like other AWS services and management consoles, AWS provides the Billing and Cost Management Console. It contains a billing section where you can see all your AWS services consumptions and up-to-date billing details. You have already navigated to this dashboard a couple of times in previous chapters. I recommend going through it and getting familiar with it.

AWS Resource and Cost Allocation Tags

AWS also provides resource tags for organizing resources and cost allocation tags for tracking AWS costs. Once you activate cost allocation tags, AWS uses these tags to organize your resource costs on your cost allocation report. This makes it easier for you to categorize and track your AWS costs. This feature is available in the Billing dashboard.

Consolidated Billing

You learned about consolidated billing in the last section. This is an AWS Organization feature that allows you to have a single bill for all of your accounts. It's easy to keep track of overall expenses and monitor spending across different accounts through a single bill. You can also trace costs from each account and get the expense data in a CSV file.

AWS Cost Explorer

By using Cost Explorer, you can view AWS costs and usage for the past 13 months, which will help you forecast future spending. Cost Explorer allows you to create customized views, which can help you analyze your AWS costs and identify areas for improvement. In addition to that, the AWS Cost Explorer provides an API that enables you to access data using your existing analytics tools.

AWS Budget

You are already familiar with AWS Budget. You can set and enforce budgets for each AWS service using AWS Budget. When budgets are exceeded or reached, you will receive messages or emails from the Simple Notification Service (SNS). A budget can be associated with specific data points, such as data usage or various instances, or an overall cost budget can be defined. This tool provides a dashboard similar to Cost Explorer, which displays how services are used with respect to their budgets.

Automated Billing

AWS automatically deducts the billing amount from the credit card you entered when signing up for an account. You do not need to pay separately.

In the next section, you learn how to use the AWS Pricing Calculator.

AWS Pricing Calculator

So far, this chapter has been looking at different aspects of cost in AWS. Once you start working with customers, you'll need to estimate the total running cost of your projects. AWS has a nice tool to do this cost calculation—the Pricing Calculator.

Go to the web browser and search for the AWS Pricing Calculator. Click it to go to the tool. To calculate the cost, click Create Estimate. You will see lots of AWS services. Search for EC2 and click Configure. As you can see, the calculator shows some options.

The pricing varies depending on your region. Verify that you have the right region. I changed mine to the Asia Pacific (Mumbai) and then clicked Accept to confirm.

You also have to choose some other options. You can use a quick or an advanced estimate. Stick to it quickly for this demo. You can also choose your operating system. I will leave it on Linux. Then you can specify the resources that you need. Let's say you need four CPUs and select 24 for memory. This new configuration is going to change the estimate.

If I put that down to 16, it says that it's a t4g.xlarge. If I change the CPU allocation to two again, it will change the requirement.

You can add requirements, like ECU or GPU. Then select the number of instances; I use 2.

Now you have a pricing strategy. You can select the different options and see the estimate.

Say you are going to reserve. You can look at the pricing advantages of using a one- or three-year pricing model. Maybe you want to pay all upfront to bring the price down even more, Or maybe you want on-demand because this is for a short-term workload.

You can see some cost estimates straight away here. Usually, the cost is $590 dollars. If you go to savings plans for three years, all upfront, you can see that you'd get a total cost for running all of these workloads over a three-year period. You can play around with these different variables and determine what will be best for you or your customers.

Maybe on-demand is what you need. And what about the storage. Well, general purpose is fine. Maybe you need a bit more storage, so let's put it up to 50. Again, you can look at the calculations. Perhaps you want to change to provisioned IOPS, and you want to specify a certain amount of IOPS. Again, you'll see the pricing implications of those changes in real-time here.

So you have this particular EC2 instance estimate. You can add that in. Suppose you want to add a service. Let's choose RDS. You want to run a MySQL workload, so you are going to choose RDS for MySQL. Again, it is asking for the quantity. You can choose which type of database instance you want based on the number of CPUs and memory. Finally, it will show you how much this will cost. You don't want this one to be multi-AZ, so you can reduce your costs a bit there. Then, you have a pricing model option here as well, which is applicable to some instance types, which are the storage layer and backup.

You simply added a couple of services, and you can see what your 12-month total is going to be. Here, you have your monthly total as well. That's pretty much it. You can go in and add whatever service, and it will show you the various parameters associated with pricing that you can configure. This gives you a great way of estimating how much you're going to pay for the services.

Summary

This chapter provided you with a good understanding of AWS pricing and billing. You also learned about the AWS pricing tools.

You learned that as a customer, if you are using the AWS services or resources, you can pay AWS with its simplified pricing models. You also learned about all the four pricing models in detail, which are Pay As You Go, Pay Less By Using More, Save When You Reserve, and Free Usage Tier.

Additionally, you learned that AWS Organization allows central management of multiple AWS accounts and has four components. You also learned that all of the charges for each account are billed against the master account in consolidated billing. That means if you have 100 accounts, you can get one bill and centrally manage bills like AWS accounts. You also learned about the different pricing tools in AWS that charge customers based on the consumption of AWS services and data usage. Finally, you took a quick tour of the AWS Pricing Calculator.

Index

A

L

S

Printed in the United States
by Baker & Taylor Publisher Services